D0016028

SAVE
САЧУВАТИ

The Future of Reputation

The Future of Reputation

Gossip, Rumor, and

Privacy on the Internet

Daniel J. Solove

Yale University Press

New Haven and London

To Papa Nat

A Caravan book. For more information, visit www.caravanbooks.org

Set in Garamond and Stone Sans types by Binghamton Valley Composition.
Printed in the United States of America by Vail-Ballou Press.

Library of Congress Cataloging-in-Publication Data

Solove, Daniel J., 1972–
  The future of reputation : gossip, rumor, and privacy on the Internet / Daniel J. Solove.
    p.   cm.
  Includes bibliographical references and index.
  ISBN 978-0-300-12498-9 (cloth : alk. paper)   1. Privacy, Right of.
2. Internet—Law and legislation.   3. Reputation (Law)   4. Libel and slander.
5. Personality (Law)   I. Title
  K3264.C65S65 2007
  342.08'58—dc22

                              2007013364

A catalogue record for this book is available from the British Library.

10 9 8 7 6 5 4 3 2 1

Contents

Preface

The idea for this book came to me soon after I began blogging in May 2005. I found blogging to be enthralling and invigorating. I was fascinated by the thrill of expressing my thoughts to a broad audience yet acutely aware of how people could be hurt by gossip and rumors spreading over the Internet.

In an earlier book, *The Digital Person: Technology and Privacy in the Information Age,* I explored how businesses and the government were threatening privacy by collecting massive digital dossiers of information about people. In that book, it was easy to take sides. I argued that information collection and use were threatening people's freedom and well-being, and that greater protection of privacy was necessary. When it comes to gossip and rumor on the Internet, however, the culprit is ourselves. We're invading each other's privacy, and we're also even invading our own privacy by exposures of information we later come to regret. Individual rights are implicated on both sides of the equation. Protecting privacy can come into tension with safeguarding free speech, and I cherish both values. It is this conflict that animates this book.

Although I advance my own positions, my aim isn't to hold them out as end-all solutions. The purpose of the book is to explore in depth a set of fascinating yet very difficult questions and to propose some moderate compromises in the clash between privacy and free speech. There are no easy answers, but the issues are important, and I believe that it is essential that we wrestle with them.

Many people helped shape the ideas in this book through conversations and helpful comments on the manuscript: danah boyd, Bruce Boyden, Deven Desai, Tom Dienes, Howard Erichson, Henry Farrell, Bill Frucht, Eric Goldman, Marcia Hofmann, Chris Hoofnagle, Orin Kerr, Ray Ku, David Lat, Jennie Meade, Frank Pasquale, Neil Richards, Paul Schwartz, Michael Sullivan, Bob Tuttle, Christopher Wolf, and David Wolitz. My research assistants, James Murphy and Erica Ruddy, provided helpful research and proofreading. A few passages in this book were adapted from my article "The Virtues of Knowing Less: Justifying Privacy Protections Against Disclosure," 53 *Duke Law Journal* 967 (2003). My agent, Susan Schulman, believed in this book from the start and helped tremendously in bringing it to fruition. I would also like to thank Michael O'Malley at Yale University Press, who also believed in this project and gave me the opportunity to bring it to life, and Dan Heaton, for his thoughtful editing of the manuscript.

When quoting from blog posts, I have occasionally corrected obvious typos and spelling errors.

Chapter 1 Introduction:

When Poop Goes

Primetime

It all began in realspace, on a subway train in South Korea. A young woman's small dog pooped in the train. Other passengers asked her to clean it up, but she told them to mind their own business. That's when it moved over to cyberspace and became even uglier.

Someone took photos of her and posted them on a popular Korean blog. A blog, short for "Web log," is a running online commentary about one's life or about the issues of the day. Another blogger, Don Park, explains what happened next:

> Within hours, she was labeled gae-ttong-nyue (dog shit girl) and her pictures and parodies were everywhere. Within days, her identity and her past were revealed. Requests for information about her parents and relatives started popping up and people started to recognize her by the dog and the bag she was carrying as well as her watch, clearly visible in the original picture. All mentions of privacy invasion were shouted down. . . . The common excuse for their behavior was that the girl doesn't deserve privacy.[1]

Across the Internet, people made posters with the girl's photograph, fusing her picture with a variety of other images. The dog poop girl story quickly migrated to the mainstream media, becoming national news in South Korea. As a result of her public shaming and embarrassment, the dog poop girl dropped out of her university.[2]

The story of the dog poop girl wasn't known in the United States until Don Park wrote about it in his blog, Don Park's Daily Habit.[3] It became even more popular when the blog BoingBoing discussed the story. BoingBoing receives nearly ten million visits per month—more than the circulations of many newspapers and magazines.[4] In no time, newspapers and websites around the world were discussing the story.

The story of the dog poop girl raises a number of intriguing issues about the Internet, privacy, norms, and life in the Information Age. Not picking up your dog's poop is bad behavior in most people's books, but was the reaction to her transgression appropriate? We all have probably engaged in rude behavior or minor wrongdoing. But is it going too far to transform the dog poop girl into a villain notorious across the globe?

The dog poop girl is just one example of a much larger phenomenon taking place across the Internet. Increasingly, people are exposing personal information about themselves and others online. We can now readily capture information and images wherever we go, and we can then share them with the world at the click of a mouse. Somebody you've never met can snap your photo and post it on the Internet. Or somebody that you know very well can share your cherished secrets with the entire planet. Your friends or coworkers might be posting rumors about you on their blogs. The personal email you send to others can readily be forwarded along throughout cyberspace, to be mocked and laughed at far and wide. And your children might be posting intimate information about themselves on the Web—or their friends or enemies might be revealing your family secrets. These fragments of information won't fade away with time, and they can readily be located by any curious individual. Like the dog poop girl, you could find photos and information about yourself spreading around the Internet like a virus.

This is a book about how the free flow of information on the Internet can make us less free. We live in an age drenched in data, and the implications are both wonderful and terrifying. The Internet places a seemingly endless library in our homes; it allows us to communicate with others instantly; and it enables us to spread information with an efficiency and power that humankind has never before witnessed. The free flow of information on the Internet provides wondrous new opportunities for people to express themselves and communicate.

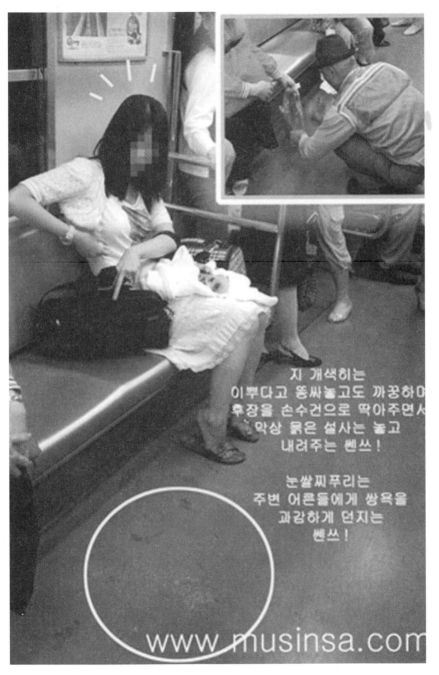

지 개색히는
이뿌다고 똥싸놓고도 까꿍하여
후장을 손수건으로 딱아주면서
악상 묽은 설사는 놓고
내려주는 쎈쓰!

눈쌀찌푸리는
주변 어른들에게 쌍욕을
과감하게 던지는
쎈쓰!

www.musinsa.com

One of the digital posters of the dog poop girl circulating on the Internet

But there's a dark side. As social reputation–shaping practices such as gossip and shaming migrate to the Internet, they are being transformed in significant ways. Information that was once scattered, forgettable, and localized is becoming permanent and searchable. Ironically, the free flow of information threatens to undermine our freedom in the future.

These transformations pose threats to people's control over their reputations and their ability to be who they want to be. Will we enslave ourselves by making it impossible to escape from the shackles of our past and from the stain of gossip and false rumors? How much information should we know about each other? How do we allow people to control their personal information without curtailing free speech or stifling freedom on the Internet?

This book will take a journey through the ways in which private lives are being exposed online, and it will examine the implications. People have profound new ways to communicate, yet the gossip, shaming, and rumors that are being spread online are sometimes having devastating effects on people's lives. Should we do something to stop the exposure of private secrets on the Internet? Can we do anything? In this book I will propose a framework for how we can address these problems—by recognizing a new and broader notion of privacy and by reaching a better balance between privacy and free speech.

THE INTERNET AS A TEENAGER

About a decade ago, the Internet in its early days was greeted with a kind of euphoria. Its potential seemed to be boundless, and people viewed it as a wondrous zone of freedom. A few years later, the giddiness dimmed with foreboding. Commentators began to point out that the Internet wasn't inherently free—it could be transformed into a radically controlled and restricted world. In 1999 the Internet law expert Lawrence Lessig declared in his famous book, *Code:* "We will see that cyberspace does not guarantee its own freedom but instead carries an extraordinary potential for control."[5]

Today, the Internet is no longer in its infancy. Although developed long ago by researchers, the Internet entered into popular usage in the mid-1990s. It is now maturing into its second decade in mainstream culture—its teenage years. The Internet indeed has proven to be a place of both rigid control and unbounded freedom.

This book focuses on the free dimensions of the Internet. The future of the Internet involves not only the clash between freedom and control but also a struggle within the heart of freedom itself. The more freedom people have to spread information online, the more likely that people's private secrets will be revealed in ways that can hinder their opportunities in the future. In many respects, the teenage Internet is taking on all the qualities of an adolescent—brash, uninhibited, unruly, fearless, experimental, and often not mindful of the consequences of its behavior. And as with a teenager, the Net's greater freedom can be both a blessing and a curse.

In the offline world, the dog poop girl would have been quickly forgotten. The incident would have ended when she left the subway train. But the Internet enabled the few witnesses of her transgression to express their outrage to millions. Indeed, the Internet affords people unprecedented new ways to communicate with others. It has blossomed into a fantastic world of free expression, teeming with chatrooms, online discussion groups, and blogs, which are proliferating at a breathtaking rate. Everyday people express themselves to a worldwide audience, something never before possible in the history of humankind.

In May 2005 I became a blogger. Within an instant, I could publish virtual op-eds to the entire world. Billions of people potentially could access my thoughts. The blog I posted on was visited thousands of times a day. A lot of people were reading. What made this so exciting was that I'd never had any success getting an op-ed published. I had tried many a time, but the editors just wouldn't give me a plot of valuable space on their pages. Suddenly I no longer need them. I can get my thoughts out far and wide without their help.

Blogging brings instant gratification. I can quickly work up my thoughts into a post and publish them to the website for the world to read. People then post comments, and I can have a discussion with them. Blogging has allowed me to explore many an idea that might have languished in a forgotten corner of my mind. In fact, this book was inspired by my blog post about the dog poop girl case.

Blogs are everywhere these days. There are blogs about virtually any topic under the sun. Dogs and poop are both popular topics for blogs. A blog called Doggie News gleefully reported the dog poop girl story.[6] There's a blog purportedly written by dogs called Blogdogs.[7] There's even a blog about poop called Poop Report.[8] Needless to say, the dog poop girl story was a big scoop for Poop Report.[9]

It is hard not to get excited about these developments, to see the great freedom and power that the Internet can provide to everyday people. But while many bloggers talk about politics, books, music, dogs, or other topics, a large number of bloggers enjoy speaking about their personal lives, their sexual experiences, the people they know, and even the girl on the train who wouldn't clean up after her dog. Details about many people's private lives are finding their way onto the Internet, often without the subjects' knowledge and consent. And in a number of cases, the consequences for these people are severe. As people use the freedom-enhancing dimensions of the Internet, as they express themselves and engage in self-development, they may be constraining the freedom and self-development of others—and even of themselves.

THE NORM POLICE

In the dog poop girl case, people harnessed the power of the Internet to enforce a norm—the obligation to clean up after one's dog. Norms are "social attitudes of approval and disapproval," the law professor Cass Sunstein writes. Norms specify "what ought to be done and what ought not to be done."[10] Norms bind societies together; they regulate everyday conduct; they foster civility. They are the oil that reduces the friction of human interaction. We need to maintain norms of courtesy so that we can all get along nicely. Imagine if we didn't have norms like first–come, first-served. Fisticuffs would quickly follow. In short, norms are a central mechanism through which a society exercises social control.

To be effective, norms must be regularly followed. If people flout norms and get away with it too often, norms can weaken and lose their influence over behavior. When somebody butts in line, many people usually just grumble under their teeth, but there are a few folks who confront that norm violator. These "norm police" help enforce norms, and they are essential to ensuring that norms remain strong.

The dog poop girl violated a norm that most people would agree with, but were the norm police too harsh in punishing her? Most norm enforcement involves angry scowls or just telling a person off. The blogosphere can be a much more powerful norm-enforcing tool, allowing bloggers to act as a cyber-posse, tracking down norm violators and branding them with digital marks of shame. Having a permanent record of norm violations is upping the sanction to a whole new level.

Don Park's blog contains some interesting comments by his readers about the dog poop girl.[11] Some commentators were sympathetic to her plight, likening the attacks on her to a "witch hunt." But others celebrated her shaming. One theme is responsibility. In the words of one commentator:

Every once in a while, it's good for someone who is an ass to be shown as an ass. Whether to a small group or large crowd. She needs to learn to be accountable, whether in front of 5 people or 5,000,000 people. It's really all the same. Manners are manners.

Another commentator opined:

In the old days, people conformed to societal expectations and norms based on the feedback they got from those around them. These days, especially in large urban areas where anonymity prevails, most people seem to be afraid to criticize anyone for anything. Maybe now technology will provide a way to reinstate that societal feedback. I doubt this episode would have occurred in a small town where everyone knows everyone and such actions would have resulted in immediate consequences.

Yet another remarked:

Lack of personal responsibility is the problem here. And it's really prevalent these days.

It is certainly true that the Internet better enabled people to hold the dog poop girl responsible for her behavior. People who act inappropriately might not be able to escape into obscurity anymore; instead, they may be captured in pixels and plastered across the Internet. They'll be held responsible for their actions. But perhaps responsibility cuts both ways. Shouldn't the cyberspace norm police also have responsibilities? What if they get out of hand? What if they wrongly accuse somebody? What if their shaming punishes a minor transgression too much?

PRIVACY

A common thread running through the comments about the dog poop girl is that she should expect no privacy because she was in public. One commentator wrote:

The initial blogger. Do I think he had every right to post her? Yep. She was in public, and it really doesn't matter if she was in front of 100 or 1,000,000 people, she was willing to act that way in the public sphere.

Under existing notions, privacy is often thought of in a binary way—something is either private or public. According to the general rule, if something occurs in a public place, it is not private. But a more nuanced view of privacy suggests that this case involved taking an event that occurred in one context and significantly altering its nature—by making it permanent and widespread.

The dog poop girl would have been just a vague image in a few people's memories if it hadn't been for the photo entering cyberspace and spreading around faster than an epidemic. Despite the fact that the event occurred in public, was there a need for her image and identity to be spread across the Internet?

Yet another commentator stated:

> I really don't think it matters that it came out on the internet. It happened in a public place so it is excusable to discuss it in a public forum. This isn't going to ruin her life, it might make her clean up her dog's mess for a month though while the story goes around. We are a fickle bunch and she will be forgotten before the end of the season.

But this comment is inaccurate. She will not be forgotten. That's what the Internet changes. Whereas before the girl would have been remembered merely by a few as just some woman who wouldn't clean up dog poop, now her image and identity are eternally preserved in electrons. Forever, she will be the "dog poop girl"; forever, she will be captured in Google's unforgiving memory; and forever, she will be in the digital doghouse for being rude and inconsiderate. The dog poop girl's behavior was certainly wrong, but we might not know the whole story behind the incident to judge her appropriately. And should people's social transgressions follow them on a digital rap sheet that can never be expunged?

The easy reaction is to steel ourselves and chalk it up to life in the digital age. But the stakes are too high for that. We perform an enormous range of activities in public. Do we want to live with the risk that people can snap our picture wherever we are and put it up on the Internet? We expose a litany of personal information as we go about our daily lives. Do we want it to be permanently posted online for the world to see? Consider the thoughts of another commentator to Don Park's blog:

> It reminds me of the struggles that editors face when deciding about what pictures to run in the newspaper. Those editors need to make a judgement call based on the value of the picture and its relevance to the story. But here, the person was outraged and ran the picture of the girl. That's totally different. It shows the dangerous flip side of citizen media. Moral outrage is easy to flame. But the consequences can be mortal. Will the ease in inciting moral outrage create a mob driven police state? It may be when the powerful realize how they can use citizen "reporters," to influence mobs. That seems to be one of the real dangers of citizen journalism.

Similarly, Howard Reingold, author of *Smart Mobs,* a book about the blistering speed of modern communications, observes: "The shadow side of the empowerment that comes with a billion and a half people being online is the surveillance aspect. . . . We used to worry about big brother—the state—but now of course it's our neighbors, or people on the subway."[12]

Compounding the problem is the fact that the norms of the blogosphere are just developing, and they are generally looser and less well defined than those of the mainstream media. The author of an article in the *Columbia Journalism Review* declares: "We've seen blogs act as media or political watchdogs, but not as aggressive watchdogs of individual violations of social norms. So this seems like a notable step. And, as with the emergence of 'citizen'journalism, it is an undefined and unregulated step in a cyberworld that lacks boundaries and standards."[13] Thus cyberspace norm police can be extremely dangerous—with an unprecedented new power and an underdeveloped system of norms to constrain their own behavior.

GENERATION GOOGLE

Generation X. Generation Y. These are yesterday's labels. They don't really capture who we are today. We are Generation Google.

Google is a search engine, a website that combs through the Internet looking for all other Web pages that contain the term you're searching for. Without search engines, the Internet would be an endless expanse of digital babble, and finding any particular piece of information would be akin to locating a specific grain of sand in the Sahara Desert. Since its creation in 1998 by Larry Page and Sergey Brin, two students at Stanford University, Google has quickly risen to become the leading search engine.[14] It can search billions of Web pages in just a fraction of a second. Google presents search results in a rank ordering calculated to put the most relevant results at the top of the list.

Want to know about a person? No need to hire a private investigator. Just go to http://www.google.com, type a name into the search box, hit the search button . . . and presto, you've got a list of Web pages with information about that individual. Google is so popular it has become a verb. To "google" someone doesn't mean anything kinky—instead, it means to do a search for his or her name on the Web. Everybody's googling. People google friends, dates, potential employees, long-lost relatives, and anybody else who happens to arouse their curiosity.

Many of us today—especially children and teenagers—are spending more of our lives on the Internet. And the more we're online, the more likely details about our lives will slip out into cyberspace. This risk is increased because it is

The Google search prompt

not just we ourselves who might leak information—data about us can be re-vealed by our friends or enemies, spouses or lovers, employers or employees, teachers or students . . . and even by strangers on the subway. We live in an age when many fragments of information about our lives are being gathered by new technologies, horded by companies in databases, and scattered across the Internet. Even people who have never gone online are likely to have some personal information on the Internet.

Details about your private life on the Internet can become permanent digi-tal baggage. For example, a story in the *Boston Globe Magazine* discusses the plight of a thirty-four-year-old professional named Michael.[15] Michael was briefly in prison when he was a juvenile. While in prison, he wrote a few ar-ticles about it in specialized journals. These articles now come back to haunt him. They are pulled up anytime somebody does a Google search for his name. Michael is single, and his Google baggage travels with him on most dates. On the first or second date, most women start interrogating Michael about his stint in prison. As Michael explains: "When you meet someone . . . you don't say, 'I had an affair one time,' or 'I was arrested for DUI once,' or 'I cheated on my taxes in 1984.'" Even when people don't ask him about his past, Michael's digital skeletons continue to affect him. Whenever there's an awkward silence in a conversation, Michael thinks the worst: "Instead of thinking, 'Was I curt last week?' or 'Did I insult this political party or that be-lief?' I have to think about what happened when I was 17." In one instance, Michael was interviewed several times for a job when, suddenly, the potential employer stopped calling him. "[Michael's] hunch: Someone Googled him. But the worst part is, he'll never know." Michael's problem is not that he is embarrassed by his past or wants to escape from it. Rather, he resents having to constantly justify himself and explain his past. Worse still, he is rarely afforded the opportunity to explain.

From the dawn of time, people have gossiped, circulated rumors, and shamed others. These social practices are now moving over to the Internet, where they are taking on new dimensions. They transform from forgettable whispers within small local groups to a widespread and permanent chronicle of people's lives. An entire generation is growing up in a very different world, one where people will accumulate detailed records beginning with childhood that will stay with them for life wherever they go. In Nathaniel Hawthorne's *The Scarlet Letter,* Hester Prynne was forced by her colonial New England village to wear a scarlet letter *A* to represent her sin of adultery. The Internet is bringing back the scarlet letter in digital form—an indelible record of people's past misdeeds. One commentator to Don Park's post about the dog poop girl said it best: "Right or wrong, the internet is a cruel historian." The Internet is indeed a cruel historian. Who wants to go through life forever known as the dog poop girl?

In this book, I discuss a litany of instances like the dog poop girl, in which rumors, gossip, or shaming on the Internet have had poisonous effects. I argue that we must protect privacy to ensure that the freedom of the Internet doesn't make us less free. But to do so, we must rethink our notions of privacy. We must also balance the protection of privacy against freedom of speech. And we must find a workable way for the law to achieve these goals. I shall propose ideas for how these goals can be achieved.

The book has two parts. In the first part I discuss how rumors, gossip, and shaming are being transformed when they take place online. In Chapter 2 I explore the new ways we're disseminating information—through blogs, social network sites, and other means. Increasingly, this information consists of personal details about people's lives. It is far too simplistic to conclude that this is good or bad—it is both. We rely upon information about people to help us assess their reputations. We want to give people some control over their reputations, but not so much that they can deceive or manipulate us. The rapid spread of information on the Internet makes establishing this delicate balance all the more challenging.

Chapter 3 is about gossip. There's a voyeur in all of us, and we often have a gluttonous curiosity about the lives of others. Gossip isn't inherently good or evil—it has its virtues as well as its vices. On the Internet, however, gossip is being reshaped in ways that heighten its negative effects and make its sting more painful and permanent.

In Chapter 4 I explore a related practice of spreading information—shaming. Like gossip, shaming has long served as a common practice to keep people from violating society's rules and norms. Shaming helps maintain order and civility. Yet when transplanted to the Internet, shaming takes on some problematic dimensions.

After examining in Part I the good and bad aspects of spreading personal information over the Internet, I turn in Part II to the question of what ought to be done about the problem. What makes the issues so complex is that there are important values on both sides. Protecting people's privacy sometimes can be achieved only by curtailing other people's free speech. Some commentators and lawmakers are quick to take sides, strongly favoring privacy or free speech. The difficulty is that we often want both. Unlike many conflicts, in which we can readily pick a side, there is no clear winner in the battle between privacy and free speech. Both are essential to our freedom.

In Chapter 5 I discuss how the law can strike a balance between allowing people to express themselves online and preventing them from revealing personal information about others. The difficulty is finding the proper role for the law to play. Too many legal restrictions or lawsuits will chill speech and stifle freedom on the Internet. On the other hand, if the law is held at bay, there will be little to prevent people from injuring others by releasing their secrets to the world. The law must take a middle path, but there's another treacherous pitfall in the road: the law can be slow and costly. In this chapter, I suggest a way for law to address the problems productively yet with moderation.

I turn in Chapter 6 to the tension between privacy and free speech. Freedom of speech is a fundamental value, and protecting it is of paramount importance. Yet, as I argue, privacy often furthers the same ends as free speech. If privacy is sacrificed at the altar of free speech, then some of the very goals justifying free speech might be undermined. Current law, unfortunately, tends to side too frequently with free speech, leaving privacy underprotected. I propose a way to balance privacy and free speech that enables them to coexist without making undue trade-offs.

The focus of Chapter 7 is privacy. One of the challenges we face in today's exposed world is that information is rarely completely hidden. Many of our comings and goings occur in public places, where technology enables them to be more easily recorded. We often share private information with others who might betray us and spread it online. Is it possible to protect privacy in public? Once we've shared information with others, can it still be private? How much control ought we to have over our personal information? In this chapter I explore these questions and propose a new way of understanding privacy, one that is more fitting to the world we live in.

I conclude the book by examining in Chapter 8 what the law can and cannot do. As important as it is to explore law's potential, it is equally important to recognize the law's limitations. The law alone cannot be the cure-all. While the law can take a more active role in preventing people from revealing the secrets of others, it will have great difficulty in stopping people from exposing details about themselves. Although the law might not be the answer in this situation, there are other ways to make headway in addressing the problem. Nevertheless, any solution will be far from perfect, as we are dealing with a social tapestry of immense complexity, and the questions of how to modulate reputation, gossip, shame, privacy, norms, and free speech have confounded us for centuries. These age-old questions, however, are taking on new dimensions in today's digital era, and it is imperative that we grapple with them anew.

Part One Rumor and Reputation in a Digital World

Chapter 2 How the Free

Flow of Information

Liberates and

Constrains Us

The Internet allows information to flow more freely than ever before. We can communicate and share ideas in unprecedented ways. These developments are revolutionizing our self-expression and enhancing our freedom.

But there's a problem. We're heading toward a world where an extensive trail of information fragments about us will be forever preserved on the Internet, displayed instantly in a Google search. We will be forced to live with a detailed record beginning with childhood that will stay with us for life wherever we go, searchable and accessible from anywhere in the world. This data can often be of dubious reliability; it can be false and defamatory; or it can be true but deeply humiliating or discrediting. We may find it increasingly difficult to have a fresh start, a second chance, or a clean slate. We might find it harder to engage in self-exploration if every false step and foolish act is chronicled forever in a permanent record. This record will affect our ability to define our identities, to obtain jobs, to participate in public life, and more. Ironically, the unconstrained flow of information on the Internet might impede our freedom. How and why is this happening? How can the free flow of information make us more free yet less free as well?

Movable type: the fifteenth century

THE BIRTH OF THE BLOG

Movable Type: Then and Now

For centuries, books had to be painstakingly copied by hand, but in the mid-fifteenth century, Johann Gutenberg's printing press revolutionized the distribution of information.[1] The printing press worked through movable type, characters and letters that could be moved into different positions. The impact of this invention was astounding.

In more recent times we have witnessed the development of new forms of media, from the radio to the television, each ushering in profound changes in the way we communicate and receive information. Along with these technological innovations, the media have grown in dramatic fashion. Even with the printing press, printed matter was still for the elites, as most people were illiterate. But as literacy became more common, and as the costs of printed material declined, the print media underwent a dramatic revolution. In the United States before the Civil War, newspapers were scarce. In 1850 about one hundred papers had eight hundred thousand readers. By 1890 nine hundred papers served more than eight million readers—an increase of 900 percent.[2]

Today, the media's size and scope are even more vast. Hundreds of magazines are published on nearly every topic imaginable. We can choose from a smorgasbord of twenty-four-hour television news networks and copious news-

Movable Type: the twenty-first century. "Movable Type" and
the Movable Type logo are trademarks of Six Apart, Ltd.

magazine shows such as *Dateline, Primetime, 20/20, 60 Minutes,* and more. But
only a select few can utilize the mainstream media to express themselves. Ordinary people might be able to get a letter to the editor in the newspaper, but
few can routinely have their thoughts printed in the papers. Most people can't
appear on CNN whenever they have something to say.

On the Internet, anybody can now communicate his or her thoughts to the
entire world. Individuals are taking advantage of this new breathtaking ability
through blogs and other websites where they can express themselves. So we're
back to movable type again, but of a different sort: one of the blogging services today is named Movable Type. We're living in the next media revolution. This time, we are the media.[3]

Blogging Hits Primetime

Blogging is the rage these days. We all can be pundits now, sharing our
thoughts and pictures with a worldwide audience. Bloggers pride themselves
in being different from the mainstream media. Unlike the mainstream media,
blogs are more interactive. Readers of blogs can post comments and have discussions. Debates occur between different blogs. In short, blogs are more akin
to an ongoing conversation than to a mainstream media publication or broadcast. As the professors and popular bloggers Daniel Drezner and Henry Farrell observe: "Blogging as an activity is almost exclusively a part-time, voluntary enterprise. The median income generated by a weblog is zero dollars; the
number of individuals in the United States that earn their living from blog-

ging is less than twenty. Despite these constraints, blogs appear to play an increasingly important role as a forum of public debate, with knock-on consequences for the media and for politics."[4]

Blogs are more egalitarian than the mainstream media. You don't need connections to editorial page editors to get heard. If you have something interesting to say, then you can say it. Many popular blogs are created not by celebrities or professional writers but by everyday people. And bloggers have served as a critical voice to the media, uncovering blunders and omissions in many mainstream media stories.[5] Drezner and Farrell note that "there is strong evidence that media elites—editors, publishers, reporters, and columnists—consume political blogs." Editors at major newspapers say (confess) that they read blogs. Drezner and Farrell explain that the media is paying attention to blogs because bloggers can provide special expertise on certain issues, blogs can be an inspiration for story ideas, and bloggers often get their opinions out faster than the mainstream media pundits.[6]

Blogging 101: How to Become a Blogger in Less than Three Minutes

Do you want to become a blogger? Well, you're in luck. You don't need to apply anywhere. You don't need to pay anything. Nobody can turn you down. All you need to do is go to one of the popular blogging websites, and you can set up an account for free (or at most, a few bucks per month). Some popular blogging websites include Blogger or TypePad. To set up your blog, you merely need to choose a name for it and a template for its look and style. In less than three minutes, you'll become a blogger, and with the click of a mouse, you can broadcast your thoughts live to the entire planet.

I still can't contain my amazement about these developments. Never before in history have ordinary people been able to reach out and communicate to so many around the globe. Of course, just because you now have the power to reach a worldwide audience doesn't mean that anybody will be reading. You need to attract some attention. To do that, you must have something interesting to say so others start blogging about it.

Each entry you write in your blog is called a "post." To post on your blog, you log in and write whatever you want. You can add pictures too. You then hit the publish button, and in a magic instant, your thoughts travel from your computer to the vast expanses of cyberspace. Each post is displayed chronologically on the website, with the most recent post appearing first.

You also can permit readers to add comments to your post. If you allow

Google's Blogger.com, which enables anyone to create a blog for free

comments, readers' reactions to your post will appear below your text. A blog post can inspire some fascinating discussions. I really enjoy reading the comments to my posts and hearing people's responses. It is a form of instant feedback I rarely receive when I publish an article.

Bloggers, Bloggers Everywhere

It seems as though everybody's blogging these days. The person you're dating might be blogging a running commentary about your relationship. Your spouse might have a blog. Your employees might have one too—or your boss. Your child might have a blog. Maybe even your dog. According to one estimate, about 20 percent of teens with Internet access have blogs.[7]

The entire universe of blogs is collectively referred to as the blogosphere. The blogosphere is big. There were about 50 blogs in 1999, a few thousand in 2000, more than 10 million in 2004, and more than 30 million in 2005.[8] By the end of July 2006 there were approximately 50 million blogs.[9] According to Technorati, a website that tracks blogs, each day brings 175,000 new blogs and 1.6 million new blog posts.[10]

Blogs in All Sizes, Shapes, and Colors

Blogs range from the profound to the frivolous and cover nearly every topic, from music to celebrities to politics to sex to health to law. Among the more colorful blogs, The Daily Rotten covers "news you cannot possibly use."[11]

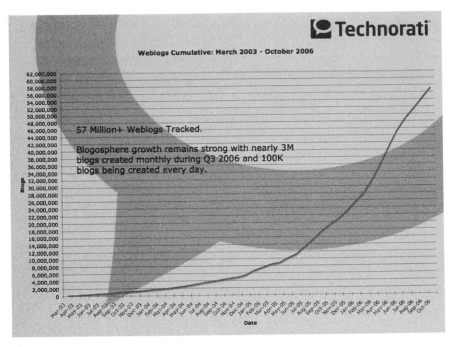

This chart from Technorati illustrates the increase in blog postings

Wonkette dishes on inside-the-beltway gossip.[12] Gawker reports celebrity gossip from Manhattan.[13] Overheard in New York supplies snippets of dialogue that bloggers overhear during the day.[14] The Superficial posts paparazzi photos of celebrities, including shots of celebrities caught in the nude.[15] And then there are blogs that are downright bizarre. One blog has a section called "Steve, Don't Eat It," in which a blogger discusses his experiences trying such unusual foods as pickled pork rinds, Beggin' Strips for dogs, breast milk, and fermented soybeans.[16] There's a blog with videos of people crying while eating.[17] If these blogs are too odd for you, there's a blog called The Dullest Blog in the World with posts entitled "scratching my knee," "looking at a wall," "moving an item from one place to another," and "turning off a light."[18]

Beyond topical blogs, many keep blogs about the various events in their lives. A high-priced London call girl created a blog called Belle de Jour chronicling her life. She parlayed it into a book deal, and her blog will be made into a television drama.[19] People are starting blogs about coping with various illnesses, such as HIV and cancer.[20] Soldiers in Iraq are blogging about their experiences. A blog called DotMoms features the experiences of motherhood by a group of women.[21] At least one blogger chronicles his entire sexual history, with details about his more than two dozen sexual partners.[22] Other bloggers write about their daily activities and whatever thoughts are buzzing in their brains at the moment.

After Hurricane Katrina devastated New Orleans and other Gulf Coast cities, blogs enabled survivors to post information about lost family members so that people could reconnect and find loved ones.[23] Blogs have even helped solve crimes. In one chilling instance, a blogger helped catch his own murderer. In a May 2005 post written just minutes before he was killed, the blogger wrote:

> Anyway today has been weird, at 3 some guy ringed the bell. I went down and recognized it was my sister's former boyfriend. He told me he wants to get his fishing poles back. I told him to wait downstair [sic] while I get them for him. While I was searching them, he is already in the house. He is still here right now, smoking, walking all around the house with his shoes on which btw I just washed the floor 2 days ago! Hopefully he will leave soon.[24]

The man didn't leave soon; instead, he stabbed the blogger and his sister repeatedly with a butcher knife. The police located the murderer by reading one victim's final blog post.[25]

Blogs are blossoming across the Internet. They are increasingly being woven into the fabric of society, and they are starting to play a profound role in our lives.

Journalists or Diarists?

By enabling virtually anybody with a computer to disclose information to world, the Internet is dissolving the boundaries between professional journalists and amateurs. Glenn Reynolds, a law professor and author of the very popular blog Instapundit, extols the virtues of the amateur journalist in his book, *An Army of Davids*. With the growth of blogs, he observes, "power once concentrated in the hands of a professional few has been redistributed into the hands of the amateur many." Known as The Blogfather because he created one of the first blogs, Reynolds argues that "technology has made it possible for individuals to become not merely pamphleteers, but vital sources of news and opinion that rival large metropolitan publishers in audience and influence." For Reynolds, these developments are marvelous: "I don't think that weblogs and flash media will replace Big Media any time soon. But I keep seeing evidence that they're doing a better and better job of supplementing, and challenging, Big Media coverage. I think that's a wonderful thing, and it's one reason why I'm such an evangelist for the spread of enabling technologies like Web video and cheap digital cameras."

"The end result of the blog revolution," Reynolds continues, "is to create what blogger Jim Teacher calls 'we-dia.' News and reporting used to be something 'they' did. Now it's something that we all do."[26] Indeed, some bloggers even received media credentials to report on the 2004 Democratic national convention.[27] U.S. senators are beginning to hold press conferences with bloggers.[28] Reynolds views blogging as a development that enhances the freedom of the little guy: "We're likely to see an army of Davids taking the place of those slow, shuffling Goliaths."[29]

But who's David? Glenn's vision of the blogger is rather romantic. The average blogger, however, isn't a journalist. According to one estimate, more than 50 percent of blogs are written by children and teenagers under age nineteen.[30] The most common blogger is "a teenage girl who uses the medium primarily to communicate with five to ten friends."[31] Many blogs are more akin to diaries than news articles, op-ed columns, or scholarship. According to one survey, bloggers most commonly write about their personal experiences (37 percent), while only 11 percent blog about politics.[32] In other words, David is more of a diarist than a journalist. And that's why there's a problem. In lieu of diaries, people are blogging. And bloggers are getting younger and younger. One news article reports that even seven-year-old children now have blogs.[33] As people chronicle the minutia of their daily lives from childhood onward in blog entries, online conversations, photographs, and videos, they are forever altering their futures—and those of their friends, relatives, and others.

SOCIAL NETWORK WEBSITES

In addition to blogs, social network websites are emerging as a way people are sharing personal information online. These websites allow users to post a profile of themselves and link to the profiles of friends. The first social network websites emerged in the mid-1990s. Today there are more than two hundred social network websites.[34] Popular sites include MySpace, Facebook, Xanga, LiveJournal, and Friendster.

" WELL, YES, WE COULD READ YOUR BLOG.... OR YOU COULD JUST
TELL US ABOUT YOUR SCHOOL DAY. "

Cartoon by Jim Borgman, © King Features Syndicate, reprinted with permission

Social network websites are designed around the concept of social networks. A social network is a web of connections, such as a group of people
who associate together.[35] Although we often cluster together in groups, our
social circles are not isolated. Some of the people we know are likely to be
friendly with people in a different social circle. We're all connected in some
way to each other. If I don't know you personally, there's still a good chance
that at least one of my friends knows one of your friends.

In 1967 a psychologist named Stanley Milgram carried out a fascinating experiment to determine just how connected two strangers might be to each
other. He selected a target person in Boston and gave letters to some randomly
selected people in Nebraska. The letters were to go to the target in Boston, but
each person could forward the letter only to people he or she knew personally.
Surprisingly, it only took an average of six steps for the letter to get from the
randomly selected recipients to the target person in Boston.[36]

This phenomenon has been described with the phrase "six degrees of separation," which originated in a play by John Guare in 1990. A character in the
play observes: "Everybody on this planet is separated by only six other people.
Six degrees of separation. Between us and everybody else on the planet. The

president of the United States. A gondolier in Venice. . . . It's not just the big names. It's anyone. A native in a rain forest. A Tierra del Fuegan. An Eskimo. I am bound to everyone on this planet by a trail of six people."[37]

Social network sites attempt to embody these concepts. Through them, networks of friends and acquaintances can interlink their profiles, share personal information, and communicate with each other. MySpace, currently the most popular social network website, was created in 2003. MySpace profiles can contain a ton of data, including phone numbers, email addresses, hobbies, religion, sexual orientation, political views, favorite television shows, and more. People can post photos and videos on their profiles. Each user has space for a blog, including a section where friends post comments. People often use their real names for their MySpace profiles.

To create a profile, a user must claim to be fourteen years of age or older. The profiles of users under age sixteen are private, but those older than sixteen can make their profiles available to the public. MySpace skyrocketed in popularity in part because it gave users a wide range of choices about how to develop their profiles. People create elaborate designs for their pages, decorating them with graphics and giving each a distinctive look and style. As one student said: "MySpace gives you more freedom to express yourself."[38]

In just a few short years, MySpace has expanded exponentially. By August 2006 MySpace had surpassed 100 million profiles.[39] It is growing by 230,000 new members each day.[40] With its viral growth and astounding size, MySpace was sold to media titan Rupert Murdock in 2005 for about $580 million.[41]

The social network component to MySpace involves the way people can link their profiles to those of their friends. There is a place on a person's profile called "Friend Space," which contains links to the profiles of a person's "friends" and often a picture of each friend. At the top of the Friend Space section is a tally of the total number of friends in the person's network. A "friend" on a social network site is not necessarily a close friend, as many people try to inflate the number of their friends by adding total strangers to the list.[42]

In realspace social networks, people have different kinds of ties with others. "Strong ties" are close connections (very close friends and relatives); "weak ties" are looser connections (acquaintances and others with whom people might have marginal contact). But according to the computer scientist Ralph Gross and the economist Alessandro Acquisti, social network websites "often reduce these nuanced connections to simplistic binary relations."[43] Few social network sites allow users to distinguish between close friends and mere acquaintances.[44]

The researchers Judith Donath and danah boyd question the quality of one's ties in social network sites; they argue that "the number of strong ties an individual can maintain may not be greatly increased by communication technology . . . [but] the number of weak ties one can form and maintain may be able to increase substantially."[45] As Gross and Acquisti note, people's online social networks may be only an "imaginary" community because "thousands of users may be classified as friends of friends of an individual and become able to access her personal information, while, at the same time, the threshold to qualify as a friend on somebody's network is low."[46] Although MySpace allows users to keep their profile private or share it only with a few friends, most have their profile set to be fully accessible to the public. Profiles also appear in Google search results.

Another popular social network site is Facebook, used primarily by high school and college students. Facebook was created in 2004 by Mark Zuckerberg, a Harvard University student, and its popularity fueled phenomenal growth. Just a few weeks after Facebook was launched, more than half the undergraduates at Harvard had created an account. Facebook soon began allowing students at other schools to sign up, and by the end of 2004 more than a million students had accounts.[47] Facebook continued to expand in 2005, adding thousands of colleges from around the world and more than twenty-five thousand high schools. By the end of 2005 it had more than eleven million accounts.[48] About twenty thousand new Facebook accounts are being created each day. In one study, more than 80 percent of college freshman signed up for Facebook accounts before the first day of school.[49] At many schools where Facebook is available, almost every student has an account.[50]

As on MySpace, Facebook users create profiles with personal information. According to one study of Facebook users at a particular school, the profiles "provide an astonishing amount of information: 90.8 percent of profiles contain an image, 87.8 percent of users reveal their birth date, 39.9 percent list a phone number . . . and 50.8 percent list their current residence."[51] Moreover, "Facebook profiles tend to be fully identified with each participant's first and last names."[52] Facebook profiles have a feature called "Photo Albums," where users can post photos. Friends can post photos on each other's profiles. According to a study of users at one university, over the course of eight weeks, the total number of pictures grew from about ten thousand to eighty thousand, averaging more than twenty pictures per person.[53]

Social network websites are fast becoming a worldwide phenomenon. The social network website Orkut, for example, is immensely popular in Brazil. Named after its creator, the Google software engineer Orkut Büyükkökten, Orkut attracted more than eleven million Brazilian users as of mid-2006.[54] Although Orkut is run by Google in the United States, the majority of its users are in Brazil. To become a member of Orkut, a person originally had to be invited by an existing member, but Orkut later dropped the invitation requirement.[55] Orkut states that its "mission" is to "help you create a closer, more intimate network of friends" and "put you on a path to social bliss."[56] Orkut allows users to form various "communities"—special forums for users with similar interests—and it lets people rank their friends based on familiarity, trustworthiness, coolness, and sexiness. Orkut is also very popular in India, where about four million people have accounts, constituting more than 11 percent of Internet users in the country.[57] Social networking is taking off in India, which has a rapidly growing number of people online and many widely used sites, such as Fropper, Jhoom, Minglebox, and more.[58] In Canada the networking sites Piczo and Nexopia are widely used.[59] Launched in Spain, the site Adoos has been spreading quickly in South America.[60]

In Europe, Passado is one of the more popular sites, providing users with "ways to interact with one another such as blogging, photosharing, forums and broadcasts." Based in London, Passado has become widely used in Germany, Spain, and Italy, where it has more than five million members.[61] In the United Kingdom, the social network website Bebo has become very trendy. As of late 2006 it had more than twenty-two million users.[62] And in 2006, along with MySpace, Bebo was one of the most frequently searched words in Google.[63]

In Asia several social network websites are hugely popular. In Japan, Mixi (meaning "I mix") has attracted 6.5 million member as of late 2006, making it one of the most visited websites in the country.[64] In China the popular sites are Mop and Cuspace.[65] In South Korea, Cyworld reigns supreme, with an astonishing 92 percent of people in their twenties having an account, as well as 30 percent of the total population.[66] Cyworld encourages its users to place their personal information online: "Upload your photos, drawings and images—we give you unlimited storage so you can save and display as many as you want."[67] Cyworld also has websites in China, Japan, and Taiwan. When

Cyworld became available in China, one million people joined within six months.[68] By the end of 2006 Cyworld had about nineteen million Korean accounts and three million Chinese accounts.[69] Frequent users of Cyworld are referred to as "Cyholics."[70]

In short, there are social network sites in all shapes and sizes, and they are sprouting up around the globe. There are social network sites for Dogs (Dogster) as well as for Cats (Catster).[71] And not to be left out of the fun, even hamsters have their own social network website.[72]

INFORMATION EVERYWHERE

With blogs and social network sites, personal information is being posted online at a staggering rate. Given the ease at which information can be recorded and spread, there will be more instances when information we want to keep on a short leash will escape from our control. There are a number of well-known instances where people have had the misfortune of sending an email to the wrong people. One such email gained Internet infamy in 2003. A law student was working for a powerful New York law firm as a summer associate, a rather cushy job where firms try to recruit future attorneys by indulging them with expensive food and drink. One afternoon, after a nice long lunch, the student fired off this email to his friend:

> I'm busy doing jack shit. Went to a nice 2hr sushi lunch today at Sushi Zen. Nice place. Spent the rest of the day typing emails and bullshitting with people. Unfortunately, I actually have work to do—I'm on some corp finance deal, under the global head of corp finance, which means I should really peruse these materials and not be a fuckup. . . .
> So yeah, Corporate Love hasn't worn off yet. . . . But just give me time.

At the bottom was his name and his contact information. Another email followed a few hours later:

> An apology
> I am writing you in regard to an e-mail you received from me earlier today.
> As I am aware that you opened the message, you probably saw that it was a personal communication that was inadvertently forwarded to the underwriting mailing list. Before it was retracted, it was received by approximately 40 people inside the Firm, about half of whom are partners.
> I am thoroughly and utterly ashamed and embarrassed not only by my behavior, but by the implicit reflection such behavior could have on the Firm.

The email goes on for several more painful paragraphs. This incident demonstrates how easy it is for private communications to find their way into the wrong inboxes. But if this wasn't enough embarrassment, the email and the apology soon became the toast of the Internet. They were reproduced in all their glory, with the person's full name included, on numerous websites. The incident became so well known that the *New Yorker* ran a story about it.[73] If you run a Google search on the person's name, you can still pull up the emails in an instant.

Of course, it is easy to say that the student should have been more careful. But we're accustomed to living at a hyper pace these days, launching emails at breakneck speed. Leaks and miscues are bound to happen. Sometimes information winds up online because we put it there intentionally; sometimes it is accidental; and other times, it is put there without our knowledge and consent.

REPUTATION

The proliferation of personal data on the Internet can have significant effects on people's reputations. As the sociologist Steven Nock defines it, a "reputation" is "a shared, or collective, perception about a person."[74] Our reputations are forged when people make judgments based upon the mosaic of information available about us.

Our reputation is one of our most cherished assets. As the Book of Proverbs states: "A good name is rather to be chosen than great riches."[75] In William Shakespeare's *Othello,* Cassio, whose reputation is ruined by the evil plotting of Iago, laments: "Reputation, reputation, reputation! O, I have lost my reputation! I have lost the immortal part of my self and what remains is bestial."[76] John Proctor, in Arthur Miller's play *The Crucible,* refuses to sign a false confession that he engaged in witchcraft, opting instead to be hanged. Similar to Cassio's lament in *Othello,* Proctor declares: "Because it is my name! Because I cannot have another in my life! Because I lie and sign myself to lies! Because I am not worth the dust on the feet of them that hang! How may I live without my name? I have given you my soul; leave me my name!"[77] Proctor would rather perish than sacrifice his reputation. Proctor recognizes that he cannot function within the community without his good name.

Our reputation is an essential component to our freedom, for without the good opinion of our community, our freedom can become empty. "The desire of the esteem of others," wrote President John Adams, "is as real a want of nature as hunger."[78] The sociologist C. F. Cooley famously pointed out that we form our own selfhood based on how we think others perceive us. Cooley's theory, which he called the "looking glass self," has become widely accepted by social psychologists.[79] Our reputation can be a key dimension of our self, something that affects the very core of our identity. Beyond its internal influence on our self-conception, our reputation affects our ability to engage in basic activities in society. We depend upon others to engage in transactions with us, to employ us, to befriend us, and to listen to us. Without the cooperation of others in society, we often are unable to do what we want to do. Without the respect of others, our actions and accomplishments can lose their purpose and meaning. Without the appropriate reputation, our speech, though free, may fall on deaf ears. Our freedom, in short, depends in part upon how others in society judge us.

Reputation and Accountability

Although we want some degree of control over our own reputation, we also want to know the reputation of others. While privacy gives people greater control over their reputations, it also "makes it difficult to know others' reputations."[80] We have a lot at stake in our relationships with others, and we are vulnerable to great loss if we are let down or betrayed. In many circumstances, we look to people's reputation to decide whether to trust them. As the sociologist Francis Fukuyama defines it, "Trust is the expectation that arises within a community of regular, honest, and cooperative behavior, based on commonly shared norms, on the part of members of that community."[81] Nock observes: "Trust and the ability to take others at their word are basic ingredients in social order. If we never knew who to trust, could never be sure that what we were told was true, or that promises made would be promises kept, there would be little to bind us together or make groups cohesive."[82]

The economist Avner Greif provides a fascinating account of reputation and trust when he discusses the Maghribi traders, a group of Jewish merchants who bartered along the Mediterranean during the eleventh century.[83] To carry out their business, the Maghribi traders depended upon agents to help store, transfer, and sell goods. There was a constant danger, however, of agents embezzling and cheating. Most relationships between agents and traders weren't based on contracts, and the law played virtually no role in regulating their relationships. Nevertheless, the Maghribi traders managed to ensure that agents rarely cheated. The Maghribi simply established a rule that they would never employ an agent who had cheated. A dishonest agent could not move to another trader after cheating a Maghribi trader because information about the agent's untrustworthiness would readily be shared. The Maghribi traders thus used gossip to keep the agents honest. Agents depended upon having a good reputation in order to stay employed, and they knew that if they cheated, they would be held accountable.

Thus, beyond allowing individuals to guard against dealing with dishonest people, reputation also functions to preserve social control. By ensuring that people are accountable for their actions, reputation gives people a strong incentive to conform to social norms and to avoid breaching people's trust.

From the Small Village to the Global Village

In earlier times, people lived in small villages, and they had firsthand knowledge of one another. All villagers were well known, people's pasts were common knowledge, little was private, gossip spread across the village quickly, and social norms were strongly enforced through shame. People could readily assess one another's reputations.

Today we live in a vast and impersonal society. People are highly mobile. Urbanization and population growth have made communities larger and more diffuse. The sociologist Robert Putnam notes that civic life has been deteriorating—we're increasingly "bowling alone."[84] People have gradually been withdrawing from involvement in community affairs. In the urban jungle, we are lost amid a sea of unfamiliar faces. We often don't even know many of the people who live on our block, let alone in our building—or even next door. Studies have pointed out a breakdown in social norms and an increase in rudeness and uncivil behavior. In a 2005 poll, for example, about 70 percent of respondents believed that people are more impolite than a generation ago.[85] Trust is declining.[86] Modern life has made various social ties more diffuse; we interact with many strangers and often lack adequate information to assess their reputations.[87]

Despite these transformations, we have nevertheless found a way to evaluate reputation in contemporary society—by assembling fragments of personal data. Credit reporting agencies, for example, provide a standardized way to assess our financial reputations. They provide reports to our creditors with an extensive compilation of information about our financial dealings, assets, and transactions. Credit reporting agencies and other companies also provide heaps of data about individuals for employer background checks. As Nock observes, these new reputations "do not depend on a particular locale or group. They follow us as we move and they are accessible when they are needed. They can be altered, or created, in a matter of minutes."[88]

At the dawn of the computer age, Marshall McLuhan predicted that new electronic media would bring the world closer together into a "global village."[89] The Internet is the fulfillment of his prophecy. People scattered across the globe can now all congregate together in cyberspace to share ideas and information. Ironically, the global village leads us toward a future that revives part of the past—life in the small village of several centuries ago. With the prevalence of cell phone cameras, people can no longer engage in social infractions without risking being caught in the act. No longer can people hide in obscurity and escape accountability for their actions. People can readily document and record each other's norm violations, and they can then post them online.

The global village not only revives features of the small village but also amplifies and alters them in profound ways. The global village is worldwide and it encompasses millions of people. The people of the global village have weak rather than strong ties; they are often known not for their whole selves but for various information fragments others hastily consume.

In the past, oral gossip could tarnish a reputation, but it would fade from memories over time. People could move elsewhere and start anew. The printed word, however, was different. As Judge Benjamin Cardozo wrote in 1931: "What gives the sting to writing is its permanence in form. The spoken word dissolves, but the written one abides and perpetuates the scandal."[90] In the past, people could even escape printed words because most publications would get buried away in the dusty corners of libraries. The information would be hard to retrieve, and a sleuth would have to devote a lot of time to dig it up. The Internet, however, makes gossip a permanent reputational stain, one that never fades. It is available around the world, and with Google it can be readily found in less than a second.

Why Should We Be Able to Control Our Reputations?

There's a paradox at the heart of reputation—despite the fact we talk about reputation as earned and the product of our behavior and character, it is something given to us by others in the community. Reputation is a core component of our identity—it reflects who we are and shapes how we interact with others—yet it is not solely our own creation. As one person in the nineteenth century put it: "A man's character is what he is; a man's reputation is what other people may imagine him to be."[91] Our reputation depends upon how other people judge and evaluate us, and this puts us at the mercy of others. Our good reputation can quickly be lost, with deleterious consequences to our friendships, family, jobs, and financial well-being. We must all cope with the fragility of reputation, the delicate porcelain vessel that carries our ability to function in society.

Since reputation plays such a dramatic role in our lives, we naturally desire to have some control over it. As the U.S. Supreme Court has noted: "Society has a pervasive and strong interest in preventing and redressing attacks upon reputation."[92] The law, in fact, allows people to protect their reputations from being sullied by falsehoods. But why? Since reputation is bestowed upon us by others in society and consists of what others think about us, why should we have a right to control it at all?

Under one theory of reputation, the law professor Robert Post observes, it is a form of property. People earn the esteem of others by "the fruit of personal exertion."[93] Indeed, people work hard at building a reputation in society; and it can often be among a person's most valuable assets. One reason to protect reputation, then, is to preserve the years of effort people put into developing it. Another theory of reputation, Post notes, is that we protect it in the name of human dignity.[94] As Post explains, the "dignity that defamation law protects is thus respect (and self-respect) that arises from full membership in society."[95] We protect people from having their reputation unjustly ruined because we respect their dignity.

Another reason to protect reputation is that the stakes are so high. In the past, a false rumor could prove deadly. Between the fourteenth and seventeenth centuries, more than five hundred thousand people were burned in Europe for witchcraft, more than 90 percent of them women.[96] In America the witch trials in Salem, Massachusetts, in 1692 were fueled by rumors and falsehoods. Today reputation still plays an enormous role in our lives, even if not for life-or-death stakes. Our reputation matters quite a lot to us, but it also matters a lot to others in society, who use it to determine whether to trust us. Wrongful and undeserved polluting of a person's reputation not only has devastating consequences for that person, but it also prevents others from accurately judging that person.

A person's reputation is often far from accurate. "Reputation is an idle and false imposition," the villain Iago asserts in Shakespeare's *Othello*, "oft got without merit and lost without deserving."[97] Indeed, Iago deviously destroys people's reputations, and he recognizes how fragile, manipulable, and inaccurate reputation can be. Good people can have bad reputations and bad people can have good reputations.

When an individual has a better reputation than deserved, it might be the result of essential facts being concealed from the calculus. We're constantly putting on a show for others, trying to hide our warts and present ourselves at our best. Judge Richard Posner contends that privacy allows people to "conceal information about themselves that others might use to their disadvantage."[98] Similarly, the legal scholar Richard Epstein contends that "the plea for privacy is often a plea for the right to misrepresent one's self to the rest of the world."[99] Is there a justification for allowing people to conceal information about themselves that will lower their reputations? It is one thing to ensure that the information factored into the assessment of a person's reputation is truthful; it is quite another to allow people to hide true information that could sully their reputations. Does privacy enable people to be seen in a better light than they deserve? Does privacy undermine our ability to know people for their true selves? We might be entitled to have falsehoods about us cleansed away, but are we entitled to a reputation free from the stain of truths? I will explore these questions in the next chapter.

We can't stop others from judging us, and ultimately, we have only a limited degree of control over our reputations. Once information about us finds its way into the minds of others, we can't control what they think about it. Our ability to exercise control consists of being able to limit the circulation of information about us. The key question is how much control we ought to have over the spread of information about us. We don't want to provide too much control, as this will allow people to trick us into trusting them when they don't deserve it. Too much control will also stifle free speech, as it will prevent others from speaking about us. Hence the conflict: we want information to flow openly, for this is essential to a free society, yet we also want to have some control over the information that circulates about us, for this is essential to our freedom as well.

DUBIOUS DATA

Although we're getting a lot more good information via the Internet, we're also getting a lot more bad information. On the Internet, we constantly live in a twilight between fact and fiction. We're often exposed to information that we can't entirely trust. In a world where it is difficult to separate the true from the false, rumor and defamation can readily spread, and the Internet can be used as a powerful tool to launch malicious attacks on people and ideas. With modern computer software, anybody can readily create convincing counterfeit images and doctor photographs. Anybody can dexterously concoct fake documents. It is now easier than ever to fabricate and forge.

With the Internet, false information can spread much more rapidly. In 1996 a false rumor about the clothing designer Tommy Hilfiger erupted on the Internet. According to the rumor, Hilfiger said: "If I had known that African-Americans, Hispanics, and Asians would buy my clothes, I would not have made them so nice." The rumor also had Hilfiger confirming on the Oprah Winfrey show that he had made the statement, leading Winfrey to demand that he leave. The rumor sent Hilfiger's company into a tailspin. But Hilfiger hadn't even appeared on *Oprah,* nor had he made the offensive remarks. Winfrey announced on her show that the rumor "is not true because it never happened. Tommy Hilfiger never appeared on this show. Read my lips, Tommy Hilfiger has never appeared on this show. All of the people who claim that they saw it, they heard it—it never happened. I've never even met Tommy Hilfiger."[100]

Katie, an eighteen-year-old who lived in a small town about two hours from Denver, Colorado, learned firsthand the power of false rumors on the Internet. An attractive blonde, Katie was an honor student and prom queen. Like almost everyone else in town, she was shocked when on July 4, 2003, Kobe Bryant was accused of raping a nineteen-year old woman from the same small community. The identity of Bryant's accuser was kept confidential. The mainstream media for the most part kept her identity secret because of a common rule of journalistic ethics not to reveal the identities of sexual assault victims. But immediately, speculation as to her identity erupted on the Internet. Then Katie became ensnared in the story.

One website named Katie as Bryant's victim. The report, however, was false. Initially, Katie thought it was simply a harmless mix-up. Katie and the victim weren't far apart in age; they went to the same high school; and they lived in the same small town. But Katie didn't realize how fast information moves on the Internet. Within a short time, the information migrated to numerous websites and chatrooms. Her picture was posted around the Internet, emblazoned on one page with the caption "WHORE ALERT." Some websites manipulated images to depict her engaging in sex with Bryant. The Internet cackled with vile and graphic comments about her. Katie said: "It didn't really hit me that hard, just because it was one site. . . . So I thought, you know, we live in the same town so maybe people just mix up the girls or whatever. But, after a couple of days it wasn't just on one site anymore."[101]

Katie was devastated by the frenzy about her on the Internet. "I was really upset by the whole situation," she lamented.[102] "It's hard knowing that when people think about Kobe's accuser, I'm the face that everyone think[s] of," she remarked in another interview. "I feel violated. I want it to be known that these pictures aren't of the right girl, and I want them removed." Katie's mother was also deeply affected: "I was furious. I'm a helpless mother and my daughter is smeared all over the Internet." Katie's mother contacted many websites asking them to remove Katie's name and photos. Some did, but others didn't. One website owner replied: "In this day [and] age, there is no privacy."[103]

"The fragments of people's lives that emerge on the Internet are somewhat haphazard," one journalist aptly observed. "They can be incomplete, out of context, misleading or simply wrong."[104] In the past, rumors and falsehoods would readily spread around the small village, but the Internet lacks the village's corrective of familiarity. In the small village, people had a long history together and knew the whole story about an individual. But now someone reading an online report about some faraway stranger rarely knows the whole story—the reader has only fragments of information, and when little is invested in a personal relationship, even information that is incomplete and of dubious veracity might be enough to precipitate ridicule, shunning, and reproach.

The rapid information-spreading power of the Internet can be a virtue too. Judge Richard Posner points out: "The blogosphere as a whole has a better error-correction machinery than the conventional media do. The rapidity with which vast masses of information are pooled and sifted leaves the conventional media in the dust. Not only are there millions of blogs, and thousands of bloggers who specialize, but, what is more, readers post comments that augment the blogs, and the information in those comments, as in the blogs themselves, zips around blogland at the speed of electronic transmission."[105]

Posner is certainly right—information does speed around the Internet at a breakneck pace. Errors can get corrected quickly. The best thing to do when faced with a malicious rumor is to spread correct information as rapidly as possible.

This works well when we clearly know the truth about something or someone. But what about when we don't? And what happens when facts are posted online that while true, are also of a private nature? With false information, the record can eventually be set straight. But with true information, there's no way to put the secret back in the bag.

THE SOBERING CONSEQUENCES

Combine all the information available about people on the Internet—some of it true, some of it false—with our insatiable curiosity and desire to glean information about others, and some troubling implications emerge. Increasingly, information fragments about people on the Internet are used to make judgments about them.

Employers are looking at social network site profiles of prospective employees.[106] Microsoft officials admit to trolling the Internet for anything they can find out about people they are considering for positions.[107] After a promising interview with a college student for a summer internship position, a company president checked the student's Facebook profile. The student listed his interests as "smokin' blunts" and having a lot of sex. He didn't get the job.[108] Facebook profiles are more restricted than MySpace profiles; access is limited to students. But some employers have kept their accounts after graduating, and other employers have students who work for them check the profiles of prospective employees.[109] Some big corporations are using software to systematically monitor employee blogs.[110]

One young woman was quite surprised when her employer began talking to her about her Friendster profile.[111] But people might never find out if an employer looked at information about them on the Internet. Many employers won't ask a person in a job interview about the story behind his or her half-naked photos on the Internet. Indeed, it can be quite awkward to confront people about the weird things you find out about them online. People just don't get the job or don't even get called in for an interview. The information about a person on the Internet can thus be a secret job killer.

A professor writing under the pseudonym Ivan Tribble notes that before hiring new professors, administrators at his college google each candidate and scrutinize the results: "Our blogger applicants came off reasonably well at the initial interview, but once we hung up the phone and called up their blogs, we got to know 'the real them'—better than we wanted, enough to conclude we didn't want to know more." Our "quirks," Tribble writes, are best kept hidden, "not laid out in exquisite detail for all the world to read."[112]

To make matters worse, the information that emerges in a Google search of a person's name might not all relate to that person—it could pertain to other people with the same name. Or it could be spoofed. In one case, students created a fake MySpace profile under their principal's name with pornographic photos and offensive comments.[113]

Dooced

One blogger, Heather Armstrong, achieved fame for being fired from her job because of her blog, Dooce.com. Her firing became so well known throughout the blogosphere that the term *dooced* was coined to describe losing one's job because of one's online postings. Today her blog is one of the most popular on the Internet, receiving fifty-five thousand visitors per day.[114] She has blogged about her family, her pregnancy, her bouts with severe constipation, and her postpartum depression.[115] But it was blogging about her work experiences which ultimately got her fired. Among other things, she wrote:

> I hate that one of the 10 vice-presidents in this 30-person company wasn't born with an "indoor" voice but with a shrill, monotone, speaking-over-a-passing-F16 outdoor voice. And he loves to hear himself speak, even if just to himself. . . . Lately, he's been an authority on patently grotesque facial hair patterns. . . .
>
> I hate that the Enabling Producer enables nothing but my never-ending agony, that she never knows what she wants and so gives directions as vague as, "Mock up something that, you know, says something," without even telling me what I'm supposed to say something about.[116]

An anonymous person emailed her supervisors about her blog, and they weren't pleased. As Heather wrote about her firing: "Essentially, they explained, they didn't like what I had expressed on my website. I got fired because of dooce.com." Heather tried to defend herself by pointing out she had never mentioned anybody or the company by name, but to no avail. In the end, however, she couldn't quarrel with her firing: "I made my bed; I'll lie in it, to quote the inimitable Courtney Love. I understood the risk when I wrote certain things about certain figures that key members of my company might discover my website and pooh-pooh my endeavors."[117]

But not everybody knows the risks of exposing themselves online. Many individuals are teenagers and college students, who may not consider the consequences. Moreover, many people are not simply self-disclosing in their blogs. Heather's blog contained information about her coworkers, and much of the information people post online involves not just themselves but their friends, teachers, parents, employers, and others. One college professor discovered to her dismay that a student filmed her class and posted it on YouTube, a popular website where people can upload videos and others can watch them for free.[118] In 2006 Google purchased YouTube for $1.65 billion.[119] Anybody can post videos of anybody else on YouTube. People can post pictures of you or write about you in their blogs. Even if you aren't exhibiting your private life online, it may still wind up being exposed by somebody else.

Doing a Background Check on My Admirer

Shortly after my book *The Digital Person* came out in 2004, I received an email from a reader who expressed great admiration for it. The reader, whom I'll call John Doe, said that he was sending copies to a few of his high-powered friends, one of whom was a U.S. senator. Needless to say, I was quite flattered. His email signature indicated he was the "spokesman" for a large data security company.

I emailed him back and thanked him for the praise. We had a number of friendly email exchanges, and he wanted to chat with me on the telephone about various privacy issues. It was at this point that I became interested in finding about more about him and his company. His email signature didn't include a website for his company, so I did a search for it online. I couldn't find an official website for his company. I thought this was quite odd, since most major companies have a website. I then did a search under John Doe's name. Google pulled up some disturbing posts about John in an online discussion group. One member of the group indicated that John had been removed from the discussion list. Among the information I found were these remarks:

> One aspect of the John Doe phenomenon is that I have never, ever seen anything—not a webpage, not a news report, not a public filing, not a friend, no nothing—that suggests anyone's seen anything from John Doe or Doe's company except for email and (sometimes) a voice on the telephone.

In another discussion thread, I found these comments:

> This is just a reminder that Doe's company does not exist, that John Doe is not to be taken seriously, and that he speaks only for himself and not for a group of over 100,000 people. Frankly it is sad, and I wish he would get help. Regular readers will ignore his inane ramblings, but new readers may be tricked into replying. Among the "nutsy-cukoo" things he has said in the last few weeks are: That he met personally with President George Bush in Waco Texas and that he is having secret email conversations with government officials. Here is the rest of the FAQ:
> Who is John Doe? John Doe has claimed in postings to various lists:

—to be the Chief Executive Officer and the Co-Founder of [a] 4.8 billion dollar privately-held employee-owned company. . . .

—to be an ex-IBM Fellow,

—to have three degrees, MBA, Masters in Computer Science and Engineering, and Law

—to have served as a judge for 7 years

—to be the author of two books and is working on a third. . . .

—to have been acting squadron commander of the Marine combat F4 squadron VMF214 (Black Sheep) at Tan Son Nhut during the Viet Nam war. . . .

—Retired Colonel, United States Marine Corps—to own 8% of eBay[120]

The comments went on and on. In some of the material I found on John Doe, there were replies by John. Here's one:

Can you prove any of these statements? I am quite sure you cannot. Please refrain form making false statements in the future.

So here I was, doing a makeshift background check on a person. Online, it's often hard to find out if people are who they say they are. There are many people I know only through email. I read blog posts by pseudonymous authors and reply to comments to my own posts that are by anonymous individuals. A lot of my interactions today are with people I've never seen or heard or met. Having information about others helps us establish trust, especially online, where we often don't meet people in person.

But can we trust the information about people that we find on the Internet? Although John seemed suspicious, the comments about him also seemed to lack credibility. Who goes through all the trouble to discredit a person in a discussion group? Was the poster of these comments about John Doe credible himself? I had to make a judgment, and I didn't trust either John or the antagonist documenting John's purported lies. The easiest thing to do was just to walk away. I ultimately decided not to call John. His background seemed too sketchy. Thus even dubious data about John deterred me from continuing to communicate with him.

Google was a useful tool for me in this situation. I was able to investigate John's reputation, and the information I learned helped me make a decision about whether to talk to him. But this incident made me realize that as strongly as I believe in privacy, the temptation to google people can be irresistible. You can certainly hope that nobody types your name into Google, but that hope is probably futile. At some point in your life, you're probably going to get googled, and the information that pulls up might affect what others think of you.

THERE'S NO GOING BACK

On December 12, 2004, a stocky nineteen-year-old teenager from New Jersey named Gary posted on the Internet a video of himself lip-synching and dancing to "Dragostea Din Tei," a Romanian techno song by the group O-Zone. Gary called his act the "Numa Numa Dance," a name based on some lyrics in the song.[121] As he sat in his chair in front of his computer, Gary danced before his webcam. In a very energetic way, he wiggled back and forth and pumped his arms enthusiastically to the techno beat of the song. The song was extremely catchy, and Gary's movements were quite humorous. He was so passionately engaged in the music that the video had a kind of charm. He submitted his video to a website where users post their videos, which are then made available on the website for anybody to view.

Almost overnight, Gary became a sensation. Soon the video had been downloaded about two million times. Gary appeared on *Good Morning America,* NBC's *Tonight Show,* and CNN. His video was shown on VH1. Soon the video had been downloaded more than seven million times. To put this number into perspective, a music CD reaches "platinum" status if it sells more than one million copies, which is a great achievement for any musician.

Then, suddenly, Gary decided that he hated the spotlight. According to a *New York Times* article ten weeks after Gary had posted the video, he "has now sought refuge from his fame in his family's small house on a gritty street in Saddle Brook. . . . According to his relatives, he mopes around the house. . . . He is distraught, embarrassed."[122]

Can he take it all back? No. There's no going back. Numerous websites now host his video. It is splashed all across the Web. There are Numa Numa Dance parodies. Wikipedia, a free online encyclopedia, has an entry for the Numa Numa dance. There's even a fan website for Gary:

> On this site I'll include everything we can find out about our favorite lip-synch icon, including photos, a biography, an annotated list of new videos, fan-created .mp3s, . . . movie posters, breaking news, and more!

What Gary did can't be undone. And he was only nineteen years old when he did it. For most of us, the foolish things we do as teenagers disappear into oblivion and are revived only when we reminisce with old friends. But in today's world, foolish deeds are preserved for eternity on the Internet. They become what a person is known for. The world will always remember Gary as the Numa Numa dancer.

Gary's story has a happy ending. He resurfaced in the summer of 2006 with a new slick website designed by a media company and a new music video—this time professionally produced.[123] Gary appears to have embraced his Internet fame. Many, however, have not.

Little Fatty

Qian was a pudgy sixteen-year-old in China. He was attending a traffic safety class when someone secretly took his photo. His face was round and plump, his cheeks were rosy, his eyes were looking sideways in a skeptical glance, and his small lips were in a pout. The photo began to circulate online, where Chinese Internet users became obsessed with it. People began to use Adobe PhotoShop to place Qian's face on a variety of different images. His face appeared on a variety of movie–poster mock-ups, ranging from the Harry Potter, Austin Powers, and Pirates of the Caribbean series to *Brokeback Mountain*, *The Da Vinci Code,* and more. Scores of celebrities were given Qian's digital countenance. He appeared on Buddha images as well as on photos of porn stars. In one image, his visage was carved into Mount Rushmore; in another picture, he was sitting next to President George W. Bush giving him rabbit ears; in yet another, his head was superimposed upon the body of Adam in Michelangelo's Sistine Chapel fresco sequence. And so on. People began to call him Xiao Pang—"Little Fatty."

One day, somebody told Qian that his photo was all over the Internet. Qian went to a cyber café and was stunned to find thousands of websites with his image. At first, Qian was devastated. "When I saw that I was angry and upset," Qian stated in an interview. "It was as if I had been struck by a thunderbolt," he said. "I felt really humiliated. I couldn't bear it and I left [the cyber café]."

Soon, Qian's fame began to spread even farther. People began to stop him on the street. At a concert, a group of girls wanted to take a photo with him. Throughout all this, Qian felt embarrassed and ridiculed.

Qian, however, later changed his perspective and began to take the events in stride. "Now my feeling has changed," he said in an interview. "If you always feel depressed, then you feel uncomfortable. Now I can view this event with a calm mind, and I feel released." Moreover, he noted, "I have tried to turn sorrow into strength. At least this makes people smile." He stated that for the most part, he had made peace with his newfound Internet fame: "I like it when they put me on the body of heroes, such as Russell Crowe in *Gladiator*. But I hate it when they place me on the shoulder of naked women or when the touch-up job is terrible."

Doctored image of "Little Fatty" (face obscured) next to President George Bush

Qian is now a star in China, though he still works at a gas station and doesn't make much money from his fame. He appeared on a popular Chinese talk show. And his fans continue to keep track of him. When Qian once mentioned in an interview that he liked the comedian Jim Carrey, people created Little Fatty posters of Carrey's movies. Without even being aware of it, Qian had become an icon throughout China. Fortunately, he made the best of it, but he had little alternative.[124]

The Star Wars Kid

Ghyslain was a stocky fifteen-year-old boy from Canada who was a fan of science fiction. You might already guess that he was classified as a nerd at school and teased. Today, Ghyslain is a worldwide celebrity, known by millions of people in all corners of the globe. Most know him as the "Star Wars Kid," although his full name readily appears on countless websites and news articles.

How did Ghyslain transform from a Canadian teenager into the Star Wars

Still shot from the Star Wars Kid video (face obscured)

Kid? It all happened quite rapidly. In November 2002 he filmed himself at his school video studio pretending to fight an imaginary foe with a golf ball retriever as a light saber.[125] The video lasted about two minutes. Ghyslain twirled around waving the golf ball retriever frantically, making his own sound effects along the way, pretending to be a character from the movie *Star Wars: Episode I, The Phantom Menace.*[126] The character was Darth Maul, a menacing villain who wielded two light sabers connected at the handles to form a staff. Unlike Darth Maul, whose movements were gracefully choreographed, the Star Wars Kid made jerky and awkward movements, stumbling at some points.

Ghyslain didn't intend the video to be seen by anyone. He left the video on the shelf of the school's TV studio. The video languished there for several months, until April 2003, when another student discovered it.[127] The student shared it with others, and soon they converted it to digital format and posted it on an Internet file-sharing network, where anyone could download it for free. What happened next was amazing. It became an instant hit. Within days, the video was being discussed and posted on numerous websites. Countless people downloaded it.

But that wasn't the end of it. One blogger created an edited version of the video with music and special effects. The edited video began with the traditional *Star Wars* opening, with text streaming across outer space. The golf ball retriever was illuminated like a light saber, with sound effects added as Ghyslain swung it around. The remix of the video was adeptly done and was quite funny. In a matter of weeks, the original video and the remix were downloaded more than a million times from around the world.

Within no time, websites were barraged by postings making fun of the kid. At Waxy.org, one of the first websites to discuss the story, countless comments were posted. The author of the blog soon stopped allowing comments:

> I've turned off new comments in this thread because of the mean-spirited tone, and deleted the most vicious comments. Yes, he's fat and awkward. We get it. Since 90% of the traffic to these videos is coming from gaming, technology, and Star Wars news websites, I'm guessing that most of you weren't any cooler in junior high school than this poor kid. All of you geeks, nerds, and dorks out there need to think twice before trashing one of your own.[128]

The worst comments have been deleted, but here is a taste of what remains:

I don't know which one is funnier, raw or remixed. . . .

How come this kid is still fat?

If there were more portly Jedis like that, I'd totally leave the dark side.

I dub thee Darth Haul.

Oh my God that is hilarious. I can't breathe!

It's like a bad train wreck . . . you don't want to look at it, but you just can't stop yourself.

Replica Jedi Staff $25; School Camera Rental Fee $5, Video Cassette $3, Making an ass out of yourself and having it spread across the internet . . . priceless.

Wow. Simply put, this kid can 1) never live this down 2) never watch any thing [*Star Wars*] related without thinking about his humiliation and 3) never run for president of any country ever. That poor poor boy.

The comments go on and on. One commentator at another website wrote: "The Internet makes fools into stars and stars into fools."[129] Soon the mainstream media found out about the story, and it was written up in numerous newspapers and magazines, including the *New York Times*. In that story, Ghyslain said: "People were laughing at me. . . . And it was not funny at all."[130] Ghyslain transferred to another school.[131] Out of sympathy for Ghyslain's troubles, a blogger collected donations to buy Ghyslain an iPod music player.

The iPod was a small consolation prize for Ghyslain, who was deeply scarred by the incident. Students at his high school would start shouting "Star Wars Kid! Star Wars Kid!" as he walked by. According to Ghyslain, the torment was "simply unbearable, totally. It was impossible to attend class." He dropped out of his high school and had to seek psychiatric care. His family sued the students who placed the video online and the case eventually settled. To this day, Ghyslain has not spoken much about the incident publicly.[132]

Forever, Ghyslain will be known as the Star Wars Kid. There's even an entry under his name in the online encyclopedia Wikipedia.[133] A search under his name or under "Star Wars Kid" pulls up countless hits on Google. Today, according to estimates, the video has become the most watched video on the Internet, having been viewed hundreds of millions of times.[134] Over at a website called The Screaming Pickle, you can watch one of dozens of versions of the video.[135] The website offers up a menu of videos to see:

Star Wars Kid	The Original Star Wars Kid Video
Star Wars Kid Remix	The FIRST Special Effects Dub of The Star Wars Kid Saga
Star Wars Kid version 1.5	Seeker Drones Added to First Dub
UnderCover Star Wars Kid	Simply the best yet made!!! You must see this.
Star Wars Kid—LOTOR	Star Wars Kid—Lord of the Onion Rings—Excellent! Edits from LOTR trailer, superimposed scenes, etc.
Bravekid	Star Wars Kid As Braveheart Trailer
Bulk	Star Wars Kid as The Incredible Hulk Trailer
Chewee	Edits from Episode IV with Chewbacca, Han and Luke on detention level of Death Star
Dancing Baby and The Star Wars Kid	Dancing Baby and Star Wars Kid Movie Trailer
R2D2 and C3P0 Witness from The Star Wars Kid	"That's funny, the damage doesn't look as bad out here . . . are you sure this thing is safe?"—Edit From Episode IV Blockade Runner Scene with Star Wars Kid

Star Wars Kong	one of many "remakes" which included no content from the original SWK video, but were re-enacted—Star Wars Kid / Star Wars Kong = SWK
Star Wars Kid—Drunken Jedi Master	Drunken Jedi Master Dub adds green saber blades deflecting blaster shots
Star Wars Kid Very Special Edition	Features Edits from Episode I referencing the Clone War—Star Wars Kid and his Clone fight each other—1 green saber, 1 red saber
Star Wars Kid Revolutions	The Matrix Trailer with spliced scenes of The Star Wars Kid
Star Wars Kid—T3 Rise Of The Machines	T3 Trailer with SWK model TX morphing from liquid metal

Believe it or not, there's more.

And although it's two years since the original video made its rounds on the Internet, the Star Wars Kid is still a topic of discussion. In 2005 there was an online petition to persuade George Lucas to include the Star Wars Kid in *Episode III, Revenge of the Sith*:

> We the undersigned, urge you to consider Ghyslain A.K.A. "Star Wars Kid" for a cameo in the upcoming Star Wars Episode III movie.[136]

The petition received more than 146,000 signatures, but it was unsuccessful.[137]

And Waxy.org recently posted a tribute to the Star Wars Kid:

> It's been almost two years since the Star Wars Kid video, but the tributes keep coming. . . . Finally, because I get asked occasionally, I have no new Star Wars Kid news. He's never tried to contact me, and I haven't tried to follow up in any way. I don't know the outcome of the lawsuits or what Ghyslain is up to. If anyone out there knows, I'd love to know how he's doing.[138]

Whether you like it or not, whether you intend it or not, the Internet can make you an instant celebrity. You could be the next Star Wars Kid.

THE GOOD AND THE BAD

We live in exciting and wondrous times. The Internet and Google bring a library of data into all of our homes. The blogosphere is profoundly democratizing, giving anybody with something interesting to say—or, for that matter, with *anything* to say—a global voice. Blogs and social network websites enable people to express themselves like they've never been able to before. They encourage people to share their lives with strangers, to open up their diaries to the world. As one blogger wrote, blogging allows you "to discover yourself while discovering about other people's [lives]."[139] Blogging allows people to exchange experiences, and it holds out the possibility that many others might find a connection. Blogging represents the very best that communication has to offer. Bloggers who are great writers and storytellers find their calling; some begin writing books. Without blogging, they might never have realized that they had stories or ideas to share. These developments are incredible and dazzling.

But not so good if you're the Star Wars Kid or the dog poop girl. As we charge headfast into the future, as more details about our lives are captured in data fragments, as the blogosphere expands and draws more attention, what are the implications for our privacy? As we move into the future, new technologies of recording sound, images, and tracking people's whereabouts will further enable even more fragments of data about our lives to be captured and potentially disseminated online. In a short essay in the *New Republic,* Eve Fairbanks writes:

> My generation is the first to have grown up with the Internet, and we see the online universe . . . as a place where anything goes, where there is neither consequence nor shame, and where concerns about protecting your reputation are less, not more important. Teens blog details, true or made up, about their personal lives that their elders would have blushed to put in their diaries. Parents and teachers . . . chalk this up to naïveté, suggesting that, when these children grow up, they will be as concerned about privacy as past generations were. But maybe not.[140]

If Fairbanks is correct, then perhaps generations in the future will no longer expect much privacy. One might envision a future where we can finally be uninhibited and honest about ourselves. When everybody's warts are exposed, maybe people will stop readily condemning others, and the social norms that people enforce yet secretly transgress will gradually fade away.

Or not. Maybe the future will be one that is less free, where society is both oppressive and uncontrollable, where people are vulnerable to having their reputations destroyed in an instant, where mistakes in one's past can forever thwart opportunities in one's future.

Chapter 3 Gossip and the
Virtues of Knowing Less

Robert was an attorney employed by a U.S. senator. He had a slight crush on Jessica Cutler, a twenty-five-year-old staff assistant to the senator who had begun working there in February 2004. Robert had briefly met Jessica early on when Jessica began working, but he rarely had contact with her since he worked in a different part of the office.

Jessica had recently moved to Washington from New York. Slender and attractive, Jessica was part Korean, part Caucasian. When she moved to D.C., she first lived with her boyfriend, but she grew bored with him and began to cheat on him. They broke up, and she moved out into her own apartment.[1]

On Thursday, May 6, a coworker told Jessica that Robert liked her and invited them both out for drinks at Union Station after work. Unbeknownst to Robert, Jessica had created a blog the day before, called The Washingtonienne, which was written in the style of a Washington "Sex in the City" column. The blog began like this:

WEDNESDAY, MAY 05, 2004

I have a "glamour job" on the Hill. That is, I could not care less about gov or politics, but working for a Senator looks good on my resume. And these marble hallways are such great places for meeting boys and showing off my outfits.

POSTED BY THE WASHINGTONIENNE AT 5:32 PM

According to Jessica, she created her blog to keep a few of her friends informed about her escapades. She didn't set up the blog so that only people with a password could read it because she thought it would be "too much trouble for my friends to have to type in a password."[2] She stated that she believed that her blog would be a needle in the electronic haystack of cyberspace.

On her blog, Jessica described the daily adventures in her life, which consisted of a lot of partying with various men. One of them was her ex-boyfriend, with whom she continued to have sex occasionally. Another was a staffer at a senator's office where she interned before getting her current job. Jessica was also sleeping with a man she described as a "sugar daddy who wants nothing but anal." And she was also involved with a married man, the chief of staff at a government agency who was paying her for sex.[3]

Before she left for drinks with Robert and their coworker on Thursday evening, Jessica dashed off a post to her blog. She wrote that Robert was a "new contender for my fair hand" and referred to him by his real initials. Jessica didn't seem all that excited about the evening, noting that it would be "full of awkward moments." But apparently the evening went better than Jessica had expected. In a post the next morning, she wrote about their sexual encounters that evening, including the fact that Robert was into spanking.

Robert began a relationship with Jessica. Things were moving fast. They were sleeping together and began seeing each other frequently. Robert wasn't aware of Jessica's other sexual exploits, and he had no idea that as their relationship began to develop, Jessica was blogging the intimate details. In one post, Jessica wrote that she and Robert went out for drinks after work and then went back to her place to have sex "every which way." That evening, Robert reported having heard that she had told a few friends in the office about his interest in spanking. Jessica confessed that she had told a few people, and Robert forgave her but told her to stop talking about it. But although Jessica stopped gossiping about it in the office, she continued to blog about her sex life with Robert. After writing about the fact that he "likes submissive women," Jessica quipped: "Good, now I can take it easy in bed. Just lay back and watch him do freaky shit."

Jessica blogged about Robert's difficulty using a condom. "I also learned that he was a cop," she wrote, "so he has scary police shit like handcuffs in his closet. He implied that we would be using them next time, which is intriguing." Jessica also recounted that they were beginning to like each other and mused about the future of their relationship, which was about a week old at the time. She wondered whether there was a future: "But can it go anywhere, i.e., marriage? I don't know. He's Jewish, I'm not. And we have nasty sex like animals, not man and wife."

May 18 was the last day of their relationship. From Jessica's post that morning, it appeared that everything was progressing satisfactorily in her relationship with Robert. They had plans to go out that evening and continue celebrating Jessica's birthday.

But Jessica's blog was about to send everything into a tailspin. That day, the popular blog Wonkette linked to Jessica's blog. Wonkette is an inside-the-beltway gossip blog started by Ana Marie Cox, "a 31-year-old self-described failed journalist."[4] Wonkette is akin to a digital tabloid. The *Village Voice* declared that Wonkette "swims in the libidinal current of American politics." The *New York Times* called it "gossipy, raunchy, potty-mouthed." The conservative pundit Michelle Malkin called Cox "profanity-laced and sex-obsessed . . . [a] vain, young, trash-mouthed skank." Wonkette's website proudly displayed these quotations and more. It received tens of thousands of visitors each day.[5]

Wonkette's posting on the morning of May 18 began like this:

A Girl After Our Own Heart (She's So Getting a Book Deal Out of This)
     We realize that some of you who follow this link will never come back: Compared to our humble blog, *Washingtonienne* has half the politics and twice the ass-fucking.

Jessica's blog went primetime. When Jessica learned that Wonkette had linked to her blog, she quickly deleted it.[6] But it was too late. Tens of thousands of people had read it. Copies of it had already been archived. Robert came into Jessica's office with a printout of her blog, told her the relationship was over, and walked away. A few minutes later, the woman who had set Jessica up with Robert for drinks came into Jessica's office. The woman was furious. She told Jessica that she should leave. Jessica quickly slipped out of the office.

Three days after Wonkette had plugged Washingtonienne, on May 21, the senator's office put out a press release: "On May 18, 2004, our office became aware of allegations that an employee had been using Senate resources and work-time to post unsuitable and offensive material to an Internet Weblog. . . . The employee has been terminated."[7] Being fired was nothing new for Jessica. One of her friends said that "Jessica has been fired from more jobs than anyone I know."[8] The same day, Wonkette posted an interview with Jessica:

> WASHINGTONIENNE SPEAKS!! WONKETTE EXCLUSIVE!! MUST CREDIT WONKETTE!! THE WASHINGTONIENNE INTERVIEW!!
>
> Wonkette spoke to Washingtonienne. Her name is Jessica Cutler. . . .
> Washingtonienne: Hello? Wonkette? This is the Washingtonienne!
> Wonkette: Hi!
> Washingtonienne: [Laughs]
> Wonkette: You certainly are in good spirits.
> Washingtonienne: Oh, this whole thing is so two days ago for me. . . .
> Wonkette: . . . Now, first of all, is there anything you want people to know?
> Washingtonienne: Uhm . . . I'm not naming names. I'm not ashamed of anything I wrote in the blog. And people are sad if they're interested in such a low level sex scandal. I wrote the blog not to ruin people's lives. It was just for the amusement of me and my friends.[9]

The incident was written up in most major newspapers, including the *Washington Post* and the *New York Times*. CNN discussed the story too. And, of course, the tabloids got into the action.

Life was good for Jessica. She was an instant celebrity, and she relished the attention. She went out partying with Ana Marie Cox, and they posed suggestively together in photos which were posted on Wonkette. She did television interviews and posed nude for Playboy. In 2005 she wrote a novel, titled *The Washingtonienne,* for which she received a $300,000 advance. A blurb on the book boasted: "The Capitol Hill aide who scandalized Washington, D.C., with her blog has now written a sharp, steamy, utterly unrepentant novel set against the backdrop of the nation's capital." Her novel was based in part on events discussed in the blog. The only drawback to Jessica's fame was that she had some trouble finding a new job in D.C., so she moved back to New York City. She also started a new blog called Jessica Cutler Online, where she currently blogs about sex, clothes, and partying. Her blog accepts donations. "I need money for slutty clothes and drugs!" Jessica implores.[10]

Life was good for the author of Wonkette, too. Her blog traffic shot up more than threefold, to more than 1.5 million visits in the month of May 2004. MTV asked Ana Marie Cox to help cover the Democratic National

Convention.[11] She later wrote a novel, *Dog Days,* and became a columnist for *Time* magazine and its website.[12]

For Robert, life was not so good. In May 2005 he filed a lawsuit against Jessica, stating:

> Cutler caused widespread publication of private intimate facts concerning Plaintiff in a manner that would be deemed outrageous and highly offensive to an ordinary reasonable person of average sensibilities, subjecting Plaintiff to severe emotional distress, humiliation, embarrassment, and anguish. . . .
>
> No reasonable person would want the intimate physical, verbal, emotional, and psychological details of his or her sexual life and romantic relationships life exposed against his or her will on the Internet for the entire world to read. It is one thing to be manipulated and used by a lover, it is another thing to be cruelly exposed to the world.[13]

The complaint was served on Jessica as she was giving a reading from her book at a Washington bookstore.

Playboy magazine asked Jessica: "What advice would you give to someone starting a blog?" Jessica replied: "With a blog, you can't expect your private life to be private anymore. You just never know. But, when you work on the Hill you find out the guy you've been sleeping with has told everyone in your office about it. So, what's the difference? It's writing on the bathroom wall."[14]

In another interview, Jessica said that she felt "really bad for the guys. They didn't deserve this." But she was enjoying her newfound fame: "Some people with blogs are never going to get famous, and they've been doing it for, like, over a year. I feel bad for them." According to Jessica: "Everyone should have a blog. It's the most democratic thing ever."[15]

Blogging School

While Jessica tells tales out of school, other bloggers are telling tales in school. In a development that sends shivers down my spine, students are beginning to blog about their professors. One of my colleagues, the George Washington University law professor Orin Kerr, tells an interesting tale. He's a blogger at the popular blog The Volokh Conspiracy. Here's what he writes:

> WHEN PROFESSORS READ PSEUDONYMOUS STUDENT BLOGS
> This fall, I came across a pseudonymous GW 1L student blog, Idle Grasshopper. Mr. Idle Grasshopper blogged a lot about his professors (appropriately anonymized, but still recognizable to an insider), and I decided to tip off one of

those professors so he could check out what the student was saying about him. That professor is one of GW's best young teachers, and Idle Grasshopper was appropriately wowed by his teaching—and also a bit nervous about getting called on given the professor's demanding Socratic style.

My colleague started to visit the student's blog on occasion to see the student's reaction to class and also to see if he could figure out the student's identity. After visiting the blog on a semi-regular basis for a few months, he was able to piece together the evidence and determine who was Idle Grasshopper. He also realized that he had never called on the student in the course of the entire year (the course was Civ Pro [Civil Procedure], a year-long class). He decided not to call on Mr. Idle Grasshopper until the very last case on the very last day of the semester. And when he did, it was with a very cleverly crafted introduction:

Professor: So, Mr. [ ].

Student: Yes sir.

Professor: You've been sitting back there idle all year, laying low in the grass, but I'd like to put this seating chart in the hopper, so I thought I'd call on you.[16]

Here's what the student blogged about the experience:

PCP called on me today. Yep, I got cold called in CivPro. On the last day. The very last person to be called. But I wasn't just called. Oh no. As you can see from above, PCP called on me in a way that let me (and a few select others that know my semi-secret identity and who were paying attention) know that he knows. About the blog. And about my identity. So I guess that makes this post an "I know that you know" post. . . .

I'm not sure how I feel, knowing as I do now, that PCP has been reading my blog. Part of me is . . . intimidated? . . .

On the other hand, how cool is it that one of the best profs I'll have in law school (if not the best, but I've only had three so far, so the sample size is still too small) takes the time to not only read what I write, but also took the time to call on me in a way that took a tiny bit of effort to craft, while knowing that few, if any, of the class would find it humorous? Pretty freakin' cool.[17]

This incident ended happily, but one doesn't need an active imagination to think of more ominous ways students might blog about their teachers.

The Phantom Professor

What if teachers started blogging about the lives of their students? Actually, it has happened. One adjunct journalism professor was fired from teaching a course at Boston University for posting his thoughts about his first day of

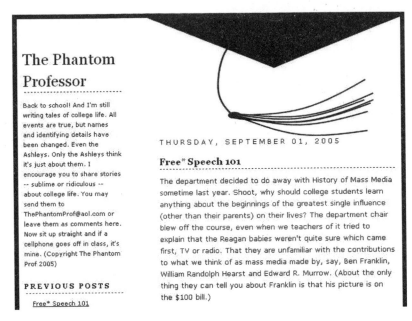

The Phantom Professor

Back to school! And I'm still writing tales of college life. All events are true, but names and identifying details have been changed. Even the Ashleys. Only the Ashleys think it's just about them. I encourage you to share stories -- sublime or ridiculous -- about college life. You may send them to ThePhantomProf@aol.com or leave them as comments here. Now sit up straight and if a cellphone goes off in class, it's mine. (Copyright The Phantom Prof 2005)

PREVIOUS POSTS

Free* Speech 101

THURSDAY, SEPTEMBER 01, 2005

Free* Speech 101

The department decided to do away with History of Mass Media sometime last year. Shoot, why should college students learn anything about the beginnings of the greatest single influence (other than their parents) on their lives? The department chair blew off the course, even when we teachers of it tried to explain that the Reagan babies weren't quite sure which came first, TV or radio. That they are unfamiliar with the contributions to what we think of as mass media made by, say, Ben Franklin, William Randolph Hearst and Edward R. Murrow. (About the only thing they can tell you about Franklin is that his picture is on the $100 bill.)

A page from the Phantom Professor blog

teaching. He wrote: "Of my six students, one (the smartest, wouldn't you know it?) is incredibly hot. . . . It was all I could do to remember the other five students."[18]

Another instance involved a pseudonymous blogger at Southern Methodist University. The blog, called The Phantom Professor, was born in the fall of 2004.

The blog chronicled the daily happenings at SMU in a frank and uninhibited way. It related the stories of students' campus lives, including their views on having sex, using drugs, dealing with stress, and coping with eating disorders. The mysterious blogger expressed her own opinions about the students, especially rich female students whom she referred to as "the Ashleys." In one post, for example, she wrote about a student whom she admired:

She's not one of the Ashleys. She's a few years older and she's a minority. She has a husband and a baby. . . .

I have no doubt that, unlike the Ashleys who half-joke about being in college to "earn a Mrs. Degree," she'll be heading to grad school and a career in the academy. This young woman is a natural teacher with a real flair for research.

She's not like them at all. And for this one day, it got to her. Their Prada handbags and their SUVs (brand new, all filled with high octane charged to daddy's plastic) and their size o derrieres kept warm with pastel Juicy Couture sweats that show just a hint of dorsal cleavage. She looked around at their perfect skin and their French manicures and it seemed suddenly unfair.[19]

In another post, she wrote about a student who had suffered a mental breakdown. In one instance, The Phantom Professor described a rich student who stopped by her office during office hours:

Kortney calls. I'd dub her one of the Ashleys—those plastic girls tottering on $500 sandals, clutching their $1500 handbags—but try as she might, she'll never quite fit the mold. Her weight for one thing. Girls on this particular campus hover at near-skeletal levels. Kortney is on the chunky side.[20]

Although the blogger tried to hide the identities of those whom she spoke about, many people recognized themselves and others. Soon, some had figured out who the blogger was: Elaine Liner, a popular writing instructor. At the conclusion of the 2005 spring semester, she was asked not to return.[21]

Why did she decide to blog about campus life? "I felt I had so many great stories to tell about students," Liner said, "and this would be a way to start writing them. . . . I just have this compulsion to tell stories. I wanted to write from deep inside, to be the person in the back of the faculty meeting or the person listening to what was going on. I wanted to write about what people don't know about colleges."[22] In another interview, she explained: "I thought I was just writing funny, odd, touching little stories about my experiences on a campus and in a classroom."[23]

Some people supported her blogging. One said: "She tells the brutal truth, and I had a lot of emotions. But she's a writer and that's what she does and it should be supported."[24]

Not everybody is pleased with what Liner wrote about them. In comments to an article in *Inside Higher Ed* describing Liner's blogging adventures, a faculty member at SMU writes:

The physical descriptions were too close for many of our faculty and students to not know who was being discussed. And the rude remarks about a particular person's physical appearance was a kind of statement that can create hostile working environments.[25]

The Phantom Professor also wrote about fellow professors. She described an attractive male professor whom she called Hot Pockets, the efforts of female students to flirt with him, and his efforts to stop it. Another of Liner's posts described an African-American professor who was prized by the faculty as an up-and-coming star:

> Wide load Professor Wideass had what she called her "Jerry Maguire" moment at the departmental faculty meeting yesterday. She's the newest tenure-tracker, fresh from a mediocre Midwestern university, with a Ph.D. in something no one cares about. She recently was named a "rising academic star" by some obscure journal. . . . Wideass is a well paid full-timer with a secure future at the university and all the health benefits her plaque-laden arteries will ever need. We adjuncts are delighted to have discovered she is widely despised by the undergrads.[26]

Professor "Wideass" wrote in the comments to the article about Liner:

> Her comments about my size, my recognition by the Chronicle of Higher Education, my alma-mater, and my values are painful, demeaning, and in all cases false (except I guess her depiction of my size . . .)
>
>   Unfortunately, our students, those who are rich, as well as those who are poor, are simply undergraduates with an average age of 19. Many of them are not as well equipped to see their faults, their personal problems or those of their family written about so cavalierly and publicly by someone they trusted.[27]

The Phantom Professor raises a number of difficult questions about blogging. Her blog was a candid account of college life, and she told stories that often remain hidden. Pull back the curtains, and a lot of very interesting things can be revealed. And there are also free speech considerations. Doesn't Liner have the right to speak freely about things she feels strongly about? Doesn't she have the right to chronicle the troubling and sometimes unseemly events she witnesses in the lives of college students and professors? According to the author of the *Inside Higher Ed* article: "Rita Kirk, the department chairwoman, says that she received complaints about the blog from students and parents, and that she consulted with university lawyers about what to do about it. Kirk describes herself as a strong First Amendment supporter, but she says she worries that the blog violated students' privacy rights and upset some students. 'People need to remember that words can hurt,' Kirk says."[28] Words can certainly sting, but what about free speech? Then again, what about privacy? These are the difficult tensions increasingly arising as more people take to the blogosphere.

By way of postscript, after being fired, Elaine took a brief break from blogging and deleted some of the posts. But she then reposted a few of her old postings, and resumed blogging. The Phantom Professor lives on.

GOSSIP MOVES ONLINE

The mainstream media have ethical rules regarding people's privacy. These rules are flexible and permissive, but they are typically followed by most media entities. One rule is to avoid naming victims of rapes and sexual assaults.[29] But bloggers come in all shapes, sizes, and ethical configurations, and many don't follow any conventional code. There are few limits in the blogosphere. Moreover, the national news media don't talk much about local gossip. The talk at the water cooler about your coworker's extramarital affair often won't be of interest to CNN. But for bloggers, it's prime fodder.

Many blogs are primarily about political issues, current events, or other topics. But a sizable number of blogs consist of people's musings about their lives. People used to tuck their diaries away in drawers or lock them up, but now, they are sharing them with the public on the Internet.

Some people blog anonymously or pseudonymously; others blog in full exposure. According to a survey: "For the most part, respondents identified themselves on their blogs. 81% of participants said they used some form of self-identification: 55% used their real names, 20% used some variant of their names (only a first name, a nickname that friends knew, initials, etc.)."[30]

As for the content of their blogs, 25 percent of bloggers in the survey noted that they frequently posted very personal details on their blogs. According to the survey, bloggers frequently wrote about other people they knew, but 66 percent never asked the permission of these people when they did so; only 3 percent routinely requested permission. Many explicitly identified other people on their blogs (21 percent) but more attempted to avoid identifying others (42 percent). As one blogger explained:

> With work-related entries, I'll sometimes use only a first initial [to identify people.] I'm not overly concerned since the people I write about don't know of my blog's existence and aren't particularly net-savvy.[31]

Schools are beginning to grapple with problems emerging from student blogging, a difficult issue since most blogging occurs outside of the schoolhouse doors. In one instance, two pseudonymous high school female students created a blog they called the Underground Newspaper, filled with the school's gossip. The students explained that they were fed up with the official school newspaper because it was too sterile. One of them said: "Everything's so positive when not everything about our school is positive."[32] The blog received 2,500 visits per month. But school officials contacted the girls' Internet service provider and had the blog shut down.

Nannies are beginning to blog too. One nanny blogged about the couple she worked for and discussed details about a squabble between them. She also revealed that she sometimes came to work with a hangover. When the couple discovered the blog, they fired her.[33]

One mother was shocked to discover that her thirteen-year old daughter had a blog. The daughter blogged about her life, included a list of her friends, and spiced it up with pictures. The mother also discovered that many of her daughter's friends had blogs too. And she was appalled at the pictures her daughter posted of herself and her friends: "Their pictures are very provocative. There's shots with their butt in the air, with their thongs sticking out of it. They squeeze their elbows together to make their boobs look bigger."[34]

WEBS OF COMMUNICATIONS

In the past, gossip advanced slowly. We share information within social circles, which have boundaries. Traditionally, it has been unusual for gossip to leap from one social circle to another, because people in one group rarely know or care about someone in a completely different group. A person's coworkers make up one such social circle. Gossip often travels quickly throughout a workplace, since people work in the same building and have frequent encounters with one another. They are interested in information about fellow group members. Therefore, if one of them hears a juicy piece of gossip, he or she is more likely to spread it to other coworkers than to tell someone outside the group. But others outside the workplace might not care anyway. They might find the details of a particular salacious story to be interesting, but unless they know the person involved, they probably don't care at all about that person's identity.

Social Epidemics and Tipping Points

In *The Tipping Point,* the writer Malcolm Gladwell describes what he refers to as "social epidemics." He writes that the spread of ideas and information resembles the spread of epidemics of diseases. Change doesn't occur gradually but instead arrives at "one dramatic moment," which Gladwell calls a "tipping point." How does this phenomenon occur?

Gladwell explains that within social networks, certain people are "connectors"—gregarious people who exist in numerous different social circles. Sociologists refer to them as "super nodes," hubs that link many clusters of people. "Most of us," Gladwell notes, "don't have particularly broad and diverse groups of friends." That's why connectors are so important. When information hits a connector, it spreads from one social circle to another. It is no longer contained within a particular group of friends but leaps into an entirely different clique. Gladwell gives the example of Paul Revere, whose famous horseback ride rapidly spread the word about the arrival of the British troops. Revere created a "word-of-mouth epidemic," spreading the news over "a long distance in a very short time, mobilizing an entire region to arms." Revere's ride was so successful because Revere knew tons of people from different social circles.[35]

As information spreads to greater numbers of people, it begins to proliferate exponentially. This process doesn't occur readily. A piece of information must be "sticky"—that is, it must inspire people to keep talking about it. The information, in other words, must be "contagious."[36] When this process occurs, the spread of the gossip might reach a "tipping point," where communication boils over into an epidemic, and a rumor can spread to thousands of people.

Linking

The Internet develops by building electronic connections. For bloggers to attract readers, they need to get referrals from popular websites. When other bloggers find a post interesting, they will link to it. A "link" is a hyperlink, text that whisks you at a click to another webpage. The Web is interlaced with links, a giant latticework of connections between websites, where Internet traffic fires like synapses in a gigantic brain.

While most blogs languish in obscurity, tucked away in the shadows of cyberspace, some blogs are becoming powerful rivals to the mainstream media. Some of these blogs have tremendous audiences—tens of thousands of visitors per day, hundreds of thousands, even millions, per month. When a link to a blog post or website appears on one of these websites, thousands of people will click on the link and read the post or site.

On Concurring Opinions, http://www.concurringopinions.com, where I blog with a group of law professors, we have a "site meter" that monitors our readership. It measures how many times our blog is visited throughout the day; what posts people read; and what websites are referring readers to our blog. The chart below displays the number of visits to our blog each day over the span of a month. Notice the big spikes—these are due to links from other blogs with big readerships.

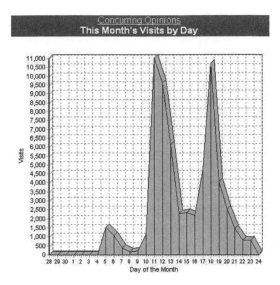

Site meter graph for the Concurring Opinions blog

An interesting post can very quickly gather attention in the blogosphere. People on the Internet often act like locusts, swarming toward the latest interesting piece of data that attracts a buzz. One of the most popular blogs is called Slashdot, which provides technology news. When Slashdot links to a website, it generates so much traffic that it can cause the website to crash due to an overload of visitors. It's like having a stampede to your website. There's even a term for it—it's called getting "slashdotted."

Gossip by Ear, Gossip by Electrons

In the offline world, rarely does gossip hit a tipping point. The process of spreading information to new people takes time, and friends often associate in similar circles, so most secrets don't spread too widely.

The Internet takes this phenomenon and puts it on steroids. People can communicate with tens of thousands—even millions—of people almost simultaneously. If you put something up on the Internet, countless people can access it at the same time. In an instant, information can speed across the globe.

Of course, the Web is gargantuan, and much gossip that finds its way online remains a needle in an enormous haystack of data. The "real issue," however, the network theorist Albert-László Barabási notes in his book *Linked*, "isn't the overall size of the Web. It's the distance between any two documents. How many clicks does it take to get from the home page of a high-school student in Omaha to the Webpage of a Boston stockbroker?" The answer: not too many—about nineteen clicks on average.[37]

But nineteen clicks is still a lot of clicks. Gossip might find its way onto the Internet, but it still might not spread widely. Imagine the small-time blogger, who has just a few friends reading her blog. She blogs about something really interesting. One of the friends might tip off a blogger at a popular blog—or that blogger might just stumble upon the story. Either way, the blogger at the popular blog might decide to blog about the information and link to it. Suppose that the popular blog gets millions of readers a week. Now the information is widely disseminated—in almost an instant. To use Gladwell's term, the popular blog is a "connector." But it isn't just a normal connector—it is a superconnector, one that can spread information much more widely and quickly than a hundred Paul Reveres.

But it doesn't end there. Many of the popular blog's readers have blogs themselves, and they blog about the story. Their readers start discussing it and blogging about it. And so on. On the Internet, gossip can more readily jump the boundaries of various social circles, because all it takes is for the gossip to come to the attention of a connector blog, where it can become contagious and spread far and wide throughout cyberspace.

IS GOSSIP GOOD?

Gossip is often thought of as unseemly, but it has both good and bad qualities. As the philosopher Aaron Ben Ze'ev observes, "Gossip is engaged in for pleasure, not for the purpose of hurting someone." He notes that most damage from gossip is minor. Gossip, Ben Ze'ev concludes, isn't "virtuous" but it is not "vicious" either.[38] Indeed, much gossip isn't malicious, and it is something that most of us engage in. Although people quickly denounce gossip, it remains ubiquitous.[39] According to one study, about two-thirds of all conversations involve gossip, and as one writer sums it up, "What people talk about is mostly other people."[40]

In countless societies, whether primitive or modern, gossip generally functions in similar ways.[41] Gossip is essential to establishing reputations. According to the psychologist Nicholas Emler: "Gossip does not merely disseminate reputational information but is the very process whereby reputations are decided. Reputations do not exist except in the conversations that people have about one another."[42] Gossip is a way to expose people's infringements of norms, and it is an essential tool for a community to ensure that its norms are respected.

Gossip helps shape people's reputations without confrontation. The anthropologist Karen Brison notes that because it often takes place behind a person's back, "gossip allows people to assess their neighbors and criticize digressions [from norms] without starting fights and breaching surface amity."[43] In other words, gossip can help enforce norms in a way that eases social tension and confrontation.

The legal scholar Diane Zimmerman argues that gossip teaches us a lot about society and human behavior: "By providing people with a way to learn about social groups to which they do not belong, gossip increases intimacy and a sense of community among disparate individuals and groups." For Zimmerman, "gossip is a basic form of information exchange that teaches about other lifestyles and attitudes, and through which community values are changed or reinforced."[44] We can learn a lot when we rip off the veil and peer into people's private lives.

In some instances, disclosing a person's secrets helps change certain social norms. Some norms persist even though many people violate them in the shadows. When this behavior is brought into the limelight, society will be forced to confront this norm more directly and realize just how often it is being violated. Society's hypocrisy will be revealed, and this might spark a change in the norm.[45]

Although gossip can help shape reputations, educate us about the lives of others, and stimulate the evolution of norms, it has some other qualities that are less savory. "People are careless when they gossip," Brison observes, "because they know they will not have to take responsibility for their words. This means that rumor spreads easily and the truth is distorted."[46] As the philosopher Martin Heidegger noted, gossip "spreads in wider circles and takes on an authoritative character. Things are so because one says so. Idle talk is constituted in this gossiping and passing the word along, a process by which its initial lack of grounds to stand on increases to complete groundlessness."[47] In other words, the problem with gossip is that it is based on unsubstantiated rumors, and people often don't bother to learn the full story. For Heidegger, gossip is a superficial way of learning information about others. It doesn't involve a serious attempt to understand another person but often remains shallow and careless. People rarely use gossip as a way to delve into the psychological depths of others, but rather consume it like a form of greasy fast food. Gossip is a delicious treat, often without much nutritional value. It certainly can inform us about the lives of others, but much gossip merely titillates without teaching. Gossip is rarely a dose of pure truth; it is often intermixed with fiction. The literature professor Patricia Meyer Spacks astutely notes that gossip "plays with reputation, circulating truths and half-truths and falsehoods about the activities, sometimes about the motives and feelings, of others."[48]

Although sociologists often point out that gossip is essential for social control, people often gossip in ways that don't benefit society but that instead further their own self-interest. According to Brison, "When people gossip they are less interested in preserving social order than in advancing their own political fortunes and slandering their rivals."[49] Gossip can thus function as a weapon to wound others without providing any significant contribution to the community.

With respect to norms, gossip works in two directions—it can undermine norms, but it can also affirm them. "On the one hand," the legal scholar Robert Post observes, "gossip threatens to subvert community norms by exposing back-stage behavior and revealing the pretensions, faults, peccadillos, and scandal of community actors. On the other hand, gossip reaffirms community norms by bringing social pressure to bear on their enforcement."[50] According to the law professor Paul Schwartz, revealing people's norm violations will not always effectively change norms.[51] The number of people whose secrets are outed is often insufficient to force a change in norms. Perhaps if the veils on our lives were all removed simultaneously, society might collectively discard certain norms. However, the process of changing norms is complicated, and it is far from certain that more gossip will effectuate change in norms. Those who seek to challenge norms they dislike by gossiping about transgressors may instead increase the oppressiveness of the norms without doing much to eradicate them. Disclosing personal secrets can create an atmosphere of coercion, blackmail, and witch hunts.[52]

In the end, we're ambivalent about gossip. Sometimes gossip is quite beneficial; sometimes it is harmless; but other times, gossip is quite malignant. Regardless of gossip's vices, we would be foolish to imagine that we can ever hush its mischievous whispers. The more meaningful question is not whether we should stop gossip, but how we should control it, how we should modulate its problematic effects.

WHEN LESS IS MORE

Some argue that the availability of more private information about people is a good thing. Indeed, the mantras of the Information Age are that "information wants to be free" and that "more information is always better." We need information about people to make judgments about them. The judge and legal scholar Richard Posner believes that people shouldn't be able to hide discreditable facts about themselves. According to Posner: "Prying enables one to form a more accurate picture of a friend or colleague, and the knowledge gained is useful in social or professional dealings with him." Posner argues that people often want to hide harmful facts about themselves for their own gain, a practice that is similar to a merchant concealing defects in a product.[53]

We need information about people to determine whether to trust them. We place our safety in the hands of others. We entrust others with our finances, our deepest secrets, and the care of our children. But establishing trust is hard these days because many people live in large communities with highly mobile populations.[54] Our neighbors are often strangers. Privacy inhibits the establishment of trust because privacy "makes it difficult to know others' reputations," and knowing reputations is a prerequisite to trusting strangers.[55]

Although the conventional wisdom of the Information Age is that more information is better than less, sometimes we're better off not biting into the bitter apple of others' private lives. Many believe that learning private information about other people will improve our understanding of them and enhance the accuracy of our judgments. But more information may not necessarily lead to more accurate judgments about others. In many cases, the disclosure of private information can lead to misjudgment based on only partial knowledge of someone else's situation.

Judging Out of Context

Judge Posner claims that a person concealing discreditable private information is tantamount to a merchant concealing defects in a product. However, the truth about a person is much more difficult to ascertain than the truth about a product or thing. People are far more complex than products. Knowing certain information can distort judgment of another person rather than increase its accuracy.

We are constantly judging other people, and we often must do so quickly. The law professor Jeffrey Rosen astutely points out that people have short attention spans and will probably not judge other people fairly: "When intimate personal information circulates among a small group of people who know us well, its significance can be weighed against other aspects of our personality and character. By contrast, when intimate information is removed from its original context and revealed to strangers, we are vulnerable to being misjudged on the basis of our most embarrassing, and therefore most memorable, tastes and preferences."[56]

People often condemn others on partial information. Indeed, necessity sometimes demands hasty judgment. We frequently don't have enough time to know the whole story. A short story called "The Last Judgment" by the Czech author Karel Čapek best captures the issue. A deceased criminal confronts a divine tribunal to determine whether he will be sent to heaven or hell. The tribunal consists of human judges. God, instead of his usual role as judge, is the witness. God testifies about the defendant's crimes but explains the causes of the defendant's behavior and declares that, under different circumstances, the defendant would have been an upstanding citizen. Nevertheless, the judges condemn the defendant to hell. Before facing his fate, the defendant asks why God has not decided his fate: "Because I know everything. If judges knew everything, absolutely everything, they couldn't judge either: they would understand everything and their hearts would ache. How could I possibly judge you? Judges know only about your crimes but I know everything about you. . . . And that's why I cannot judge you."[57]

The story nicely illustrates the difference between human and divine judgment. Human judgment is imperfect; we make judgments based on fragments of information taken out of context. If we knew everything, we might find it hard to judge others at all. Because human judgment is bound to be incomplete and flawed, we should approach it with humility. Our knowledge of other people is riddled with gaps. The novelist and essayist William Gass, writing about literature, observes: "Characters in fiction are mostly empty canvas. I have known many who have passed through their stories without noses, or heads to hold them; others have lacked bodies altogether, exercised no natural functions, possessed some thoughts, a few emotions, but no psychologies, and apparently made love without the necessary organs."[58]

Similarly, our knowledge of other people is often "empty canvas." There's a lot we don't know about our coworkers, our friends, and even our family members. When we discover new information about people, we can fill in the canvas, but we still often have only partial understanding. It is easy to leap to conclusions prematurely. Although more information about a person might help enrich our understanding of that person, it might also lead us astray, since we often lack the whole story.

The Complicated Self

William James, a philosopher and pioneer in psychology, observed that people often show different sides of themselves in different contexts: "Many a youth who is demure enough before his parents and teachers, swears and swaggers like a pirate among his 'tough' young friends." Moreover, James explained, "we do not show ourselves to our children as to our club-companions, to our customers as to the laborers we employ, to our own masters and employers as to our intimate friends. From this there results what practically is a division of the man into several selves."[59]

The sociologist Erving Goffman advanced a similar notion of selfhood. He remarked that we live our lives as performers; we play many different roles and wear many different masks.[60] For example, parents present themselves as role models to their children, and society deems it quite appropriate for parents to portray themselves in this idealized manner. Each role enables us to display different aspects of ourselves. People even play roles in which they seem improperly cast, hoping to grow into the part. One plays a role until it fits, becoming transformed in the process. The self is always growing and developing; it isn't fixed in one place.

Countless psychological studies indicate that we behave very differently when in public than when in private.[61] As the novelist Milan Kundera observes, "Any man who was the same in both public and intimate life would be a monster. He would be without spontaneity in his private life and without responsibility in his public life."[62] In our public roles, we often strive to meet the expectations of others.[63] We groom and clothe ourselves before emerging in public. We are often more careful in our behavior, for we are concerned about the impressions we create. In private roles, we express aspects of ourselves that are often inappropriate in public roles.[64] We're more relaxed and at ease. As Kundera notes: "In private, a person says all sorts of things, slurs friends, uses coarse language, acts silly, tells dirty jokes, repeats himself, makes a companion laugh by shocking him with outrageous talk, floats heretical ideas he'd never admit to in public, and so forth."[65]

There's a popular myth that the public self isn't as genuine as the private self. People's true colors come through in private, when they're offstage. In the words of MTV's reality television show *The Real World*, people "stop being polite and start being real." But the private self wasn't always thought of as more genuine. Indeed, according to the philosopher Hannah Arendt, to the ancient Greeks public life was more representative of one's authentic self than life in private.[66]

Neither the public nor private self represents the "true" self. We're too complex for that. Our public and private sides are just dimensions in a complex, multifaceted personality, one that is shaped by the roles we play. We express different aspects of our personalities in different relationships and contexts. The psychiatry professor Arnold Ludwig debunks the myth that the self displayed in private is more genuine than the self exhibited in public: "Each self is as real to the person experiencing it and as much the product of natural forces as the other. All that the distinction between a true and a false self signifies is a value judgment."[67] As a result, uncovering secrets will not necessarily reveal who people "truly" are or enable more accurate assessments of their character. Instead, these disclosures can often be jarring, for they display people out of the context in which others may know them.

Revealing private facts when first getting to know a person can be even more distorting. According to Goffman, people need time to establish relationships before revealing secrets.[68] Immediate honesty can be costly. When we first meet somebody, we have little invested in that person. We haven't built any bonds of friendship or developed any feelings for that person. So if we learn about a piece of that person's private life that seems bizarre or unpleasant, it's easy to just walk away. But we don't just walk away from people we know well. With time to gain familiarity with a person, we're better able to process information, see the whole person, and weigh secrets in context.[69]

Does the awareness that we play different roles in different contexts mean that we should actively promote this behavior through privacy protection? Who trusts people who are too chameleon-like, radically changing their personalities in every situation? Although too much dissonance may be troublesome, Arnold Ludwig argues that "when you play various roles you're not necessarily being artificial or phony. These roles let you accentuate different aspects of yourself."[70] Society has come to accept the fact that there is dissonance between public and private selves. For example, people not only accept the telling of white lies but even deem them necessary in many contexts. As the philosopher Thomas Nagel notes: "One of the remarkable effects of a smoothly fitting public surface is that it protects one from the sense of exposure without having to be in any way dishonest or deceptive, just as clothing does not conceal the fact that one is naked underneath."[71]

Nagel's observation suggests a key point—society recognizes and accepts the fact that the public self is a partly fictional construct. The public self is constructed according to social norms about what is appropriate to expose in public. People may even feel uncomfortable when other people reveal "too much information" about themselves. In short, society expects the public self to be more buttoned-up than the private self.

The Trouble with Irrational—and Rational—Judgment

Besides judging based on partial information, people are also prone to making irrational judgments. Certain traits and conditions carry great stigma, which is often the result of incorrect assumptions and faulty knowledge. According to Goffman, stigma is "an attribute that is deeply discrediting." Certain stigmatic facts about a person include addiction, alcoholism, suicide attempts, mental disorders, unemployment, and illiteracy. People with stigma are often shunned or not fully accepted by society. Stigma can spread to family members, as when a child feels stigmatized by a parent's criminal past.[72]

People protect certain secrets because disclosure might lead to stereotyping and discrimination toward them and their families. For much of history, there were widespread beliefs that people who contracted particular diseases did so because of their character flaws. Even education has a difficult time cleansing stigma. People used to believe that the disease cholera was caused by sin. Later on, the cause of cholera was discovered to be poor sanitation. But even after this discovery, during the cholera epidemic of 1866, people still clung to the belief that the disease was "the scourge of the sinful." People with noninfectious illnesses, such as cancer, still find themselves shunned by friends and family. Susan Sontag contends: "Nothing is more punitive than to give a disease meaning—that meaning being invariably a moralistic one. Any important disease whose causality is murky, and for which treatment is ineffectual, tends to be awash in significance. First, the subjects of deepest dread (corruption, decay, pollution, anomie, weakness) are identified with the disease. The disease itself becomes a metaphor."[73]

Furthermore, the disclosure that people have certain diseases engenders assumptions. Discovery that a person has AIDS often results in speculation that the person has engaged in drug use, promiscuous sex, or homosexual sex.[74]

Several surveys reveal that many employers have incorrect views of cancer's effects and treatment, and cancer patients lose their jobs five times more frequently than employees without cancer.[75] Irrational judgments have existed throughout history and continue to exist. Even in the face of high costs, employers continue to engage in racial and other forms of discrimination. Market pressure cannot always rectify strongly held beliefs or subconscious prejudices.[76]

Not all judgments made based on people's personal information, however, are irrational. Suppose a person has a genetic predisposition to develop cancer. An employer might rationally decide not to hire that person, instead opting to hire another person with similar qualifications. The employer might reason that if the person at risk for developing cancer did, in fact, develop the disease, then he or she would miss many workdays. But even if it's rational for an employer to refuse to hire a worker because of a genetic condition, society should not necessarily condone that choice. And beyond genetic data, there is a lot of information—such as an employee's off-hours activities—to which society does not believe employers should be entitled, even when relevant to job performance.[77]

Freedom from Society's Oppressive Glare

In 1996 Jennifer Ringley, a twenty-year old student, set up a Web camera in her dorm room to broadcast an ongoing video of her life over the Internet on a website called JenniCam. The camera was always on, capturing her in the nude, masturbating, and having sex. Most of the time it captured the mundane, such as her writing, reading, or doing daily chores. During the time while JenniCam was running, a scandal erupted when Jennifer had sex with her friend's fiancé. Her friend found out about it from watching JenniCam. Jennifer's website became immensely popular, at one point receiving more than a million visits per day. Mainstream media began to pay attention too, and she made it onto the David Letterman show. According to Ringley: "I keep Jennicam alive not because I want or need to be watched, but because I simply don't mind being watched."[78] JenniCam moved to Jennifer's home when she left college. She kept it going for seven years, officially ending it in the beginning of the year 2004.

Most of us, I bet, would not want to live like Jennifer Ringley. Few people can live in front of the camera like Jennifer without feeling inhibited and self-conscious about everything they do. Privacy gives people space to be free from the scrutiny of society. The sociologist Alan Westin observes that privacy protects "minor non-compliance with social norms."[79] Many norms are routinely broken, and privacy permits society to ignore these small transgressions. Protecting privacy often means that we allow people to violate social norms without getting caught or punished for it, without having their peccadillos ascribed to their reputations. The sociologist Amitai Etzioni views privacy as a "realm" where people "can legitimately act without disclosure and accountability to others."[80]

Why do we want to allow people to transgress in private and get away with it? Why do we want to foster situations where people are not accountable for their actions? Some view privacy as protecting the individual at the expense of society. According to the law professor Fred Cate, "privacy may be seen as an antisocial construct. It recognizes the right of the individual, as opposed to anyone else, to determine what he will reveal about himself."[81] However, privacy need not be understood as something that thwarts social norms. Robert Post notes that privacy protects "rules of civility" that shape life in the community.[82] We have social norms about respect for each other, and from these norms privacy emerges.[83] Thus privacy doesn't just allow people to flout norms; privacy itself is a set of norms about how intrusive we should be into each other's lives. Just as it is rude to bump into people or crowd their space, it is also rude to intrude into their private business. As the historian Peter Gay observes, granting privacy to others reflects "a capacity to respect people with ideas and ideals at odds with one's own; in short, a liberality of temper."[84] We might not like what some people may do in private, but we respect their freedom to do it so long as it remains out of the public eye. Too much judgment by others about us can lead to an oppressive amount of social control. The psychiatrist Arnold Modell notes that for many people, private space might even be central to "psychic survival."[85] Most of us desire a limited realm where we have a reprieve from the judgment of others, which otherwise might become suffocating.

Even when people are not transgressing norms or engaging in deviant behavior, they may still desire privacy. People want privacy even for their mundane daily activities. Without privacy, people might experience significant unease at everything they do, constantly wondering how others might interpret their actions. Innocent behavior might appear suspicious out of context.

The Land of Second Chances

Another reason why people ought to be able to conceal private information is to enable them to recover from past mistakes and misconduct. Most of us have disgraceful moments in our past. We have done many things we might have regretted. In childhood we may have acted with great immaturity, been cruel to others, or done things that make us ashamed. There is a value in allowing individuals the opportunity to hide these past indiscretions in their skeleton closet.

America is the "land of second chances," the saying goes. As the legal historian Lawrence Friedman puts it: "American society is and has been a society of extreme mobility, in every sense of the word: social, economic, geographical. Mobility has meant freedom; mobility has been an American value. People often moved from place to place; they shed an old life like a snake molting its skin. They took on new lives and new identities. They went from rags to riches, from log cabins to the White House. American culture and law put enormous emphasis on second chances."[86]

We grow and change throughout our lives. According to the philosopher John Dewey, the individual is not "something complete, perfect, finished, an organized whole of parts united by the impress of a comprehensive form," but is "something moving, changing, discrete, and above all initiating instead of final."[87] A person is a life process from cradle to corpse. At any given moment, we are seeing just a snapshot in time, a slice of this lifelong process. As the playwright and author Friedrich Dürrenmatt eloquently wrote: "What one commonly called one's self was merely a collective term for all the selves gathered up in the past, a great heap of selves perpetually growing under the constant rain of selves drifting down through the present from the future, an accumulation of shreds of experience and memory, comparable to a mound of leaves that grows higher and higher under a steady drift of other falling leaves."[88]

Protection against disclosure permits room to change, to define oneself and one's future without becoming a "prisoner of [one's] recorded past."[89] Society has a tendency to tie people too tightly to the past and to typecast people in particular roles. The human personality is dynamic, yet accepting the complete implications of this fact can be difficult.

But in several circumstances, people find it important to know about the checkered pasts of others. For example, people may not want to risk trusting an individual with a criminal past because recidivism rates are quite high—many ex-convicts commit crimes again.[90] Society benefits, however, when people can rehabilitate themselves and start new, more productive lives. We have a long-standing commitment to providing opportunities for rehabilitation in this country. Indeed, some of this country's colonial settlers were convicted criminals, transported here for their crimes.[91] Most states have laws that expunge juvenile criminal records when the juvenile reaches adulthood.[92] As one court observed, "an unexpunged juvenile record may create a lifelong handicap because of the stigma it carries."[93] Our criminal justice system engages in frequent and extensive efforts to rehabilitate, such as prison education programs and boot camps. We must balance the value of rehabilitation against the value of the disclosure of the information.

GOSSIP THEN, GOSSIP NOW

In the past, gossip occurred backstage; it was fleeting and localized. The anthropologist Sally Engle Merry observes: "Gossip flourishes in close-knit, highly connected social networks but atrophies in loose-knit, unconnected ones."[94] Before the rise of the blogosphere, Jessica Cutler's gossip about her sexual experiences with Robert would probably have remained within her small circle of friends. But today details about people's private lives are increasingly migrating to the Internet. Jessica's blog was read by hundreds of thousands of people—perhaps millions. It is becoming harder and harder for people to escape their pasts. For example, in her book *Slut! Growing Up Female with a Bad Reputation,* Leora Tanenbaum relates that she suffered intense emotional damage because of being labeled a "slut" in high school. She finally escaped in college: "I sliced off the experience from my memory when I went away to college, where no one knew." "While a girl can almost instantly acquire a 'slut' reputation as a result of one well-placed rumor," Tanenbaum observes, "it takes months, if not years, for the reputation to evaporate, if it does at all."[95] With the Internet, however, escaping a bad reputation can be impossible. Moreover, traditional gossip occurs in a context, among people who know the person being gossiped about. But the Internet strips away that context, and this can make gossip even more pernicious.

The Internet is transforming the nature and effects of gossip. It is making gossip more permanent and widespread, but less discriminating in the appropriateness of audience. Suppose, for example, John and Jane Doe are a married couple. John Doe is having an affair with another woman. If Jane Doe's brother were to tell her about the affair, many people would think that the brother acted appropriately. As the law professor Anita Allen observes, people are accountable to others even in their private lives.[96] Many of us believe that Jane should know about John's affair. But that doesn't make it acceptable for him to write about John's affair on his blog. Audience matters. The information is of concern to Jane, but not to the entire world. Another consideration is the purpose of the disclosure. Disclosures made for spite, or to shame others, or simply to entertain, should not be treated the same as disclosures made to educate or inform. When we determine whether gossip is good or not, we must look at the who, what, and why of it. We should ask: Who is making the disclosure? Is the disclosure made to the appropriate audience? Is the purpose behind the disclosure one we should encourage or discourage? The problem with Internet gossip is that it can so readily be untethered from its context.

I believe that it is imperative that we do something to address the developments inherent in the marriage of traditional gossip to the technology of the Internet. But what? How do we protect privacy in a world where information is flowing ever more freely, where anybody can publish information to a worldwide audience? I will explore this issue later. First, though, let us turn to the practice of shaming—which, like gossip, has taken on new and troubling dimensions in the digital age.

Chapter 4 Shaming and the Digital Scarlet Letter

Laura had to write a five-page college paper on Hinduism in a hurry. She had little to work with and knew nothing about the topic. So she decided to cheat. She sent an instant message to Nate Kushner, who listed Hinduism in his online profile with AOL. She offered him money if he would write her paper for her on short notice. Nate was appalled by what Laura was trying to do, so he hatched a plan. He would agree to write her paper but would fill it with silly errors and copied passages that could readily be found by searching on the Internet. Kushner also had a blog, and he dashed off a post about his plan with the title: "Laura [lastname] is a Plagiarist."[1] Kushner referred to the student by her real name, and he also mentioned the college she attended. According to his plan, once she turned the paper in, he would email her as well as her college dean with a link to his blog post.

What he didn't expect was that his blog post began to attract significant attention. Other bloggers began linking to Kushner's blog post. Hundreds of people wrote comments to it. Some criticized Kushner as being too harsh on Laura. Others approved of Kushner's plan. "I can't wait to see this chick get her comeuppance," one commentator gleefully declared. "You do the crime, you do the time," another wrote, "She is absolutely getting everything she deserves."

The biology professor PZ Myers of the blog Pharyngula observed: "Here's a fine object lesson: a student solicited a term paper via instant messenger, and got more than she expected. Like her name up in lights on a web page and the information forwarded to the president of her university. I like it. It's a great little poison pill to make students more reluctant to attempt this sort of thing."[2]

In a follow-up post, Kushner wrote:

> God, I honestly had no idea this would become an internet-wide thing. My imagination had told me that this could be a funny story kept between me, her school, and a couple dozen friends of mine who visit this site.

People began calling Laura's school and her home. In a subsequent post, titled "The Saga Is Over," Kushner wrote:

> First of all, everybody, this is a cease and desist order to stop calling Laura and stop calling her university. Everybody knows now.

In a post the following day, Kushner wrote:

> Alright, here's how it ends, people. Brace yourselves for disappointment, because you're going to find out where I failed to show you blood when you wanted it.
>
> Also, let's reiterate. Nobody call Laura or her school anymore. Everybody knows now. . . .
>
> I do want this to be over. . . .
>
> I had thought I could make her sweat (as had been my plan practically since the paper solicitation fell into my lap) by sending her the link to the original story sometime on Wednesday, after she'd handed the paper in. . . .
>
> So it became Monday, and instead of finishing off my nice prank I was going to share with two or three dozen real-life friends, I was faced with all of you people looking for blood. I didn't want blood. What I wanted was irony.

Laura called Kushner and begged him to take down the post. Laura's mother got involved, pleading with him to take Laura's name off the Internet. Kushner wrote about the conversation in his post: "I explained another three times that I couldn't erase her from the whole internet, and that everybody knows." Kushner agreed, however, to edit his posts to substitute a fictitious last name for Laura.

Is the story true or just a hoax? One difficulty with the information on the

Internet is that it is hard to know how true it really is. If CNN ran the story, we'd trust that the facts were checked and verified; we'd believe that CNN would not deliberately fabricate the story. We'd be assured that if CNN's story were wrong in any way, CNN would suffer reputational harm. Reporters might get fired. Retractions and corrections would be made. But Kushner is an amateur. He's not a professional journalist. He doesn't have fact checkers. He doesn't have much of a journalistic reputation at stake. He might be concocting this entire scenario for amusement. Or he might be telling the truth. We just don't know for sure.

Whether true or false, this incident demonstrates how fast information can speed across the Internet. Kushner's blog posts attracted a large audience within a matter of hours. Numerous bloggers linked to it, and the Internet's bright spotlight moved over to Kushner's blog for a short while. Kushner appeared to be quite surprised by the sudden interest. He thought he was writing for the amusement of a few of his friends. And once the story broke out around the Internet, Kushner was unable to stuff it back into the bottle. His posts indicate how quickly it spiraled out of his control. When one puts information on the Internet, it can easily become like Frankenstein's monster, escaping the dominion of its master.

This incident also demonstrates the growing phenomenon of shaming people via the Internet. Shaming is nothing new—we've been doing it for centuries. But Internet shaming creates a permanent record of a person's transgressions. And it is done by amateur self-appointed investigative reporters, often without affording the target a chance at self-defense. Numerous others then join in to help shame the victim, creating the cyberspace equivalent to mob justice. Recall the dog poop girl incident, a classic example of the Internet's profound power to shame an individual. What are the virtues and vices of using the Internet to shame others? What, if anything, should be done about Internet shaming?

CYBERCOPS

Peoria is a city of slightly more than one hundred thousand people in Illinois. It is frequently used as a symbol of mainstream America. The question "How will it play in Peoria?" has become a formula for assessing the reaction of the average American citizen. So perhaps Peoria's entrance into the shame game is especially significant. The local government began shaming campaigns for property owners who owned blighted properties. Soon residents got into the shaming business. The anonymous creators of one new website, Peoria Crack House, attempt to publicly shame people suspected of owning drug dens.³ A sample post contains the address of the property, the name of its owner, and a picture of the owner's relative who was an ex-convict. The post is written in the form of a letter to the owner:

> Dear Angela [last name]:
>
> I'm not bothering to introduce myself, but that is only fair, considering you did not bother with introductions when you moved into the neighborhood and began to re-introduce it to young thugs dressed in getto [sic] attire, conducting their drug activity. . . .
>
> It's ironic that someone who was smart enough to qualify for a $61,000.00 loan from GSF Mortgage Corp . . . is too stupid to realize that in a neighborhood where most homes are at least twice the value of yours your neighbors are not going to put up with the sort of illegal, property devaluing crap with which the inhabitants of your property think they can engage.
>
> And here is what we already know about you, Angela [last name]:
>
> 1. You used to live on the East Bluff, in a house subsidized by a PHA affiliated Not for Profit Corporation . . . where you apparently liked to threaten and intimidate your neighbors by letting your Rottweiler run loose;
>
> 2. You also had a child at that address, Jamar [last name], that like [sic] to run around loose at night after curfew.
>
> 3. Last year you moved into [address], and then you got married to a Christopher [last name] when he was paroled from the Illinois Department of Corrections in January of 2005.

The post continues with more personal details about Angela.⁴ In a follow-up post later that day, the blogger wrote:

> Parole was contacted and advised of the information on this blog. Promptly, Parole agents swarmed the house, arrested and tested Mr. [last name], who was found to be positive for illegal drugs. Upon questioning, Mr. [last name] admitted that he had been smoking crack in the shed behind the house. He claimed he had not smoked it in the house, because he did not want to dis his woman.
>
> But now there are three young thugs . . . that are hanging off of the porch.
>
> Wanna bet that Angela is going to lose her house before the year is out!

Peoria Crack House fashions itself as a citizen's way to eliminate neighborhood crime and blight. At least from the blog's description of the events, it played a role in bringing the information to the attention of the authorities. But how did the blogger obtain all the information? What if it weren't correct? And what if it led to others in the neighborhood trying to take the law into their own hands?

The New York City Subway Flasher

On a hot day in August 2005, a twenty-two-year-old woman was riding on a New York City subway train. A man seated nearby on the train unzipped his pants, exposed himself, and began to masturbate. But the young woman was ready to fight back. She snapped his photo with her cell phone camera and posted it on the Internet. More than forty-five thousand people viewed the photo. "He made me feel creepy," the woman said. "I want to embarrass him."[5]

The *New York Daily News* reprinted the photograph on its front page and later published an editorial which stated: "The perv in her picture looks much more like a regular citizen than the flasher of myth. The difference is that nothing of the pre-cyber age could generate disgrace such as [the woman] so justly imposed when she posted the photo on the Internet."[6] Shortly afterward, the man was arrested. He was a forty-three-year old man who owned a restaurant in New York City.[7]

The Cell Phone Thief

In August 2005 John's expensive Sprint cell phone was stolen from his car. Sprint provides a website where people can upload the photos they take with their cell phone cameras, so John went to the site and saw that somebody had taken nearly forty photos and made some videos. They were mostly of a young man who appeared either alone or with his girlfriend and family members.[8]

John was angry. He sent a message to the man who apparently took his phone: "Like to steal cell phones and use them to take pics of your self and make videos. . . . HA! guess what pal . . . i have every pic you took and the videos. I will be plastering the town with pics of your face." The young man, named Danny, texted an indignant reply, but he carelessly exposed his full name in the process. John posted the information and photos on an electronic bulletin board—a website where users can have online discussions. He also took the information to the police.[9]

Comments erupted on the website. One person proclaimed: "Hope that the fool that took the camera gets what is coming to him." Another cackled: "I absolutely love this! ! ! ! ! ! ! ! ! ! ! ! !" Yet another snorted: "HAHAH! This is spreading on the internet like wild fire!" One commentator did a search under Danny's name and listed the results, which included the addresses for six people with Danny's full name. Comments poured in from around the world.

"He's now famous in Germany too," one person wrote, "cause a well known German board posted the link and the stor[y]."[10]

Kevin Poulsen, a reporter for the magazine *Wired,* wrote a story about the incident. He contacted Danny and learned that he was a sixteen-year-old. Because of Danny's young age, Poulsen "elected not to report his name."[11]

When John found out that Danny was a minor, he regretted posting the pictures and his name on the Internet. Now, commentators were reposting Danny's name and photo across the Internet. John removed what he had posted and wrote:

> THE PICTURES HAVE BEEN REMOVED TO PROTECT THE PRIVACY OF MINORS. WHEN I FIRST POSTED THIS STORY I DID NOT REALIZE THE PERSONS IN QUESTION ARE MINORS. I ENCOURAGE ALL OTHERS WITH PHOTOS OF THESE PEOPLE TO DELETE THEM FROM THEIR WEBSITES AS WELL.[12]

Others, however, didn't remove the photos. In fact, many plastered the photos in the comments to John's post. Some morphed the picture into a wanted poster with Danny's name.

Responses grew much nastier. Others posted pictures of Danny's face superimposed on various images, including pornographic photos. Comments on various electronic bulletin boards devolved into bigoted slurs and insults lodged against Danny.[13]

Back at the electronic bulletin board where John originally wrote about Danny, comments continued to pour in. One commentator said:

> And I encourage everybody that has the pictures to keep on spreading them so this little thieving idiot will be infamous, and if you live in his neighborhood to make a poster and warn EVERYBODY of this little rotten bastard. I hope he rots in prison, but most probably he will get a slap on the wrist, the spoiled brat.[14]

Another asked: "WHO THE HELL CARES IF THEY ARE MINORS OR NOT????" John wrote in reply:

> Because minors do really stupid things without even thinking of the consequences and how other people will be affected.
>
> When I was kid I did absurdly stupid things. . . . Now by no means is that statement I just typed meant to be a pardon to Danny. This has been reported to the police and I WILL be following through to make sure this punk learns that there are consequences for stealing another person's property.
>
> What has gone on here is just as wrong. In another time this would be described as a lynching and you people would be called a lynch mob. Yes, I know I'm the one who

Photo of the cell phone culprit morphed into a
wanted poster (last name and face obscured)

started this, it was bad judgment on my part. People who . . . had nothing to do with
this have been dragged in just due to the fact that they keep extremely bad company.
Does anyone realize that they could be creating another victim of this crime?[15]

Incensed by John's change of heart, commentators began posting John's personal information on the comment board. One commentator wrote:

Now you've had some moral dilemma and want to recant, well I have some bad news
for you. You may not find Danny's persecution funny, but we sure do. . . . [We] have
no pity on thieving punks like Danny and I bet he's learned quite a lesson.

Consider our work a community service. Danny could have gone from boosting
phones to jacking cars, thug life and all. I would venture to guess that he'll keep his
hands to himself. . . .

Behold the power of the internets! ! ! ! ! ! ![16]

This incident raises several difficult questions. A stolen cell phone is probably not high on the priority list of the NYPD. Perhaps the Internet is a great new tool to aid in law enforcement. It can enable people to help enforce laws that police aren't sufficiently enforcing.

On the other hand, in Danny's case, the photos posted included not only himself but his teenage girlfriend and family. These other people were not engaged in any crime, but their pictures were plastered across the Internet. Danny was just a juvenile, too. John regretted his decision to post Danny's pictures and information on the Web, but the situation spiraled out of John's control. Although the illegal conduct of the subway flasher is scarcely open to question, perhaps Danny wasn't the thief. Perhaps he just found the phone or perhaps somebody gave it to him. What happens when people think that they have found the culprit but are mistaken?

Self-Deputized Police on the Internet

The Peoria Crack House website and the pillorying of the subway flasher and the cell phone thief are just a few examples of how the Internet is being used by people to shame others. In these cases, people frustrated that others were getting away with crime attempted to take the law into their own hands and expose the wrongful conduct. In some instances, they got salutary results—the wrongdoers were caught and punished. Can the Internet serve to enhance people's ability to help the cops catch criminals? Is this a good thing?

NORMS AND SHAMING

In a San Francisco Apple computer retail store, customers noticed a vaguely androgynous person spending a lot of time there with a computer. The Apple store had free wireless Internet service, and the person apparently was taking advantage of it by frequently hanging out at the store. Some people became annoyed at the person, and they blogged and posted pictures online. One blogger noted:

> The photo, taken on July 7, appears to show the same person: same hair, same earbuds. And it appears that he is a she.
>
> Her tenure at the store is now approaching at least one month. Given that the average monthly rent for an apartment in San Francisco is currently about $1700 (not including wireless Internet access), I'd say she's getting a pretty good deal.[17]

Another blogger wrote:

> [Other bloggers] have been razzing the so-called Apple Store Squatter—a PC-toting woman who allegedly spends hours, if not days away at the San Francisco Apple Store slurping up the free wifi. Just a reminder to y'all that no one's privacy is safe from the blogosphere—especially if you spend any time in public![18]

Was the Apple Store Lady breaking the law? Perhaps she was loitering, but the store employees apparently didn't seem to care. Why were others so concerned about such a trivial thing as one woman who overused free wifi in a store?

Norms

Although not breaking the law, the Apple Store Lady was violating a norm. She was using a free service "too much," which is to say beyond the amount of time that some people thought reasonable. To understand shaming, it is essential to understand norms. Every society has an elaborate lattice of norms. A norm is a rule of conduct, one less official than a law, but sometimes as improper to transgress. If you break a law, you can be punished by the government or be sued by another person. Norms generally are not enforced in this manner. Nor are they written down in a book of legal code. Nonetheless, norms are widely known and widely observed rules of social conduct.[19]

Norms and law overlap to some extent; many crimes are violations of social norms that we have agreed through legislation and adjudication to enforce through formal punishments. But norms cover a wider range of conduct. For example, there is no law against picking one's nose in public or against being rude, but both are norm violations. Norms encompass a litany of rules involving manners and etiquette that law doesn't cover. A poem from the seventeenth century humorously illustrates the rules of etiquette:

> Let not thy privy members be
> layd upon to be view'd
> it is most shameful and abhord,
> detestable and rude.
>
> Retaine not urine nor the winde
> which doth thy body vex
> so it be done with secresie
> let that not thee perplex.[20]

Norms develop and change over time. Consider, for example, the norms of cell phone use. In the United States, the number of people using cell phones grew by more than 350 percent from 1993 to 2003, from 34 million users to 159 million.[21] Worldwide, there are more than a billion cell phone users.[22]

Bystanders are especially irked by the disruptiveness of cell phones. According to one poll, 59 percent said that they would rather go to the dentist than sit beside a cell phone user.[23] In a popular commercial shown in movie theaters, an obnoxious man uses his cell phone in a myriad of outrageous ways. A jingle plays in the background with lyrics that begin: "It's inconsiderate cell phone man." At the end of the ad, he boasts to another person over the phone: "I've got a million minutes."[24]

Generally accepted rules of etiquette for cell phones have quickly developed. Turn them off at the theater. Don't speak in a loud voice on the phone when in public. If you get a call during dinner at a restaurant, excuse yourself from the table if you need to take it. Few people would argue with these norms. Within a relatively short time following the wide acceptance of this new technology, there appears to be considerable consensus about cell phone norms. The extent of compliance with these norms, however, still lags.

Norms are often good things. As Henry David Thoreau observed, "We live thick and are in each other's way, and stumble over one another." Thus we "have had to agree on a certain set of rules, called etiquette and politeness, to make this frequent meeting tolerable and that we need not come to open war."[25] Norms enable us to get along smoothly and to resolve many situations that could lead to disputes.

But norms can be bad things, too. For instance, they can be riddled with double standards. Throughout much of Western history, for example, adultery by women was viewed as vastly more culpable than that by men.[26] Additionally, some activities are common but hidden, such as certain sexual practices. As Anita Allen notes, society can be quite hypocritical about sex. Society's attitudes toward sex are a complex stew of "conflicting physical, emotional, and social imperatives."[27] There are also many norms we now recognize as unjust.

Norm Enforcement

When somebody violates a norm, a few others might try to confront that norm violator. I call these people the "norm police." Just as we need police to enforce the law, we need norm police to enforce norms. If a norm never gets enforced, then it will gradually cease to be a norm.

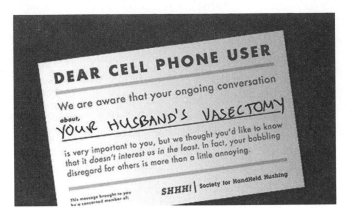

Sample SHHH card. Designed by Aaron James Draplin,
http://www.draplin.com, based on an idea by Jim Coudal's wife,
Heidi, http://www.coudal.com

Regarding cell phones, the designers Jim Coudal and Aaron Draplin, inspired by an idea from Jim's wife, Heidi, created free cards that people could download from the Internet and hand out to obnoxious cell phone users.[28]
According to the website,

> After reading a story in the NYT, Jim's wife Heidi came up with a method to fight back against the obnoxious cell phone users that we all have to deal with in stores, restaurants, trains and pretty much everywhere else. Can design ride to the rescue? Jim and the incomparable Aaron Draplin think it can. So, as a public service, we introduce the reasonably polite SHHH, the Society for HandHeld Hushing.

In many cases, norm police help us maintain an orderly society. We want to keep cell phone users from becoming too obnoxious. We want norms to develop and for them to be enforced. Shame makes us self-aware in an often painful and uneasy way.[29] It can serve as both an external and an internal check on behavior. The tough issue, however, is just how much norm enforcement we want.

The Internet is quickly becoming a powerful norm-enforcement tool. A plethora of websites now serve as forums for people to shame others. For example, a website called Rude People allows users to post reports of their encounters with impolite individuals.[30] On the website PlateWire, people post information about bad drivers, identified by their license plate numbers. The site declares: "Report and flag bad drivers, award good drivers, and even flirt with cute drivers. PlateWire was born out of frustration from years of driving alongside drivers who seem to have no concern with anyone's safety, including their own."[31] And on the website Flickr, where people post photos, there are countless snapshots of individuals accused of talking too loudly on their cell phones.[32] Some post pictures of "the annoying guy behind us," the "rude man," "obnoxious people," or anybody else who acts in an uncivil manner.[33]

This new norm policing technology raises all sorts of difficult questions. To explore these questions, let's look at an example of how the Internet can be used to enforce norms of tipping.

Bitter Waitress

For quite a long time, sociologists, psychologists, and economists have been fascinated by tipping. Scores of scholarly papers have examined the practice.[34] The practice is less common in Europe and in many other countries than in the United States, where people tip for a variety of services. We tip servers in restaurants, doorpeople at hotels, concierges, cab drivers, and more. The general rule of thumb is that one tips between 15 and 20 percent. Tipping in the United States generates $27 billion per year in income.[35]

One reason why scholars find tipping so fascinating is that people often tip servers whom they will never encounter again. Of course, if we will see a server again, it makes good sense to tip that person well. After all, if we tip poorly, the server might treat us badly next time. But in many cases, we'll never see a particular waiter or waitress again. Why bother tipping? Why not just keep the cash? We could save a lot of money this way, and there would be few consequences to us. After all, who would find out?

Certain traditional economic theories of human behavior have a difficult time explaining tipping. If there's no external sanction for not tipping well, and there's no continuing relationship between the tipper and server, then the rational self-interested person shouldn't bother tipping. Yet the majority of us tip anyway.

For those who don't, there's little that can be done to punish them for it. By the time the server finds out about the measly (or nonexistent) tip, the diner has left the restaurant. Nobody else might find out either—it's something known by the server and the tipper and anyone the server happens to complain to.

But now something can be done about lousy tippers. A website called BitterWaitress allows servers to enter information to a "Shitty Tipper Database."[36] It contains the names and locations of bad tippers, the tip, the percentage, as well as a description of the tipper. The website declares:

> Welcome to the Shitty Tipper Database (beta). OK, so here's how the fun works. Very simply, you click *submit to the STD* and enter the name, total check, and tip of somebody who left you a shitty tip.

The database looks like this:

Shitty tipper	Location	# in party	Total bill / tip amount	Percentage	
[full name]	Minneapolis, MN	5	$58.73 / $8.00	13%	*Read details*
[full name]	Orlando	4	$125.00 / $0.00	< 1% you cheap fuck	*Read details*
[full name]	Los Angeles	1	$19.00 / 0.50	2%	*Read details*

The database goes on and on. People can search the database for specific names. According to the website's author, "A shitty tip is, by my definition, any gratuity under 17% for service which one's peers would judge as adequate or better (e.g. Orders are correct, on time, special requests are honored, etc.)." Offenders are also offered a rare online opportunity: "If you see your name here and would like to apologize, click *submit an apology.*"

When you click "read details" in the database, you get a short narrative about each bad tipper. Here's an example:

> Tipper's Name: [full name]
>   Where it happened: Virginia
>   Total bill / Tip amount / Percentage: $40.93 / $0.00 / 0%
>   What happened: If you get this girl, watch out! She is the type to use the excuse that you are rude to not leave a tip. I was working cocktail (by myself) the night she came in, and had just got sat with a party of 10 that wanted 10 separate checks. I brought their food out, and was particularly nice to them, and thanked them for coming in etc. In the tip space of the credit card slip, she wrote "Don't be rude." . . . Is this your pathetic excuse not to tip me because you are a ghetto piece of shit?? Fuck you then . . . be careful next time that there is not a big pile of spit in your stupid well done steak.[37]

The author of a comment about another patron gripes: "Cheap dirt buckets! Maybe they should spend a little less money on their grody tattoos and a little more money tipping for exceptional service. Cheap, unattractive, ignorant jerks."[38]

Malcolm Gladwell, author of the best-sellers *The Tipping Point* and *Blink,* found himself in the website's database for leaving only a 10 percent tip. Gladwell denied that he is a bad tipper: "I could have sworn I was reliably in the 15-to-20 percent range."[39] There is no attempt to verify the information on the website, and any server can submit a name and an entry. The website has a disclaimer that states: "Please note that all submissions are printed with minimal or no editing. We are not responsible for submissions to the [database]. Uh-uh, no way, not in the least."

Bad Boys Getting Their Due

Some of the new shaming websites allow women to publicly shame men who engage in bad behavior. One of these sites is a blog called Holla Back NYC, to which people submit cell phone pictures of men who make crude remarks to them.[40] At the top of the website are pictures of women confidently holding cell phone cameras like loaded pistols pointed at the viewer. The site declares:

> HOLLA BACK NYC EMPOWERS NEW YORKERS TO HOLLA BACK AT STREET HARASSERS. WHETHER YOU'RE COMMUTING, LUNCHING, PARTYING, DANCING, WALKING, CHILLING, DRINKING, OR SUNNING, YOU HAVE THE RIGHT TO FEEL SAFE, CONFIDENT, AND SEXY, WITHOUT BEING THE OBJECT OF SOME TURD'S FANTASY. SO STOP WALKIN' ON AND HOLLA BACK: SEND US PICS OF STREET HARASSERS!

Incidents described range from coarse pickup lines to gawking to flashing to reading porn in public.

Another website, Don't Date Him Girl, provides a forum for women to denounce men who cheat on them. The website's motto is "investigate before you date."[41] Don't Date Him Girl describes itself as "an online community of powerful women from around the world who choose to exercise their rights to free speech on the Internet by boldly sharing their bad dating experiences with other women."[42]

The website's mission statement offers a utopian vision:

> Wouldn't it be great if your next paramour came with a list—Secrets I'm Keeping From You? Or, how fabulous would it be if you could get all your new boyfriend's exes in a room and cross-examine them, Gloria Allred-style? You could really learn how your new man operates. You'd have information you could use to discern whether you're making the right choice in love. Of course, you can do a criminal

background check, but no one's invented a way to do a personality check. Is he or she attentive, caring and ambitious? Or does he cheat and lie? Is he controlling or is he a mama's boy? A criminal background check cannot answer these questions.[43]

The website has a database with profiles under the name of each errant man. The profiles describe the man's detestable behavior, often in great detail. Several of the profiles include pictures. The misbehavior chronicled at Don't Date Him Girl ranges from the mild to severe. For example, one entry reads:

> His name is Cliff. He's a charmer. A doctor, musician, athlete, good looking guy! He is on (or has been on) Match.com, Yahoo!, AmericanSingles, JDate, eHarmony. . . .
>
> Basically, he cannot remain loyal to one woman. During our brief dating time he gave me the impression we were exclusive. A friend of mine spotted him online and after some browsing I found him on several sites. When I confronted him he lied. He's not a bad guy but just cannot respect women. . . .
>
> I just want to warn others not to be taken in by his initial charm as I was. Just ask him about his background with woman and about his relationship with his mother and you'll have the full picture. And lastly, he seems to be growing! Last year he was 5'11" in his profile. . . . this year he's 6'0"!

Another profile asserts:

> This man should be avoided AT ALL COSTS! He lures women into his web of deceit and lies through Cupid dot com, and other online dating sites. He has a violent criminal past which includes beating up his ex wife and sending her to the hospital!

Is There a Problem?

Should we see websites like BitterWaitress and Don't Date Him Girl as a positive revolution in norm enforcement? Perhaps the Internet enables more effective norm enforcement than people can achieve in realspace. The Internet can enable norm violators to be shamed in many instances where it would be difficult or impossible to do otherwise. Without BitterWaitress, bad tippers could continue with impunity, undetected and unpunished. Now, on the Internet, their stingy souls can be bared for everyone to see. Is this a good thing?

THE DEATH AND REBIRTH OF SHAMING PUNISHMENTS

From Salem, Massachusetts, in the year 1674, comes this account of how one transgressor was punished:

Hannah Gray, according to one of her neighbors, was a "lying little devil." Another neighbor said she had seen Hannah in the company of Andrew Davis, acting in a lascivious manner. A seventeen-year-old girl testified that her brother had told her how Hannah used to entice "the scoller boys" (from Harvard, presumably) and use "baudly language." The court ordered her to stand at the meetinghouse at Salem and later at Beverly with a paper on her head on which was written in capital letters; "I STAND HEERE FOR MY LACIVIOUS & WANTON CARIAGES"[44]

In the past, shaming punishments were common. The ancient Romans would brand a letter signifying the crime onto the wrongdoer's forehead—the Latin equivalent of M for murder, V for vagrancy, and F for fighting.[45] Branding was also performed in colonial America. Burglars were branded on the face with the letter B, and someone who stole another's hog was branded with an H.[46] Bodily mutilation was also common. As the legal historian Lawrence Friedman observes about the American colonies, "Dozens of detached ears . . . litter the record books."[47]

Another popular punishment was the pillory. A transgressor was forced to stand in public with head and hands locked between two wooden boards. The device was used for dishonest merchants, libelers, adulterers, drunkards, thieves, and many others.[48] Women were subjected to the "ducking chair" for "scolding": tied to a chair, the woman was dunked into a river.[49] Other punishments included being whipped in public, being paraded around with a sign proclaiming one's offenses, or being forced to do humiliating labor.[50]

Nathaniel Hawthorne's 1850 novel *The Scarlet Letter* provides a powerful illustration of a colonial shaming punishment. During the seventeenth century, in a small Puritan community, Hester Prynne is forced to wear the letter A stitched to her clothing as a punishment for her adulterous affair. This symbol serves as a form of public identification, "fantastically embroidered and illuminated upon her bosom," that links her to her breach of community norms. It serves as an inescapable reminder of her past misdeeds: "It had the effect of a spell, taking her out of the ordinary relations with humanity, and inclosing her in a sphere by herself."[51]

Over time, these colorful punishments disappeared. Why? One reason is that shame lost some of its power as the population expanded, as towns turned into cities, and as people more frequently moved from one place to another. In colonial times, shaming was a severe punishment. People were not very mobile in seventeenth-century America. Communities were close-knit; most people in town knew one another.[52] Public humiliation could be devastating in such tight communities: "Colonists both dreaded this humiliating exposure and were repelled by the threat of enduring the judgmental, jeering eyes of community peers."[53]

Urbanization and mobility changed the nature of communities. Today, in large urban areas, people are surrounded by strangers; they go about their days in relative anonymity. They can readily move to different cities and become part of new communities. These facets of modern life make it easier to escape the sting of shame.

Another reason that shaming subsided was the rise of prisons. Since there were few prisons during colonial times, other forms of punishment had to be used. The more serious crimes were punishable by execution, but for the less serious ones, shame was enough of a sanction. Incarceration provided an alternative means for punishing people.[54] No longer exposed to public scorn, criminals were locked away in institutions that the public rarely saw. Punishment used to be a public spectacle; now it is hidden from public view.[55]

Today, however, shaming punishments have returned—with a vengeance. Localities are publicizing photographs of men who solicit prostitutes. In 1997 Kansas City began broadcasting on television the names, photos, and addresses of people arrested for soliciting prostitutes. It was called *John TV*. Oakland is placing images on large billboards of people caught soliciting prostitutes.[56] Judges are requiring thieves to wear T-shirts referring to their crimes. Other judges have forced people to wear "brightly colored bracelets that read 'DUI Convict,' 'I Write Bad Checks,' and the like."[57] In 2004 two states—Massachusetts and Rhode Island—began posting the names of delinquent taxpayers on a website.[58]

THE VIRTUES OF INTERNET SHAMING

The shaming sanctions I have described are being undertaken by the government to enforce the law. Internet shaming, in contrast, is often done to punish not just violations of law but also transgressions of norms. Moreover, the Internet allows shaming not only by the government but also by everyday citizens.

Internet shaming has many benefits. Without shaming, people like the dog poop girl, the subway flasher, and the creep who harasses women in the street would often go unpunished. In a world of increasingly rude and uncivil behavior, shaming helps society maintain its norms of civility and etiquette.

Online shaming also gives people a chance to fight back, to voice their disapproval of inappropriate behavior and even of poor customer service. A growing segment of online shaming is devoted to corporations that mistreat their customers. For example, the law professor Eugene Volokh of the popular blog The Volokh Conspiracy complained about the customer service he received from Dell for his laptop computer:

> Dell gets the dubious honor of having given me what's likely the most ridiculously bad customer service experience I've had in years. I have a simple problem: The hard drive for my Dell notebook crashed after my computer was out of warranty. I bought a new hard drive, but now I need a boot disk for the Microsoft XP Professional operating system that I originally bought loaded onto my computer. I suspect this happens very often; there ought to be a standard procedure for it.
>
> I've now spent over an hour trying to get this straightened out—almost all of it navigating through the voice-mail menus, waiting on hold, or being transferred to some other department. I got cut off during the transfer process twice. I've probably talked to eight different people. I was transferred to spare parts, who told me I had to talk to customer support, who then tried to transfer me back to spare parts, except at that point the call was cut off.[59]

The Volokh Conspiracy receives thirty thousand or more visits each day, so it would be wise for Dell to take notice. Ordinarily, if a company treats a customer badly, it takes a while for word to work its way around. But the blogosphere makes it much easier to give customer complaints some sting.

In another incident, a blogger sparked a public relations nightmare for Sony BMG after the company put hidden antipiracy software on Sony CDs that would be installed on the hard drives of users who played the disks in their computers.[60] Sony had been using the software for about eight months until Mark Russinovich, a computer expert and blogger, discovered it and blogged about it in October 2005.[61] Mark explained that the software made affected computers less secure, and his post ignited an uproar across the blogosphere. The mainstream media soon picked up the story, and Sony quickly responded by releasing a patch to remove the software.

Across the Internet, people are shaming companies into providing them better service, into fulfilling the promises of their glitzy ads that tout prompt and reliable assistance for their products. This kind of shaming allows the little guy to fight back against the big corporation rather than go through the typical channels of writing a complaint letter and getting a formulaic "we appreciate your concerns and we'll do better next time" reply. As a spokesperson for Consumer Action declared: "To get back at people who are out to steal or swindle, shaming may be a reasonable response. . . . Anything that produces more information, anything that penetrates this slickly manicured image, is useful information."[62]

Like companies, individuals can have "slickly manicured" reputations, and shaming might expose these reputations as a façade. People might find it useful to know about the dog poop girl, for they might not want to associate with her. Shaming can thus provide valuable information to help us assess each other's reputations.

Moreover, without the Internet shaming, people would easily be able to get away with rude and wrongful behavior. Internet shaming makes it harder for people to escape their transgressions. And people like the dog poop girl, the cell phone thief, and the subway flasher deserve to be punished. The law professor Lior Strahilevitz points out the virtues of marshaling the public to report on the infractions of others. Programs such as "How's My Driving?" which encourage people to call a toll free number to register complaints about bad driving by truck drivers, have reduced driving accidents significantly.[63] Strahilevitz recommends expanding such programs to all drivers and even to other contexts.[64] If "How's My Driving?" programs work well in the offline world, perhaps we should celebrate the development of similar programs online. Shaming can empower people to enforce laws and social norms that increasingly go unenforced because our vast and impersonal society allows transgressors to remain obscure and anonymous, unaccountable for their vile conduct.

THE VICES OF INTERNET SHAMING

Although Internet shaming can have many benefits, it unfortunately also can raise some very severe problems. The primary trouble is that Internet shaming is hard to keep under control, and this fault can be particularly pernicious.

Permanent Alienation

One of the chief drawbacks of Internet shaming is the permanence of its effects. Internet shaming creates an indelible blemish on a person's identity. Being shamed in cyberspace is akin to being marked for life. It's similar to being forced to wear a digital scarlet letter or being branded or tattooed. People acquire permanent digital baggage. They are unable to escape their past, which is forever etched into Google's memory. For the philosopher Martha Nussbaum, shame is more than simply an expression of displeasure at particular acts; rather, it is an enduring reduction in social status to a lesser kind of person:

"Shame punishments, historically, are ways of marking a person, often for life, with a degraded identity. . . . Guilt punishments make the statement, 'You committed a bad act.' Shame punishments make the statement, 'You are a defective type of person.'" Nussbaum contends: "Tattoos, brands, signs—these mark a person as having a deviant identity, and their role historically has been to announce that spoiled identity to the world." For Nussbaum, shaming is too degrading to a person's dignity for a respectable society to encourage it.[65]

Certain forms of temporary shaming, in which a person is humiliated for a short period of time and then reintegrated into the community, are much less problematic than everlasting shaming. Shame has a way of alienating people, inhibiting their ability to rehabilitate and reintegrate themselves into the community.[66] Shame creates an impulse to cover up and hide.[67] Perhaps the best-known image of shame is that of Adam and Eve covering themselves as they are expelled from the Garden of Eden. Shame is about hiding; it is about exile; it is about withdrawal. Shame's tendency to lead to withdrawal and alienation makes it troubling. Without allowing a wrongdoer to reenter community life, shame becomes quite destructive. Wrongdoers are not educated or simply taught a lesson. Their reputation is wounded, and they are left without a chance to become part of the community again. People alienated from society often have little to lose and a lot of bitterness—a recipe for their continuing to engage in wrongdoing.

Lack of Proportionality in Punishment

Generally, we believe that punishment should be proportionate to the crime. The problem with Internet norm enforcement is that it often spirals out of control. Offenses that deserve a mild scolding are punished with digital equivalent to branding. When someone makes a grievous mistake, he or she ought to be punished. But disproportionate punishment risks creation of an oppressive society. Even desirable norms can be enforced to an excessive degree.[68] Internet shaming has a tendency to become overzealous. Often the punishments don't fit the crime, and people's lives can be ruined for relatively minor transgressions.

Unlike the shaming of businesses, the shaming of individuals is often more difficult to ameliorate. Companies can readily reinvent themselves, and they routinely do so after their reputation suffers damage. Institutions can change their management, their personnel, and their business philosophy. We often more readily accept change in institutions than in individuals. Before online shaming, individuals could also reinvent themselves, but a tarnished reputation on the Internet is hard to escape from. Often, the information fragments about a person that appear in a search will not include the person's redemption. When shaming occurs online, it ceases to be a temporary mark of disgrace and becomes a lasting inscription of stigma. Permanent shame can be unproductive. It punishes people for longer than necessary and it prevents them from building new lives.

Lack of Due Process

In medieval towns and villages, long before the dawn of police, justice would be carried out by posses. Victims would raise the hue and cry, and posses would hunt down the suspected offender and carry out punishment on the spot (typically execution). We've come a long way from those days. But Internet shaming resurrects dimensions of the posse.

Internet shaming falls outside the control of the legal system. Indeed, as Nussbaum argues, shaming involves a sanction that the state cannot entirely control:

> In shaming, the state does not simply mete out punishment through its own established institutions. It invites the public to punish the offender. This is not only an unreliable way to punish, but one that is intrinsically problematic, for it invites the "mob" to tyrannize over whoever they happen not to like. Justice by the mob is not the impartial, deliberative, neutral justice that a liberal-democratic society typically prizes.[69]

Internet shaming is farther removed from the state's control than government-sponsored shaming punishments. In the ordinary criminal justice process, a person is innocent until proven guilty. The world of shaming works differently, as people are punished without a hearing. In one incident, the University of Colorado used a website to post surveillance photos of students and other individuals it wanted to identify for smoking marijuana on Farrand Field. It was long a tradition at the university for students to smoke pot on Farrand Field each year on April 20—a party called "420 Day." The university wanted to stamp out this tradition, so it created a website on which it posted pictures of 150 students captured in the act of smoking pot.[70] According to the website:

> The University is offering a reward for the identification of any of the individuals pictured below. After reviewing the photos (click on a photo for a larger image), you may claim the reward by following the directions below:
>   1. Contact the UCPD Operations section at (303) 492-8168

2. Provide the photo number and as much information as you have about the individual.

3. Provide your name and contact information.

4. If the identity is verified to be correct, you will be paid a $50 reward for every person identified.

5. The reward will be paid to the first caller who identifies a person below, multiple rewards will not be paid for individuals listed below.[71]

The website consisted of a grid of thumbnail photos that people could click on to get larger, high-resolution images. Pictures of students who were identified were stamped with the word IDENTIFIED in large capital letters.

The Farrand Field website purported to investigate "trespassers" on the field. But it really appeared to be an attempt to use shaming to try to snuff out the embers of 420 Day. Soon after the website was created, it was taken down. The reason why is unknown.

The Farrand Field website exposed students engaging in a minor infraction to being forever memorialized as drug users, and it did so even before students were convicted of any wrongdoing. Some of the students might have been smoking cigarettes; some might have just been there with friends. But their inclusion on the website implicated them.

Norm enforcers can be mistaken. There are no rules and procedures to ensure that the Internet norm police are accurate in their assessments of who should be deemed blameworthy. An example by the mainstream media illustrates the problems with mistaken attempts to shame. In one incident in 2005, a Fox News commentator gave out the home address of a man believed to have ties to the London subway bombing. The man wasn't charged with any crime and hadn't been officially identified as a suspect. But in any case the harm wasn't suffered by the suspected terrorist. He had vacated the house three years before. Instead, a couple with three children currently occupied the home. After the broadcast, the Internet shaming brigade sprung into action. People posted satellite photos of the home online. They provided directions to the home. For several weeks after the broadcast, the couple was harassed and threatened. Their home was spray-painted with the word *Terrist* [*sic*]. The couple attempted in vain to contact Fox News to complain about the error. Eventually, Fox News issued an apology. A Fox spokesperson stated that the commentator was "reprimanded for his careless error." The commentator explained that "mistakes happen" and that he had used "the best information we had at the time."[72]

It is tempting to shame, especially when we are convinced that we have seen something blameworthy. But what if we're wrong? What if we don't know the whole story? We have developed procedures in the law to protect against such errors. No such procedures exist in the world of shaming.

Vengeance and Bullying

Some people are shamed even when they did nothing wrong. Recall what happened to the Star Wars Kid. He didn't do anything improper, yet that didn't absolve him from being shamed. Sometimes people are just mean, and a joke can get out of hand.

One person's shaming is another's personal revenge or yet another's bullying. For example, a website called Revenge World provides a forum for spurned lovers to take vengeance by writing about their exes and posting nude pictures of them.[73] According to the website's introduction:

> RevengeWorld.com is an online community which allows its users to vent and post pictures and stories on the world wide web, viewable by the RevengeWorld.com community. This site is FREE, and will remain that way always.[74]

Some, but not all, of the people chronicled on Revenge World allegedly cheated during relationships. Many pictures posted are just the result of a bad breakup. Is this kind of revenge ever justified, no matter how unfaithful a person might have been? And even if you think it is justified in some cases, who determines when it is and isn't? One problem with shaming is that we can't always agree on who deserves to be shamed and to what degree. While we all agree on some norms, we don't agree on many others. Who controls what norms are being enforced?

Moreover, some forms of shaming can deter legitimate activities. Websites are emerging to create blacklists of individuals who file medical malpractice claims. One site started in 2004, Doctors Know Us, listed the names of malpractice plaintiffs.[75] After a *New York Times* article chronicled the plight of a man who was blacklisted at the site and had trouble finding physicians, the site was taken offline.

How Much Shaming Do We Need?

Although Internet shaming can help enforce norms, norms can often take care of themselves without the help of external enforcement. The law professor Robert Cooter observes that norms often work through a process called "internalization"—people follow norms not because they fear external shaming by others but because they would feel ashamed of themselves if they violated a norm.[76] Returning to tipping, one explanation why most people tip even when there will be no penalties if they don't is that they feel as if it's the right thing to do. As the economist Ofer Azar explains, "People tip because it is the social norm; if they deviate from it they feel unfair and embarrassed."[77] Tipping norms work internally, and this internal pressure often suffices. Of course, for some norms, we may desire the added benefit of external norm enforcement, but for many norms internal self-enforcement works quite nicely on its own. As the law professor Lawrence Mitchell puts it, people "not only want to avoid blame, but blameworthiness."[78] Even if we're never caught, we can never escape from ourselves, and our internal judges are often our most stringent.

FROM SHAMING TO VIGILANTISM

Beyond the problems I have discussed, Internet shaming can devolve into vigilantism and violence. In 2004 two commuters in San Jose, California, became fed up with single drivers who were using carpool lanes. One morning, a driver kept tailgating them in the carpool lane trying to pass. They let him pass only to discover that he had no passengers and shouldn't have been in the lane.

At that moment, the idea was born. One of the commuters explained: "We looked at each other and said, 'Somebody ought to have a Web site and post these clowns' pictures.' Then we realized, we're a couple of Web heads. We can just do it ourselves."[79]

That's how Carpool Cheats came into being:

This website is dedicated to all those who abide by the rules and brave the traffic on our freeways everyday. Many of us who commute everyday aren't able to avail ourselves of the carpool (HOV) lanes for one reason or another. When I don't have passengers, I stay out of the HOV lanes and slog along at a snail's pace to get to work or home.

I've talked with hundreds of other commuters that are annoyed by those individuals that think they're above the law or better than the rest of us, or privileged . . . or something . . . and can consequently drive solo in the HOV lane.

Using a high-quality digital camera, the two commuters posted photos of carpool cheats. The photos included pictures of license plates and the faces of the scurrilous motorists.

But Carpool Cheats didn't last very long. The website's content was soon removed and replaced with this notice:

NOTICE TO OUR FAITHFUL READERS

CarpoolCheats.org website is temporarily out of service.

This is due to several threatening communications from an individual or individuals presently (but not for long) unknown to us.

We are investigating this situation with the aid of our legal advisors and the California State Bar Association, and law enforcement officials.

We wish to thank our loyal supporters and fellow commuters who continue to use the commuter lanes in the intended manner.[80]

On the surface, Carpool Cheats sounds like sweet justice to the people who brazenly take advantage of carpool lanes. But it involves private citizens engaging in their own form of vigilante justice. What if they're wrong about a driver and there really is another passenger—perhaps a child that they can't see? And because private citizens are taking matters into their own hands, it can incite people subjected to the shaming to retaliate in return. That's what happened with Carpool Cheats. It's what can happen any time people try to take justice into their own hands.

The Nuremberg Files

Carpool Cheats involved enforcing norms that people generally agree with. But the Internet can also be used to facilitate vigilantism by fringe groups seeking to enforce their own norms. One of the earliest attempts at Internet vigilantism was the website known as the Nuremberg Files.[81] Created in 1997 by Neal Horsley, the website listed the names and personal information of abortion doctors and their families. This was part of a campaign by a group known as the American Coalition of Life Activists (ACLA) to terrorize abortion doctors. The website included data on more than two hundred individuals, including names, addresses, photographs, driver's license numbers, and information about family members, such as the schools their children attended.[82] The name of the site alluded to the Nuremberg trials of Nazi officials following World War II. The site listed doctors who had been wounded by antiabortion activists in grey and those killed with a line through them. Another part of the website listed the names of clinic owners and workers, and spouses of abortion doctors.

After Horsley created the website in January 1997, two abortion doctors were shot at their homes that year. In 1998 an abortion clinic in Alabama was bombed and another doctor was killed by sniper fire at his home in New York. Shortly afterward, a strikethrough was placed through his name on the Nuremberg Files website.

Planned Parenthood and a group of doctors sued, contending that the website caused them to live in fear, to require police protection, and to wear bulletproof vests. The case went to trial in 1999. One doctor stated that he switched his driving route to work and rode in a separate car from the rest of his family.[83] "Every time I get a package, it makes me nervous," a doctor declared. "It's a creepy thing to have to live with, thinking every time, 'Is this something I ordered or is it a bomb?' "[84] One doctor began to wear wigs to conceal herself in public.[85] A jury awarded the doctors more than one hundred million dollars in damages. The case was appealed, with Horsley and the ACLA contending that the verdict violated their right to free speech. The court of appeals affirmed, concluding that the website involved threats of violence with the intent to intimidate rather than articulating a position to debate.[86]

SPIRALING OUT OF CONTROL

Shaming is an important tool for social control, yet it can be dangerous if unchecked. When people can report on the misdeeds of others, they eliminate the anonymity that often facilitates the transgressions of norms. "How's My Driving?" programs, for example, have led to improvements in road safety. But such programs work best when under tight controls. In the "How's My Driving?" program, complaints about drivers are investigated and drivers are given feedback, training, and instruction.[87]

Much Internet shaming, in contrast, occurs without any formal procedures, investigation, or direct feedback to the accused offender. As a result, Internet shaming can readily get out of hand. Because the Internet allows thousands to communicate quickly, it makes it easier to form the digital equivalent to a mob. Gustave Le Bon, in his famous 1896 work *The Crowd,* observed that crowds have a different psychology than individuals do: "A crowd is as easily heroic as criminal."[88] Crowds can be impulsive and excitable. Psychologists describe a related phenomenon known as "group polarizing effect." As groups converge on particular issues, they tend to polarize in their opinions, resulting in more extreme points of view.[89]

People on the Internet often move quickly, like a swarm of killer bees. They often behave in moblike fashion. In China, for example, a person used an online bulletin board to shame a college student who he believed was having an affair with his wife. Readers of the bulletin board quickly exacted punishment on the student. One reader wrote: "Let's use our keyboard and mouse in our hands as weapons to chop off the heads of these adulterers." Thousands of people joined in the attack, causing the target to leave school and making his family hide away in their home. In a similar case in China, a man caught a college student having an affair with his wife. He posted the student's name online and described the affair. People quickly rallied to support the husband, providing more information about the student, including his address and phone number. The student denied the affair, even posting a short testimonial video. But the attacks didn't stop. Some people even began seeking out the student at his school and home. The husband was so surprised by the quick and vigorous reaction that he came to the defense of the student and urged a halt to the vigilantism. One of the shamers proclaimed: "What we Internet users are doing is fulfilling our social obligations. We cannot let our society fall into such a low state."[90]

The shamer's explanation for attacking another person, somebody he probably didn't even know, stems from a belief that shame is necessary to ensure social order. Without the threat of shame, people would transgress norms, making society less orderly and civil. But as some of these incidents demonstrate, although shaming is done to further social order, it paradoxically can have the opposite result. Instead of enhancing social control and order, Internet shaming often careens out of control. It targets people without careful consideration of all the facts and punishes them for their supposed infractions without proportionality. Shaming becomes uncivil, moblike, and potentially subversive of the very social order that it tries to protect.

Part Two **Privacy, Free Speech,**

and the Law

Chapter 5 The Role of Law

With so much data being collected about us and with anybody being able to disseminate it around the globe, is there anything we really can do to protect privacy? According to the science fiction writer and essayist David Brin, it is too late: "Light is going to shine into nearly every corner of our lives."[1] Scott McNealy, CEO of Sun Microsystems, has famously quipped: "You already have zero privacy. Get over it."[2] His stance reflects a view that many are increasingly sharing. Privacy is dead, they believe, and there's not much that can be done except deliver a eulogy and move on. Can anything be done? Is it possible for the law to protect us? Or should we just get over it?

A TRIP BACK TO THE NINETEENTH CENTURY

New technologies rarely give rise to questions we have never addressed before. More often they make the old questions more complex. Gossip, rumor, and shaming have been with us since the dawn of civilization. Although modern information technology has revolutionized how we record and spread information, we have experienced similar revolutions in the past. More than a century ago, in the second half of the nineteenth century, we were in the throes of another information revolution—the rise of the newspaper. This revolution had its roots in the 1830s in England, with the innovation of the "penny press." New printing technology enabled newspapers to be sold much more cheaply than ever before—for just a penny. These new papers were filled with news of scandals, family squabbles, public drunkenness, and petty crimes.[3] They were tabloids, and people loved them.

It didn't take long for the penny press to come to America. In 1833 in New York, Benjamin Day published a newspaper called the *Sun* modeled on the English penny papers. With a cheap price and a heavy dose of sensationalism, the *Sun* quickly attracted many readers. When true lurid tales couldn't be found, *Sun* reporters would just make them up. One series of stories about creatures on the moon became known as the "moon hoax." Circulation rates exploded, quickly surpassing those of the more traditional newspapers, which were referred to as the "qualities" or the "respectables." Imitators soon followed—the *New York Herald*, the *New York Transcript*, and the *New York Graphic*, to name a few. And penny press papers sprung up in Boston and Philadelphia and other big cities as well.[4] Charles Dickens depicted this frenzy of newspapers in his novel *Martin Chuzzlewit*. When Martin steps off a steamer from England to New York in the 1840s, he encounters a crowd of paperboys: " 'Here's this morning's New York Sewer!' cried one. 'Here's this morning's New York Stabber! Here's the New York Family Spy! Here's the New York Private Listener! Here's the New York Peeper! Here's the New York Plunderer! Here's the New York Keyhole Reporter! Here's the New York Rowdy Journal!' "[5]

This new breed of sensationalistic reportage, called "yellow journalism," proliferated after the Civil War, when newspaper circulation continued to rise exponentially.[6] Newspapers vigorously competed to capture the public interest and sell papers. The age of yellow journalism soon became dominated by Joseph Pulitzer and William Randolph Hearst, two titans who lorded over vast newspaper empires.

In the novelist Henry James's *The Reverberator,* written in 1888, a character proclaims the prevailing attitude of the media: "It ain't going to be possible to keep out anywhere the light of the press. Now what I'm going to do is to set up the biggest lamp yet made over and make it shine all over the place. We'll see who's private then."[7]

The press came under sharp criticism for invading privacy. For example, when journalists converged around President Grover Cleveland's cottage while he was there on his honeymoon with his new wife and watched him with binoculars, the president complained that the press "in ghoulish glee desecrate every sacred relation of private life."[8]

The media went into overdrive during the 1875 adultery trial of the Reverend Henry Ward Beecher, which one commentator describes as "one of the first great American media/privacy stories."[9] A masterful speaker during a time when the public was captivated by oratory, Beecher was one of the most famous and revered figures in America.[10] To expose social hypocrisy about sex, the free-love proponent Victoria Woodhull revealed that Beecher was having an affair with Elizabeth Tilton, a member of his congregation and the wife of his friend Theodore Tilton.[11] The story received unprecedented media coverage. Before the trial, the Associated Press dispatched thirty reporters to cover Beecher's address before his church commission. Nearly all newspapers covered the trial, and some even printed daily transcripts. The trial ended with the jury deadlocked. Just fourteen minutes after the verdict was announced, one newspaper was already on the streets with the news.[12] A year afterward, Beecher lamented: "I have not been hunted as an eagle is hunted; I have not been pursued as a lion is pursued; I have not been pursued even as wolves and foxes. I have been pursued as if I were a maggot in a rotten corpse."[13]

In addition to the voraciously sensationalistic press, other new technologies were posing an increasing threat to privacy. In 1876 Thomas Edison invented the telephone, allowing people to converse over great distances. A short time afterward, technology to wiretap phone conversations was developed.[14]

In 1884 Eastman Kodak Company came out with a new invention called the "snap camera." Photography had been around since the mid-nineteenth century, but cameras were large and difficult to operate. People had to pose for a long time to have photos taken. Cameras were also expensive. As Robert Ellis Smith observes: "In the years before the development of photography in the mid-1800s, even mirrors were not universal in British and American home life. Imagine the realization that for the first time the very essence of your being—your visage—could be captured by someone else—used and controlled by someone else."[15] Kodak's snap camera was cheap and portable. Many more people could afford to own their own camera, and for the first time, candid photos of people could be taken.

In 1890 E. L. Godkin, a famous social commentator, complained that these developments were threatening privacy. According to Godkin, curiosity was

An advertisement for the Kodak camera in 1889

the "chief enemy of privacy in modern life." Godkin noted that for a long time in history, gossip was oral and only slightly wounded the individual. But "gossip about private individuals is now printed, and makes its victim, with all his imperfections on his head, known to hundreds or thousands miles away from his place of abode." Godkin was not optimistic about finding a solution to these new threats to privacy. "In truth," he wrote, "there is only one remedy for the violations of the right to privacy within the reach of the American public, and that is but an imperfect one. It is to be found in attaching social discredit to invasions of it on the part of conductors of the press." Godkin did not foresee any plausible way to alter the current sensationalism of the press: "At present this check [of social discredit] can hardly be said to exist. It is to a large extent nullified by the fact that the offence is often pecuniarily profitable."[16]

Samuel Warren and Louis Brandeis were concerned about the same privacy problems as Godkin. Warren was a well-known Boston lawyer and socialite. Louis Brandeis was a brilliant young attorney who would later become a Supreme Court justice. Warren and Brandeis met in law school, where Warren read aloud Brandeis's law school assignments because Brandeis had poor eyesight.[17] Brandeis finished first in his class, and Warren was second. They began practicing law together in Boston and cowrote a few law review articles in the late 1880s. Their first two articles were entitled "The Watuppa Pond Cases" and "The Law of Ponds"; not surprisingly, these essays on pond law sank into obscurity.[18] But for their third article, Warren and Brandeis turned to a much more gripping topic—privacy—and this would become one of the most famous law review articles of all time.

"The Right to Privacy" was published in the *Harvard Law Review* in 1890.[19] The reason for their switching topics from ponds to privacy has long been the subject of a contentious debate. According to William Prosser, one of the most famous tort law scholars, the article was prompted by Warren's outrage over the media's snooping on his daughter's wedding. Prosser quipped that Warren's daughter had a "face that launched a thousand lawsuits."[20] But there's a problem with this theory: Warren's daughter was only about six years old in 1890.[21] Instead, Warren and Brandeis's interest in privacy was probably sparked by a series of articles about Warren's dinner parties in a Boston high-society gossip rag.[22]

More broadly, Warren and Brandeis were concerned about the sensationalistic press and new technologies such as the snap camera. "The press is overstepping in every direction the obvious bounds of propriety and of decency," Warren and Brandeis complained in the article. "Gossip is no longer the resource of the idle and of the vicious, but has become a trade." They observed that the problem of the increased commercial exploitation of the private life would be vastly heightened by the impact of new technologies: "Instantaneous photographs and newspaper enterprise have invaded the sacred precincts of private and domestic life; and numerous mechanical devices threaten to make good the prediction that 'what is whispered in the closet shall be proclaimed from the house-tops.' "[23]

At the time of their article, however, the snap camera was just a recent development and the media's use of candid photos wasn't much of a threat. In the late nineteenth century, few daily newspapers printed drawings, let alone photographs.[24] Warren and Brandeis, however, astutely recognized the potential for these new cameras to be used by the already sensationalistic press. Warren and Brandeis looked into the future and foresaw the paparazzi.

Unlike Godkin, Warren and Brandeis believed that law could provide a solution to these privacy problems. They observed that privacy invasions caused "mental pain and distress," an "injury to the feelings." The law didn't adequately protect against these kinds of injuries.[25] But they argued that the law could evolve to protect privacy. They explained that the law already protected "the more general right of the individual to be let alone," and that this right could be the foundation for new protections for privacy to develop. Warren and Brandeis recommended a tort remedy for people whose privacy is invaded. A tort is a legal cause of action where people can sue others who have wronged them. If I wrongfully injure you, you can sue me for damages. Warren and Brandeis argued that a tort remedy should be available for privacy invasions—if I wrongfully invade your privacy, you should be able to sue me.

Warren and Brandeis's article was a big hit in the legal world. Between 1890 and 1900, more than ten articles examined Warren and Brandeis's proposal to create privacy torts.[26] Throughout the twentieth century, states began to recognize privacy torts as Warren and Brandeis had suggested. Today the vast majority of states have created tort actions in response to the Warren and Brandeis article.[27] Many commentators consider the article to be one of the primary foundations of privacy law in the United States. One famous scholar even declared that it was the "most influential law review article of all."[28]

The debate in 1890 has many similarities to that of today. Warren and Brandeis were concerned about the incursions into privacy by the burgeoning print media, the most rapidly growing form of media in the late nineteenth century. Today we are experiencing the rapid rise of a new form of media— the Internet. There are those like Godkin, who say that there is little to be done. And there are those like Warren and Brandeis, who call for action. I side with Warren and Brandeis.

TYPES OF LEGAL APPROACHES

What can and should the law do? From the bird's-eye view, there are three basic approaches the law might take. First, the law could take a libertarian approach and remain as "hands off" as possible. Second, the law could adopt an authoritarian approach and attempt to radically limit the ability of people to spread information on the Internet. Or, third, the law could take some middle-ground approach between these extremes.

The Libertarian Approach

The law could adopt a libertarian approach, exercising great caution about hindering the flow of information. The libertarian approach reflects deeply rooted norms that developed among Internet users in the early days of the technology. At that time, the prevailing view was that the Internet was a free zone, and the law should keep out. People analogized the Internet to the Wild West.[29] One of the most famous and extreme statements of this view was John Perry Barlow's Declaration of the Independence of Cyberspace:

Governments of the Industrial World, you weary giants of flesh and steel, I come from Cyberspace, the new home of the Mind. On behalf of the future, I ask you of the past to leave me alone. You are not welcome among us. You have no sovereignty where we gather.

We have no elected government, nor are we likely to have one, so I address you with no greater authority than that with which liberty itself always speaks. I declare the global social space we are building to be naturally independent of the tyrannies you seek to impose on us. You have no moral right to rule us nor do you possess any methods of enforcement we have true reason to fear.[30]

Commentators celebrated the openness and freedom that the Internet provided. For example, the cyberlaw scholars David Johnson and David Post argued that it was best to leave the government out of regulating the Internet, which would function best on its own.[31]

Although these attitudes have mellowed over time, the general view that the flow of information should remain free still persists. Consider the case of Laurie Garrett. A Pulitzer Prize–winning journalist, she attended the World Economic Forum in 2003 and wrote a candid email to a few friends about her experience.[32] Among other things, she described her "hobnobbing with the ruling class":

> A day spent with Bill Gates turned out to be fascinating and fun. I found the CEO of Heineken hilarious, and George Soros proved quite earnest about confronting AIDS. Vicente Fox—who I had breakfast with—proved sexy and smart like a— well, a fox. David Stern (Chair of the NBA) ran up and gave me a hug.

With uncommon candor, Garrett concluded: "The world isn't run by a clever cabal. It's run by about 5,000 bickering, sometimes charming, usually arrogant, mostly male people who are accustomed to living in either phenomenal wealth, or great personal power."

Somehow, Garrett's email got forwarded around to others, and eventually made it onto the Web, where it was reproduced on numerous websites and widely read and commented upon. Why did the email become so popular? One of the primary reasons was that Garrett was so frank and direct. These were Garrett's personal sentiments, not the kind of prose found in the typical journalism article. Ironically, the email's popularity stemmed from its not being written for popular consumption.

Garrett was aghast that her personal email had been broadcast to the world. She wrote a public letter to MetaFilter, one of the blogs where her email was being discussed. Garrett noted that when she found her email on the Internet and "read the remarks, paranoid fantasies, speculations, derisions, insults, and Internet din," she felt "considerable humiliation." She further declared:

> Let me be as clear as possible about this: The letter you are all clamoring over, parsing, deriding and fantasizing about was a personal note. It is a private letter that someone among my friends thoughtlessly, yet I am sure without any malice, forwarded to a couple of people who are strangers to me. And they, in turn, passed it on to more strangers, and so on. Now, to my deep embarrassment, and acute sense of invaded privacy, all of you—thousands of strangers—are dissecting my personal letter. I would never have written for public consumption in such a sloppy, candid, opinionated flip tone. This was never intended for your eyes.[33]

The reaction she received from many online, however, was unsympathetic. One commenter replied:

> Personally, I'm not sorry I read your email, but I'm sorry it was posted without your knowledge, and that some people said careless things about you. If you're looking for somewhere to shove the "blame" though, you may want to start closer to home.

Another commentator observed:

> For a professional journalist, Ms Garrett has a pretty slip-shod approach to protecting her own privacy. Because email is as insecure as it is, responsibility falls to the end user to protect their own privacy.

"Welcome to the 21st century," yet another person wrote, chiding Garrett to stop "pining for a mythical 1979 in which privacy was universally respected and photocopiers didn't exist."

As the cyberlaw scholar James Grimmelmann aptly points out, the comments embodied a "classically techno-libertarian viewpoint" that holds that it is impossible to contain the spread of information and that the rapid dissemination of data is a good thing.[34]

The problem with the libertarian approach is that it fully embraces the free flow of information and does little to protect privacy. The result of this "hands off" approach is that people who suffer the stings of gossip and rumor on the Internet have little redress. As I will show in the next chapter, gossip and rumor have substantial effects on people's freedom, autonomy, and self-development—the very same values that free speech protects.

The Authoritarian Approach

At the other end of the spectrum, the law could adopt an authoritarian approach. Such an approach is designed to employ strict controls over the spread of information. Authoritarian approaches employ censorship in an attempt to halt the circulation of problematic information. Lawmakers often find such approaches appealing. For example, a bill in the United States House of Representatives would ban social network sites from public schools and libraries.[35] Some state legislatures are considering similar bills. Other authoritarian attempts at regulation have included bans on anonymous speech or criminal penalties for impersonating another online. For example, back in the mid-1990s, Georgia made it a crime to send any data through a computer network and falsely identify oneself. A federal court struck down the law as violating the constitutional right to free speech.[36]

Authoritative approaches often wind up being more symbolic than effective, since the First Amendment stands in the way of many attempts at censorship. The authoritative approach can be oppressive and far too stifling of free speech. Attempts to ban social network sites from schools do little to stop students from using them. The use of the sites will simply migrate to places outside of school, where schools have even less control. In short, authoritative approaches attempt to address the problem in a broad and crude manner that is inconsistent with the U.S. Constitution.

Finding a Middle Ground

We need to find some middle ground between the libertarian and authoritarian approaches. A more moderate role for the law to take would be to help shape the norms that govern the circulation of information. As people are discovering the profound power to disseminate information across the planet, they often continue with gossip as if there were no difference between realspace and cyberspace. The law should ensure that people better understand the dramatic difference between gossip offline and online.

Tort law remedies—lawsuits—represent one possible middle-ground approach. They aren't authoritarian because they are initiated by individuals and are not systematic in their reach. There are many problems with lawsuits, which I will discuss, but we must evaluate any approach not in the abstract but as a practical choice among a set of imperfect alternatives.

The law currently protects the flow of personal information about people's reputations through defamation law as well as the invasion-of-privacy torts spawned by Warren and Brandeis's article. For this body of law to work effectively, however, two seemingly contradictory changes must be made. First, the law must be broadened significantly—especially the law of privacy. Second, the law must be restricted so that the lawsuit is employed only rarely to redress privacy invasions.

LEGAL PROTECTIONS OF PRIVACY
AND REPUTATION

Throughout history, people have found some mechanism for vindicating their reputations. For centuries, European aristocrats defended their honor by dueling.[37] The duel, which originated in Italy around 1500, became immensely popular among European gentlemen, especially in the 1600s and 1700s. As one commentator observes: "In France alone, in just the twenty-one years of Henri IV's reign, 1589 to 1610, perhaps ten thousand gentlemen died for their honor."[38] Although today we think of dueling as barbaric, it was long considered to be a civilized and urbane way of resolving disputes, since the alternatives were sneak attacks and brawls.

A duel could be provoked by insult, defamation, or gossip. Even the slightest of insults could spark a duel. An elaborate set of rules, the "code duello," governed the practice. The offended person would issue the challenge, which involved the use of swords or pistols. Before a duel was fought, the parties exchanged letters and engaged in negotiations to see whether a reconciliation could be achieved. Each party had a "second," who functioned as his agent throughout the process. In many cases, the parties reached a settlement, with the offender admitting, for example, that a rumor was spurious without conceding that he had deliberately spread a lie.[39] Skillful seconds were adept at helping the parties reconcile, and one contemporary observer even remarked that "nine duels out of ten, if not ninety-nine out of a hundred, originate in the want of experience in the seconds."[40] "It is not the sword or the pistol that kills," another stated, "but the seconds."[41]

When dueling migrated to America, it became especially popular in the South, where lawyers, judges, politicians, and wealthy elites frequently engaged in the practice. Andrew Jackson allegedly engaged in more than a hundred duels before becoming president and even killed a man during one duel.[42]

Although both the church and the law banned it, dueling persisted. As the eighteenth-century English legal scholar William Blackstone observed, until an alternative method could be found to redress the offended person, "the strongest prohibitions and penalties of the law will never be entirely effective to eradicate this unhappy custom."[43] In America every state prohibited dueling, but nobody seemed to care. A duelist who killed his opponent could face murder charges, but even this was an ineffective impediment, as juries would rarely convict.[44]

One reason dueling was so difficult to stop was the tremendous social pres-

The duel between Alexander Hamilton and Aaron Burr

sure to defend one's honor. If a person wasn't willing to duel, he was thought to be spineless.[45] As Samuel Johnson once said, the gentleman duels "to avert the stigma of the world, and to prevent himself from being driven out of society."[46] Alexander Hamilton perished in a duel he didn't want to fight. When Aaron Burr challenged Hamilton to a duel in 1804, Hamilton wrote that he "abhor[red] the practice of dueling" but that he felt a "peculiar necessity not to decline the call." He explained that to remain "useful" in public affairs, he had to protect his reputation, which would be impugned if he refused Burr's challenge.[47] During the duel, Hamilton's shot missed (by some accounts his intention), but Burr's shot mortally wounded Hamilton.

An alternative to the duel was the courtroom. Lawsuits constituted a peaceful way to resolve disputes and keep people from resorting to violence. They substituted money for blood.[48] But many still believed that squabbles over reputation were "best resolved by extralegal means," and courts were a "last resort."[49] In the days of dueling, going to court was seen as cowardly and ineffective.[50] As one commentator has observed, "Duels were the only court available for retrieving your reputation with your peers."[51]

The historian Cynthia Kierner's fascinating account of a scandal in the 1790s involving Richard Randolph (brother of the famous politician John Randolph) reveals a lot about how people attempted to vindicate their reputation in postrevolutionary America. The Randolph family was one of the most elite families in Virginia. Rumors circulated that Richard Randolph had engaged in an adulterous affair with his unmarried sister-in-law, Nancy, resulting in an unwanted pregnancy. Although the infant may have been miscarried or stillborn, Richard and Nancy were suspected of having aborted it.

Richard thought that Nancy's brother William was spreading these rumors. To defend himself, Richard published an open letter to the public in the principal newspaper of Virginia (it appeared just after news of King Louis XVI's beheading in Paris).[52] In the letter, he indicated that he would be willing to duel to defend his reputation.

Richard didn't bring a defamation lawsuit because, as Kierner notes, "slander was a deeply gendered offense in eighteenth century America." For men, the most damaging attacks on their reputation impugned their honesty and trustworthiness; for women, the most harmful reputational assaults focused on their sexual activities. Therefore the sexual dimension to the scandal "undoubtedly deterred Richard from initiating legal proceedings against William Randolph."[53] Instead, Richard "waited for the local authorities to act and faced a criminal charge instead." Richard and Nancy were charged with the murder of their baby. They were acquitted, but the trial may have "enhanced the authority of the gossip and innuendo that he sought to discredit. . . . The court proceedings, far from silencing the rumors about him and Nancy, facilitated their circulation among a wider audience."[54]

The Richard Randolph scandal illustrates the benefits and limitations of using the courts as an alternative to dueling. The courts could provide a more orderly and fair way to vindicate one's reputation, but they also could further spread the offensive information.

Courts eventually won out over the duel as the way to redress reputational harm. The death of Hamilton had a sobering effect on dueling in the North, where it largely ceased by 1850. Dueling in the South lasted longer but finally began to fade away after the Civil War. Many theories have been proposed for why dueling ended. One of the more convincing theories is the legal historian Alison LaCroix's contention that dueling diminished because the norms of honor governing gentlemen changed with increased commercial activity and industrialization. The qualities that people deemed important to reputation transformed from a more aristocratic sense of honor to factors that mattered in the marketplace. Impugning one's honor no longer was a big deal; instead, what mattered was damaging one's reputation for "creditworthiness." Dueling persisted longer in the South in part because the South remained more agrarian and honor-based than the North.[55] After the Civil War, another commentator explains, many in the Southern aristocracy had been killed, and the South became "more urbanized and commercial, more open to ambitious businessmen" and "less hospitable to dueling."[56]

For all their crudeness and barbarism, duels did serve an important function. As the historian David Parker notes, "The duel offered a highly effective tool for repairing a damaged reputation" because others in the aristocracy viewed one's willingness to duel as "evidence" of his "integrity and conviction" and because "an agreement to duel was also an agreement to end the polemic that gave rise to the duel." As Parker writes, "Ideally, a well-fought duel reconciled the two adversaries, reestablished mutual respect, and 'cleansed' the stain caused by the original insult. No lawsuit or libel prosecution was capable of producing the same effect."[57] Moreover, the law could not redress all of the harms redressed by duels. The kinds of insults that provoked duels would strike many of us as rather silly. Merely calling a person a "puppy," a "liar," or a "coward" could spark a duel.[58] South Carolina Governor John Lyde Wilson, in his 1858 guide to dueling, declared that "in cases where the laws of the country give no redress for injuries received, where public opinion not only authorizes but enjoins resistance, it is needless and a waste of time to denounce the practice [of dueling]."[59]

But as America modernized, mere insults no longer seemed as damaging. Instead, what mattered to people's reputations were harms that would diminish their employment opportunities and economic success. Courts in defamation cases understood reputation more narrowly as "damage to an individual as a commercial actor" rather than more broadly as gentlemanly honor.[60]

If there's a moral to the story of the demise of dueling and the rise of litigation, it is that every society needs some mechanism to resolve reputational harms. Duels served this function for centuries (albeit only for elites). Duels thus satisfied a social need. With the rise of the modern economy, honor ceased to be the core of a person's reputation, and dueling faded into obscurity. But something still had to serve as the vehicle for people to safeguard their reputations, and the courts became the main option.

Today, instead of guns and swords, people use lawyers. There are two main bodies of law available to people who sue because of information (or misinformation) being circulated about them—the law of privacy and the law of defamation. These two bodies of law serve as a primary tool for people to vindicate their reputations.

Defamation

The ancient law of defamation has long protected against spreading false rumors about a person. Defamation "exposes a person to hatred, contempt, ridicule, or obloquy, or causes him to be shunned and avoided."[61] President John Adams once stated that the "man . . . without attachment to reputation, or honor, is undone."[62] As one U.S. congressman remarked in 1794, "Slander is in a moral what poison is in a physical sense; it is the resource of cowards. It is a species of attack against which it is impossible to defend ourselves."[63]

Defamation law developed over the course of thousands of years. It existed in ancient Rome, which made certain kinds of defamation criminal offenses.[64] In the early Middle Ages, defamation was punished by cutting out the offender's tongue. Later on in the Middle Ages, ecclesiastical courts began to punish defamation by requiring public penance.[65] Eventually, the state required defamers to pay damages and publicly admit to their lies.[66]

Today, defamation law consists of two torts—libel and slander. Libel involves written or recorded words (newspaper articles, television broadcasts, and writing on the Internet). Slander involves oral communications and speech between individuals. For the law to kick in, a statement must be false and it must harm a person's reputation.[67] The person making the defamatory statement must be at fault—if she reasonably believed the fact to be true, then she isn't liable. It is up to the plaintiff to prove that the statement was false, and the speaker doesn't have to vouch for its truth. If the statement is true, the plaintiff loses. Someone can be liable for defamation even for just spreading information originated by someone else.[68]

Defamation law is a complicated and uncertain body of law. Entire treatises have been written on it. Critics call it a "forest of complexities, overgrown with anomalies, inconsistencies, and perverse rigidities."[69] Another First Amendment scholar writes: "The law of defamation is dripping with contradictions and confusion and is vivid testimony to the sometimes perverse ingenuity of the legal mind."[70] Beyond these complexities, defamation law has been limited by the Supreme Court in order to protect free speech. Even though these limits are substantial, the defamation torts remain quite powerful. For defamation on the Internet, however, the law is much more restricted. These restrictions, which I will discuss in the next chapter, make defamation law a relatively ineffective tool to protect against the spread of rumors on the Internet.

Invasion of Privacy

The second body of law available to protect reputation is the law of privacy. A number of torts evolved to protect privacy in response to the Warren and Brandeis article of 1890. These torts are referred to collectively as "invasion of privacy." The privacy torts are a relatively young body of law, just over a century old. There are four torts in all: (1) intrusion upon seclusion; (2) public disclosure of private facts; (3) false light; and (4) appropriation.[71]

The tort of intrusion protects against the intentional intrusion into one's "solicitude or seclusion" or "his private affairs or concerns" that "would be highly offensive to a reasonable person."[72] This tort primarily redresses intrusive information gathering activities. The tort of false light protects against the spread of false, distorted, or misleading information about an individual that is "highly offensive to a reasonable person."[73] False light has many similarities to defamation law.

The two most relevant privacy torts for addressing the spread of information online are appropriation and public disclosure. Appropriation protects against the use of a person's name or likeness for the benefit of another.[74] For example, the tort allows someone to sue if her name or image is used in an advertisement without her consent. To be liable for appropriation, "the defendant must have appropriated to his own use or benefit the reputation, prestige, social or commercial standing, public interest or other values of the plaintiff's name or likeness."[75]

Another of the privacy torts is the tort of public disclosure of private facts, which provides a remedy when somebody widely discloses another person's private information. The disclosure must be "highly offensive to a reasonable person" and "not of legitimate concern to the public."[76] This tort can potentially be helpful in protecting our private lives from being splattered across the Internet. In contrast to defamation, which makes people liable for spreading falsehoods, the public-disclosure tort remedies the dissemination of truths.

Courts are uneasy about the privacy torts and have limited them in two fundamental ways. First, in the name of free speech, privacy law (as well as defamation law) has been severely restricted. Second, the law of privacy is being held back by narrow understandings of privacy. Many courts throw out lawsuits because they do not recognize a privacy violation. As a result, people suing under the privacy torts frequently lose their cases. The First Amendment scholar Rodney Smolla observes that if the Warren and Brandeis privacy torts "were a stock, [their] performance over the last century would not be deemed impressive."[77]

FINDING THE RIGHT ROLE FOR LAW

Although lawsuits based on defamation law and the privacy torts are key components of a middle-ground approach, we don't want to encourage a blizzard of lawsuits. Lawsuits are frightful monsters. They are expensive, imposing, and stressful. Merely being subjected to a lawsuit can be traumatic, let alone losing and having to pay damages. The threat of a lawsuit—even a lawsuit which a speaker or writer will ultimately win—can be damaging enough to make the potential defendant extra cautious.

One problem with lawsuits is abuse. For example, people can misuse defamation as a way to attack critics. Defamation law does not protect one from being the target of negative opinions, criticisms, satire, or insults. It protects one from having falsehoods spread that damage one's reputation. But people merely insulted by criticism or satire can overreact by filing an inappropriate defamation suit. Likewise, people may misuse invasion of privacy torts to attack speakers because they dislike criticism, not because of any privacy violation.

Lawsuits can chill speech. If it is too easy to win a lawsuit, people will sue too readily, causing people to refrain from engaging in candid robust speech for fear of being sued. The effect of too many lawsuits resembles that of the authoritative approach, impeding speech far too much. But without the threat of lawsuits, online speakers have no legal incentive to remove posts or to resolve disputes informally. And for egregious cases, we want the law to be involved.

Lawsuits hurt not only the speaker but also the person who is suing. Judge Richard Posner notes that privacy cases are rare because such a suit results in further publicizing the privacy violation.[78] When people sue, American courts are reluctant to allow them to conceal their names. As one court declared, "The use of fictitious names is disfavored" and will be allowed only under "exceptional circumstances."[79] In contrast, courts in many European countries are more willing to allow people to conceal their identities when suing, thus protecting plaintiffs from bringing more attention to the gossip they are trying to stop.

The American approach, however, penalizes people for using the law to protect their rights. In one recent defamation lawsuit, a man named Todd sued the website Don't Date Him Girl for false statements about him appearing on the site. His profile contained his picture and the following comment:

> This guy is a trip. In fact, screw trip, he's a DOG. He dated one of my friends. . . . that was before she found out he had dated half of Pittsburgh. . . . Often dresses shabbily for a lawyer—probably part of his disguise. He's in his 30s; AND he is believed to have HERPES. Stay away!

Another commentator stated:

> Do NOT DATE HIM. He gave me an STD and dated 2 people at a time.

Yet another chimed in:

> Dark and handsome ladies, he looks like a chocolate dream. Until you get to know him. His crib is a dump. He wears dirty clothes all the time. He's an attorney but you would never think so cause he complains about paying child support for his kids. He got hook-ups in every zipcode in the USA. He's hot. . . . DON'T LET HIM FOOL YOU GIRL!

Todd sued, claiming that these were lies, and he wanted to set the record straight. His decision to sue, however, was met with disdain in the blogosphere. One blogger wrote that before the lawsuit, he had never heard of Todd, but now "thousands of people who never would have seen the comments are left wondering if they're not true." The moral of the story, the blogger concluded, was: "Don't sue for defamation, because even if you win, you'll lose."[80] On another blog, one commentator wrote: "To me it is like rumors and people talking smack; the more you yell about it the more truthful it seems to others. Better to post a rebuttal on [Don't Date Him Girl] and let it die a more silent death."[81] Yet another commentator said: "Hey Todd, I went to the website and read the comments about you. Big deal! You must be very thin-skinned. By suing you've brought the whole world's attention to the fact that four women don't like you. And believe me, bro, you're not helping yourself. My advice: just lay low for awhile so people will forget."[82] Reaction to Todd's lawsuit in the blogosphere is similar to the reaction to many people who sue for privacy and defamation. Some people are sympathetic, but others ridicule the plaintiffs for bringing more attention to themselves.

The American rule is unproductive, and it cuts against people's right to obtain redress for damage to their reputation. More people should be allowed to sue without having their real names appear in the record. This would allow people to seek a remedy for the spread of information about them without having to increase the exposure of the information.

Even if this problem is resolved, other problems make bringing a lawsuit a losing strategy for a plaintiff. Unlike the mainstream media, many bloggers are amateurs without a lot of money to pay damages to an injured person. In one recent incident, a woman won an $11.3 million verdict against another woman who posted messages on the Internet stating that the plaintiff was a "con artist" and a "fraud." But the woman who posted the comments had no money to pay. She had lost her home in Hurricane Katrina, she couldn't even afford a lawyer, and she didn't even bother to show up for trial. So why did the victim bother to sue? Indeed, it cost her money to sue and she wound up losing money by pursuing the case. She explained: "I'm sure [the woman] doesn't have $1 million, let alone $11 million, but the message is strong and clear. . . . People are using the Internet to destroy people they don't like, and you can't do that."[83] As one lawyer candidly observes: "Rarely does a good defamation case walk in the door."[84] Few plaintiffs win their cases in defamation suits. According to one estimate, only about 13 percent prevail in the end.[85] If you're suing for the money, then defamation and privacy lawsuits are not particularly effective. So in cases where there isn't a lot of money at stake, why would people sue?

The reason, I posit, is that people need to protect their reputations, and there are few alternatives besides bringing a lawsuit. Although in several cases, the law doesn't provide financial redress, it establishes a forum for people to seek vindication. In one study of people suing for defamation, only 25 percent were primarily interested in getting money.[86] The law professor Jerome Barron notes: "Individuals increasingly use libel actions for purposes such as vindication, reprisal, response, and publicity."[87] Lyrissa Lidsky, a defamation law scholar, notes that people sue primarily "to salve hurt feelings and express outrage at the misbehavior of defendants who publish false statements."[88] Many plaintiffs want the gossip or rumor-mongering to stop and to be removed from the site. They want to be issued an apology. In other words, people resort to the law because they want a way to vindicate their reputations.

Ideally, the law can spur people to work out these disputes amicably before the lawsuit is brought. If we find a way to allow people to vindicate themselves, express their anger, and have the damage patched up at least to some degree, we can avoid a lot of litigation. People resort to lawsuits because of a lack of informal means to find resolutions, because there are no other good options.

The goal of the law should be to encourage the development of norms and to spur people to work out their disputes informally. Ideally, most problems would be dealt with between the parties without resort to law. We need some legal remedies, however, for more extreme and harmful cases. We also need remedies for systematic infringers—those who repeatedly invade others' privacy or facilitate shaming. The law should encourage websites to develop a process by which problems can be adjudicated and resolved, where bad information can quickly be taken down, and false statements can be corrected.

At its best, the law can achieve control without having to be invoked. This might sound paradoxical, but it is a rather obvious point. The best laws for addressing harms are ones that not only help fix the damage but also keep the harms from occurring in the first place. The most effective law rarely needs to be used, as the legal process is expensive and time-consuming. The law works best when it helps people resolve disputes outside the courtroom.

TOO MUCH LAW, TOO LITTLE LAW

In short, the law works best when it can hover as a threat in the background but allow most problems to be worked out informally. The threat of the lawsuit helps to keep people in check. Without the lawsuit threat, people who defame other people or invade their privacy can just thumb their nose at any complaints.

The problem, of course, is how to have lawsuits serve as a credible threat without being brought inappropriately. Under our current legal system, we have remedies for defamation and invasion of privacy, but as we have seen, these remedies are currently quite limited in their effectiveness, especially the law of privacy. The current law is too limited and restricted to serve as a tenable threat in many situations.

One problem with expanding the scope of legal protection, however, is that it might encourage more lawsuits. Make it too hard to sue, and the law ceases to be a credible threat. Make it too easy to sue, and lawsuits multiply like rabbits. How can we maintain the law as a credible threat yet keep lawsuits in check? I propose a requirement that a plaintiff first exhaust informal mechanisms for dealing with the problem. If the defendant agrees to remove the harmful information from the website, then this should be the end of the lawsuit unless the victim can demonstrate that merely taking down the offensive speech won't sufficiently patch up the harm.

Under this system, before proceeding in a lawsuit, a plaintiff must prove that she first attempted to seek informal redress and that the defendant didn't adequately attempt to provide a resolution. Or a plaintiff could also proceed if she established that the damage done was severe and irreparable—for example, gossip that had already wreaked havoc that couldn't be undone by quietly removing the material from the site. In many cases, the gossip or rumor has not yet gone viral—it has not spread too far beyond the originating speaker. Although the Internet allows information to proliferate much faster than before, it has the virtue of allowing for an easier cleansing of gossip and rumor than does print, where retractions can be printed but the uncorrected publication still exists in circulation. Online postings, in contrast, can promptly be edited. The law should serve to induce people to edit their postings to eliminate harmful information about others.

Although in many cases, problems can be resolved before they spiral out of control, in other situations, it is too late. In several cases the information has become infectious and has spread far and wide, such as the video of the Star Wars Kid and the gossip by Jessica Cutler in her Washingtonienne blog. In these circumstances, there is no way to remove the information from the Internet. The damage is irreparable, and the lawsuit should be allowed to proceed even if the speaker subsequently removes the information from her site.

The law should also create incentives for parties to use what is known as "alternative dispute resolution." Parties can go to a mediator or arbitrator rather than go to court. In mediation and arbitration, a neutral person or group of people resolves the case. Mediation and arbitration are similar, but they differ in that mediation is nonbinding and arbitration is binding. Alternative dispute resolution might cut down considerably on the legal costs and allow disputes to be resolved more quickly.

Another possible method of cutting down on law's expense is to limit damages. Most people posting online have little money to pay. The threat of massive damages can unduly chill speech and make lawsuits more contentious. Limiting damages is designed not to trivialize the harm some people suffer to their reputations but to steer litigation toward resolving disputes more quickly and inexpensively. The primary goal of the law should be imparting a sense of responsibility on those who post online, deterring the spread of gossip and rumors in cyberspace, and creating incentives for parties to resolve their disputes informally. Large damage awards are not necessary to accomplish these goals. Exceptions could be made, however, for especially egregious cases or for speakers who demonstrate a pattern of abusive conduct.

Therefore the law should expand its protection against irresponsible Internet postings, but only after disputes have been proven insoluble via informal means or alternative dispute resolution. In other words, the law should cast a wider net, yet have a less painful bite.

Chapter 6 Free Speech, Anonymity, and Accountability

Gossiping. Shaming. Rumor-mongering. All have pernicious effects on people's lives, yet they all involve acts of expression. When the law restricts the circulation of information, it creates potential threats to free speech. This is one of the main reasons that the law of defamation and privacy are limited in scope. If the law's goal is to restrict the spread of information when it causes harm, how can the law do so without unduly infringing upon freedom of speech?

GOOD SPEECH, BAD SPEECH

Freedom of speech is an essential right in a democratic society. As the poet and essayist John Milton put it eloquently in 1644, "The liberty to know, to utter, and to argue freely according to conscience [is] above all liberties."[1] Reflecting this wisdom, the First Amendment to the U.S. Constitution guarantees that "Congress shall make no law . . . abridging the freedom of speech, or of the press."[2] Freedom of speech gives us the right to express ourselves even if our speech is trivial, despicable, crass, and repulsive. We don't allow the government to regulate "matters of taste and style" in speech, the Supreme Court has ruled, since "one man's vulgarity is another's lyric."[3] As the Court also declared, we have a "profound national commitment to the principle that debate on public issues should be uninhibited, robust, and wide open."[4]

The Supreme Court has held that the First Amendment right to freedom of speech places some limits on defamation law. The Court had originally viewed defamation as not being protected by the First Amendment because it has "no essential part in the exposition of ideas."[5] Speech that defamed a person was not a key part of public debate, so it didn't warrant constitutional protection. However, the Court changed its position in the famous case of *New York Times v. Sullivan* in 1964, when it concluded: "Erroneous statement is inevitable in free debate, and . . . it must be protected if freedoms of expression are to have the 'breathing space' they need to survive."[6] Instead of wiping out defamation law, the Court crafted a compromise to balance the protection of free speech with the ability to seek redress for defamatory statements. In later cases, the Supreme Court left the defamation tort largely intact for "private figures" but limited it significantly for "public figures."[7] A "public figure," one who has achieved a general level of "notoriety" or who has come to the "forefront of particular public controversies," must prove that the speaker acted with "actual malice."[8] "Actual malice" requires that the person who made the statement knew that it was untrue or acted "with reckless disregard of whether it was false or not."[9] Basically, famous people have to prove that the defendant intentionally told lies about them or simply didn't care whether rumors were true or not. Actual malice is hard to establish, and most plaintiffs who have to prove it lose their cases.[10] Private citizens need only show the defendant to have been negligent when he told lies, a much easier standard to establish.

The Supreme Court could have simply abolished the defamation torts of libel and slander in the name of free speech, but it compromised and preserved much of defamation law. One reason, the Court noted, was that falsehoods are "not worthy of constitutional protection" and that the "First Amendment requires that we protect some falsehood in order to protect speech that matters."[11] In other words, the First Amendment protects false speech not for its own sake but as a means of protecting true speech. Moreover, the Court observed, it is important also to preserve the "individual's right to the protection of his own good name," which "reflects no more than our basic concept of the essential dignity and worth of every human being."[12]

The law of privacy clashes more directly with free speech. As we have seen, unlike defamation law, which applies only to falsehoods, privacy law allows people to redress harms caused by the spread of true information about themselves. Truth is one of the primary defenses to a defamation case, but the fact that information is true will do nothing to halt a privacy case. The famous tort law scholar William Prosser viewed the privacy torts as creating "a power of censorship over what the public may be permitted to read, extending very much beyond . . . the law of defamation."[13] Many scholars have argued that it is difficult or even impossible to square the privacy torts with freedom of speech. As the First Amendment scholar Thomas Emerson argues: "Any individual living among others is, by the very nature of society, subject to an enormous amount of comment, gossip, criticism and the like. His right to be left alone does not include any general right not to be talked about."[14] Similarly, another First Amendment scholar, Eugene Volokh, contends: "The difficulty is that the right to information privacy—my right to control your communication of personally identifiable information about me—is a right to have the government stop you from speaking about me." Volokh concludes that the First Amendment "generally bars the government from controlling the communication of information."[15]

If Emerson and Volokh are right, then there's little the law can do. The First Amendment gives people the right to say whatever they want so long as it is true. It gives you and me the right to blog our thoughts without fear of reprisal. How can the public-disclosure tort—which would make someone liable for saying true things about someone else—be constitutional under the First Amendment? Although the privacy torts can be squared with the First Amendment, the issue is a difficult one, and it requires a bit of explanation.

Absolutism

A popular view of the First Amendment is that its protection of free speech is absolute. This means that if somebody is engaging in speech, then the First Amendment bars any attempt to regulate or prohibit that speech—no matter how odious or harmful the message might be.

Justice Hugo Black became famous for adopting this position.[16] Black argued that the First Amendment is an "unequivocal command that there shall be no abridgment of the rights of free speech and assembly."[17] In one lecture, Black declared: "It is my belief that there are 'absolutes' in our Bill of Rights, and that they were put there on purpose by men who knew what words meant and meant their prohibitions to be 'absolutes.'"[18] An interviewer once asked Justice Black what precisely he meant by these words. Black replied by taking out the copy of the Constitution that he always carried in his pocket. He read the First Amendment: "Congress shall make no law . . ." And then he said: "That's the First Amendment—I would think: Amen, Congress should pass no law. Unless they just didn't know the meaning of words."[19]

If you're a free-speech absolutist, much of the law protecting privacy becomes difficult to defend. The First Amendment forbids the law from restricting people from saying what they want to say.

Balancing

Justice Black's absolutist approach didn't win the day. Instead, the Supreme Court currently resolves free-speech cases by balancing speech against opposing interests.[20] Under a balancing approach, the value of free speech is high, but it's not absolute. If there's a good enough reason, then free speech can be trumped. So the balancing approach views free speech as important, just not sacrosanct.

Even under a balancing approach, critics of privacy protections argue that free speech has a high value that will trump privacy except under exceptional circumstances. When balancing, courts analyze any law—including a tort law—under a level of constitutional "scrutiny." The highest form of constitutional scrutiny is strict scrutiny. Under strict scrutiny, to "outweigh" a First Amendment interest, a law must be the "least restrictive means" to achieve a "compelling" government interest.[21] Laws restricting speech rarely survive strict scrutiny, which has been referred to as " 'strict' in theory and fatal in fact."[22] Volokh argues that many laws protecting privacy should be subjected to strict scrutiny: "Political speech, scientific speech, art, entertainment, consumer product reviews, and speech on matters of private concern are thus all doctrinally entitled to the same level of high constitutional protection, restrictable only through laws that pass strict scrutiny."[23] This means that the Warren and Brandeis tort of public disclosure is probably unconstitutional if we apply the strict-scrutiny standard.

Contrary to Volokh's stance, current case law holds that not all forms of speech are worthy of being protected with strict scrutiny. Some forms of speech are less important than others. If we look at current Supreme Court law, not all forms of speech are protected equally.[24] For example, the Supreme Court gives less protection to commercial speech, which occupies a "subordinate position in the scale of First Amendment values."[25] Since commercial speech isn't protected with strict scrutiny, the law can more readily regulate it.

Speech of private concern should be given less protection than speech of public concern. The Supreme Court has endorsed this view to a limited extent. In one case, the Supreme Court concluded that "not all speech is of equal First Amendment importance. It is speech on 'matters of public concern' that is 'at the heart of the First Amendment's protection.' . . . In contrast, speech on matters of purely private concern is of less First Amendment concern."[26] In short, the Supreme Court ruled that speech of private concern should be given much less protection than speech of public concern.[27] The Court has never held that Warren and Brandeis's public disclosure of facts tort is unconstitutional. The tort has been around for more than one hundred years, so if the Court were to suddenly strike it down, it would be a bolt out of the blue.

The Supreme Court has thus left open an area for the public-disclosure tort to thrive. Recall the last element of the public-disclosure tort—the "newsworthiness test"—that the speech cannot be of "legitimate concern to the public." If it is, then the case is dismissed. If the speech involves matters of private concern, then the lawsuit proceeds. The newsworthiness element of the public-disclosure tort is designed to protect free speech. The tort was, after all, designed by Louis Brandeis, who after becoming a Supreme Court justice, was a champion of the First Amendment. He is considered one of the great heroes of free speech. But he also believed in the importance of protecting privacy, and he reconciled free speech and privacy with the newsworthiness test.

BALANCING FREE SPEECH AND PRIVACY

Several scholars think that the Supreme Court should abolish the privacy torts when they conflict with free speech. The law professor Diane Zimmerman, for example, argues that the public-disclosure tort should be "scuttled" because the costs to free speech are too high; potential litigation will have a chilling effect on speech and the tort inhibits the "free exchange of personal information."[28] Zimmerman raises a valid point—the privacy torts definitely have the potential to chill speech.

There are compelling reasons, however, why the Supreme Court is right not to eliminate the privacy torts, especially the public-disclosure tort. In fact, protecting privacy—and restricting free speech in some cases—can actually advance the reasons why we protect free speech in the first place. Since this sounds paradoxical, some explanation is in order.

We first need to begin by looking at why free speech is valuable. We're so used to assuming that free speech is important that we often don't take the time to think about why. But the why of it really matters. Those pondering the issue have come up with a number of reasons. I will discuss three of the most popular ones: individual autonomy, democracy, and the marketplace of ideas.

Individual Autonomy

One of the most frequently articulated rationales for why we protect free speech is that it promotes individual autonomy.[29] We want people to have the freedom to express themselves in all their uniqueness, eccentricity, and candor. Stopping Jessica Cutler from speaking about Robert in her Washingtonienne blog limits her freedom. The autonomy of listeners is also involved. Many people enjoyed Cutler's blog. Stopping Cutler from writing her blog will take away stories that many people might want to read.

But the autonomy justification cuts both ways. As the law professor Sean Scott observes, "The right to privacy and the First Amendment both serve the same interest in individual autonomy."[30] The disclosure of personal information can severely inhibit a person's autonomy and self-development.[31] Julie Cohen notes that lack of privacy can "chill the expression of eccentric individuality."[32] The risk of disclosure can inhibit people from engaging in taboo activities.[33] From Cutler's blog, it seemed as though she fully consented to Robert's spanking and kinky sex. She liked being with him. So why shouldn't Robert be able to have sex the way he wants to with another consenting adult? The risk of disclosure, however, might prevent people from doing things they enjoy because of fear of social disapproval. Privacy allows people to be free from worrying about what everybody else will think, and this is liberating and important for free choice.

Privacy protects more than just people's freedom to engage in an unconventional sex life. Privacy permits individuals to express unpopular ideas to people they trust without having to worry how society will judge them or whether they will face retaliation.[34] Without privacy, it is hard for many people to sound off about their bosses or express their honest opinions. All of these activities are central to people's autonomy. Protecting privacy can promote people's autonomy as much as free speech can.

Democracy

Free speech is also vital to democracy. The famous First Amendment scholar Alexander Meiklejohn argued that free speech is important not because we should protect the individual's desire to speak but because free speech is necessary for a robust political discourse. According to Meiklejohn, "What is essential is not that everyone shall speak, but that everything worth saying shall be said."[35] As the law professor Owen Fiss observes: "On the whole does [speech] enrich public debate? Speech is protected when (and only when) it does, and precisely because it does."[36] In other words, free speech is most valuable when it contributes to public discussion on issues of policy and politics. Under this view, speech of private concern is relatively unimportant. Reporting people's secrets rarely contributes much to politics. Was Jessica Cutler's Washingtonienne blog about her sexual exploits on Capitol Hill really useful for a political debate? It's a titillating and engrossing read, but our democracy probably isn't going to suffer without it. As Benjamin Franklin asserted: "If by the Liberty of the Press were understood merely the Liberty of discussing the Propriety of Public Measures and political opinions, let us have as much of it as you please. But if it means the Liberty of affronting, calumniating, and defaming one another, I for my part . . . shall cheerfully consent to exchange my Liberty of Abusing others for the Privilege of not being abus'd myself."[37]

In fact, privacy protections can strongly promote democratic discussion and debate.[38] Political discussions often take place between two people or in small groups rather than at public rallies or nationwide television broadcasts. More discourse about politics occurs in personal conversations than on soapboxes or street corners. Without privacy, many people might not feel comfortable having these candid conversations. Protecting privacy can actually promote free speech, not just restrict it.

The Marketplace of Ideas

A third justification for free speech is that it contributes to the promotion of truth. This justification was most famously propounded by the philosopher John Stuart Mill, who observed that it is best not to censor speech, because that speech might be true, and censors can't infallibly distinguish between the true and the false.[39] Justice Holmes drew from this theory when he articulated the notion of the marketplace of ideas: "When men have realized that time has upset many fighting faiths, they may come to believe even more than they believe the very foundations of their own conduct that the ultimate good desired is better reached by free trade in ideas—that the best test of truth is the power of the thought to get itself accepted in the competition of the market, and that truth is the only ground upon which their wishes safely can be carried out."[40] Under the marketplace theory, free speech enables us to find the truth. The law should butt out and let people decide for themselves what's true and false.

But truth isn't the only value at stake.[41] Truth must be weighed against other values. As one nineteenth-century English judge put it: "Truth, like all other good things, may be loved unwisely—may be pursued too keenly—may cost too much."[42] There are many "truths" that are not worth much effort to find out. For example, there is a true answer to the number of paperclips I have in my office, but this information does not have much value. Much true information is trivial and useless. The value of the quest for the truth depends upon what information one is seeking. The truth about a private person's personal life is often worth little or nothing to the general public.

On balance, privacy furthers many of the same interests that free speech does. Free speech is indispensable because it promotes autonomy, democracy, and the quest for the truth. But these interests also depend upon protecting privacy. A balance between free speech and privacy might achieve these interests more effectively than merely protecting speech at all costs.

NEWSWORTHINESS

To reconcile the public disclosure tort with free speech, the tort doesn't apply when the information is of "legitimate concern to the public."[43] This is referred to as the "newsworthiness test." If a particular disclosure is newsworthy, then a public-disclosure tort case is dismissed. This newsworthiness limitation is included in the tort to protect free speech.

Information is of public concern when "the public has a proper interest in learning about [it]."[44] For example, the Restatement of Torts distinguishes between "information to which the public is entitled" and "morbid and sensational prying into private lives for its own sake, with which a reasonable member of the public, with decent standards, would say that he had no concern."[45] What is of interest to most of society is not the same question as what is of legitimate public concern. It is possible that people will want to hear a story even when they do not consider it of legitimate public concern. For example, a video of Pamela Anderson having sex with Bret Michaels was sold over the Internet, generating hundreds of thousands of dollars in revenue.[46] A video of the president giving a speech would be much less lucrative. Does this make the sex tape more newsworthy? Ample public curiosity doesn't make a piece of gossip newsworthy, as such interest can stem from a hunger for prurient entertainment instead of from a desire to learn about the news and current events. Therefore information that involves matters of public concern is protected; information that merely provokes our prurient curiosity is not.

Identifying Information

In many instances, there is little need for a story about a person's private life to identify the person. The facts of the story may be of legitimate concern to the public, but the identification of the people involved might not further the story's purpose. In one case, for example, a woman suffered from a rare disease that caused her to continue to lose weight no matter how much she ate. A reporter wrote an article about her called "Starving Glutton," and it contained a photograph of her in a hospital bed. The court found the facts of the woman's disease to be newsworthy, yet the court still let the case proceed because the story could have been told effectively without identifying the woman: "While plaintiff's ailment may have been a matter of some public interest because unusual, certainly the identity of the person who suffered this ailment was not."[47]

Contrast the "Starving Glutton" case with that of Ruth, who was involved in a horrible car accident. The car was so badly mangled that she had to be cut from the car with the "jaws of life" device. Ruth was rushed away in a helicopter. A while later, lying in her hospital bed as a paraplegic, Ruth was watching *On Scene: Emergency Response,* a reality television show featuring real medical rescues. She was shocked when she saw that this episode was about her. Scenes from her rescue were vividly featured, including images of her mangled body in the car. Ruth was appalled. She said: "It's not for the public to see this trauma that I was going through."

Ruth sued for public disclosure of private facts. The court, however, dismissed her case because Ruth's rescue and treatment were of legitimate concern to the public. Ruth argued that the show's producers should have edited the episode to obscure her identity. The court, however, rejected her argument: "That the broadcast could have been edited to exclude some of Ruth's words and images and still excite a minimum degree of viewer interest is not determinative. Nor is the possibility that the members of this or another court, or a jury, might find a differently edited broadcast more to their taste or even more interesting. The courts do not, and constitutionally could not, sit as superior editors of the press."[48] Here, the court simply deferred to the media, an approach that I believe is dodging the issue. The show could have readily been edited to protect Ruth's privacy by blocking her face and not revealing exact details about Ruth's identity. Why not require a few small steps to protect people like Ruth?

One common argument against shielding people's identities is that doing so erodes the credibility of an article.[49] Identifying people in news stories certainly allows people to verify the stories independently. But many stories of paramount importance have employed anonymous sources. In exposing the Watergate break-in and cover-up, for example, Bob Woodward and Carl Bernstein relied on the well-known pseudonymous source "Deep Throat." When journalists protect confidential sources, they engage in a balancing determination, sacrificing the public's ability to verify for the importance of protecting confidentiality. Public verifiability is not sacrosanct; it can be outweighed by privacy interests. Of course, concealing identities cannot work for all stories, especially those about public figures, since it is the identity of the person that gives the story its relevance. But in many cases, there is no need to identify.

Speaking About One's Life

Bloggers like Jessica Cutler do not have an unfettered free-speech right to talk about other people's private lives. People like Robert should be able to sue bloggers like Cutler when they reveal private details that are not of legitimate concern to the public.

However, there is one other important issue involved in the case that must be addressed—Cutler's right to speak about her own life. Our lives are intertwined with those of others. If you want to write an autobiography, you're probably going to have to talk about other people, unless you spent your life living in a shack in the woods on a mountainside. Telling Cutler not to speak about her relationship with Robert—even though it may be of private concern—seems rather stifling to her freedom to express herself. It would be one thing for a stranger to talk about Cutler and Robert's sex life, but it's another if either Cutler or Robert wants to talk about it. Shouldn't we be extra careful to preserve people's ability to tell their own life stories?

Oddly, few cases address the issue of who is doing the talking. The focus is on whether the information is of legitimate concern to the public regardless of whether Cutler is speaking about her own life or whether some reporter is talking about it. A better approach would be for the law to pay attention to who is divulging the secret. It is essential for autonomy that a person be able to talk about her own life—even when what she's describing isn't newsworthy. It's one thing to silence a person from speaking about a piece of juicy gossip about someone else, but it is quite an extreme step to stop a person from talking about her own life.

But even if Cutler has a special right to speak about her own life—whether newsworthy or not—that doesn't mean that she can do so irresponsibly. The law should still require her to be careful not to damage the lives of others like Robert. To better think about these issues, let's look at a similar case. Susanna Kaysen was a well-known author, having written the book *Girl, Interrupted*, which was made into a movie costarring Angelina Jolie, who won an Oscar for her role.[50] Kaysen started having an affair with Joseph, a married man. She ultimately persuaded him to leave his wife, and he divorced in 1996 and moved in with Kaysen. At some point afterward, Kaysen started to experience severe vaginal pain. She went to doctor after doctor, but none was able to help her. Kaysen began to write a book about her experiences. She didn't tell Joseph about the subject of her book. In 1998 Kaysen broke it off with Joseph. Three years later, in 2001, she published her book, *The Camera My Mother Gave Me*, an autobiographical account of her terrible vaginal pain and how it affected her relationship with Joseph. She referred to Joseph at all times only as her "boyfriend" and altered some details about his life, such as where he was born and his occupation.

The book contained some graphic descriptions of their sex. In the book Joseph becomes impatient with Kaysen's condition and continually pesters her for sex, even resorting to "whining and pleading." Kaysen depicts Joseph in an unflattering light, as insensitive to her plight. In one scene where Joseph tries to have sex with Kaysen, she writes: "I felt he was trying to rape me. Because he hadn't seen how willing I was. All he could see was what he wanted."

When the book came out, many of Joseph's friends, family, and business clientele read the book and knew that Joseph was the "boyfriend." Joseph sued under the tort of public disclosure of private facts, claiming that his reputation was severely harmed. The court dismissed Joseph's case, concluding that the book was newsworthy. The topic of the effects of Kaysen's vaginal pain on her relationships was a matter "of legitimate public concern, and it is within this specific context that the explicit and highly personal details of the relationship are discussed." The court also noted that Kaysen had a "right to disclose her own intimate affairs." She was "telling her own personal story— which inextricably involves [Joseph] in an intimate way."[51]

The court was right that Kaysen's and Joseph's lives were intertwined and that Kaysen has a right to talk and write about her own life. The most important consideration, however, should have been whether it was possible for Kaysen to avoid identifying Joseph. She did indeed take as many steps as possible to conceal the identity of Joseph, not only omitting his name but even altering details about his life to further prevent his identification. It wasn't possible to do much more. Therefore Kaysen appears to have exercised the appropriate level of care in the steps she took to protect Joseph from being identified. She should win for this reason.

Turning back to the Washingtonienne case, there's no need to stop Cutler from talking about her sex life. She just needs to do it a bit more thoughtfully, with more attention to the rights of the other person involved. All Cutler had to do was avoid using Robert's initials and avoid mentioning where he lived, as these were key clues that would make it possible to identify him.

But she's just a twenty-something amateur, one might say, so why should we expect her to exercise the care of a professional journalist? The answer is that the line between amateur and professional journalists is dissolving. The Internet gives amateurs a power similar to what professionals have—to reach thousands, perhaps millions, of people. And with power should come some responsibility. While we can't expect bloggers to be perfect in all the steps they take to shield others' identities, we should hold them to a reasonable standard of care. Cutler was sloppy in handling Robert's identity when she blogged. As a result, she upended his life. This didn't have to happen. Cutler could still have written her story. And Robert's sex life could still have remained private. In many cases—as in this one—with a little bit of care, free speech and privacy can peacefully coexist.

ANONYMITY

Article III Groupie wasn't the typical groupie, obsessed with rock stars. Instead, her fixation was on federal judges. Named after Article III of the U.S. Constitution, which establishes the powers of the federal judiciary, Article III Groupie was a young law school graduate who created the blog Underneath Their Robes. Article III Groupie blogged about "scrumptious tidbits of news and gossip about federal judges."[52] She also dished out gossip about law clerks, recent law school graduates who assisted judges for yearlong stints. As Article III Groupie described her blog:

> This weblog, "Underneath Their Robes" ("UTR"), reflects Article III Groupie's interest in, and obsession with, the federal judiciary. UTR is a combination of People, US Weekly, Page Six, The National Enquirer, and Tigerbeat, focused not on vacuous movie stars or fatuous teen idols, but on federal judges. Article III judges are legal celebrities, the "rock stars" of the legal profession's upper echelons.

Article III Groupie's electronic
face

This weblog is a source of news, gossip, and colorful commentary about these judicial superstars!

According to her self-description, Article III groupie graduated from a top law
school and worked for "a large law firm in a major city, where she now toils in
obscurity." She described herself as a "diva" and as a "federal judicial
starf**ker."

Little more was revealed about the elusive Article III Groupie. She said that
in "her free time, she consoles herself through the overconsumption of luxury
goods" and that her "goal in life is to become a federal judicial diva." Article
III Groupie's identity was shrouded in secrecy. The only picture of the mysterious Article III Groupie was a small hand-drawn sketch.

Who was this Sex-in-the-City-type diva? How bizarre that she would be
starstruck by the nerdy world of the federal judiciary! How exciting that
someone—anyone—was even interested in this lonely corner of the world in
the same way that groupies were into rock stars! Suffice it to say that Article III
Groupie's blog was quite quirky and entertaining. She seduced the online legal
world with her exuberance and audacity. Who else but Article III Groupie
would dare to hold "hottie" contests for male and female judges?[53] Who else
had the moxie to use such catty phrases as "judicial divas," "bench-slappery,"
"litigatrix," "bodacious babes of the bench," "judicial hotties" and "judicial
prima donnas"?

Article III Groupie's gossipy blog was a big hit. It attracted an impressive
array of readers, including federal judges themselves. It was U.S. Appeals
Court Judge Alex Kozinski who anointed Article III Groupie with the nick-

name A3G. And U.S. Court of Appeals Judge Richard Posner admitted that he enjoyed the site: "It's occasionally a little vulgar, but this is America in 2005."[54]

One day, rather abruptly, A3G decided to unmask herself. The opportunity came when Jeff Toobin of the *New Yorker* wanted to interview A3G in person. A3G agreed to meet him for lunch. When Toobin saw A3G, his jaw dropped.

"So you're a guy?" Toobin gasped.

Yes, A3G was a man. His name was David Lat. Lat was a graduate of Yale Law School who had clerked for a conservative federal judge on the U.S. Court of Appeals for the 9th Circuit. I knew Lat personally; he was a classmate of mine at Yale Law School. But I had no idea Lat was A3G until I read it in Toobin's *New Yorker* article. To make matters more interesting, Lat worked as a federal prosecutor in Newark, New Jersey.[55] He regularly appeared in court before federal judges.

When Toobin's article revealed to the world A3G's true identity, it sent shockwaves throughout the legal community. This amazing disrobing quickly drew the attention of the mainstream media, and Lat's story was featured in scores of newspaper articles.

Lat had decided to be anonymous as a way of protecting his job while maintaining such a salacious blog. In an interview, Lat explained: "The law is a fairly conservative profession, and being known as a legal gossip-monger would not be good for my professional advancement. It also wouldn't help me in my lifelong ambition to become an Article III judge. Issuing snarky commentary about sitting federal judges won't put me on a fast track to the federal bench."[56] Beyond the inherent difficulties of juggling the blog with his law career, Lat regularly appeared in federal court representing the United States government. Without anonymity, the very judges he was calling "your honor" in the courtroom would know he was referring to them as "hotties" in the blogosphere. It was difficult to imagine how he could continue to represent the federal government in court.

Moreover, Lat's anonymity provided a sense of mystery to the blog. Now that mystery had vanished. The blog just wouldn't be the same without Lat's unique alter ego, A3G. One commentator wrote in a post about A3G at another legal blog: "This is terrible. I can't read that site knowing the author is a man."[57] Anonymity had allowed Lat to assume a new identity, a persona he carefully designed to be as distinct from himself as possible. One reader of his blog who knew him stated in an interview in the *New York Times:* "David was on this one side a hard-core Federalist Society type, who clerked for an extremely hard-right judge, and was way to the right of most of his associates. And he had this whole other side of flamboyant, theater-watching, Oscar-watching, shoe-loving, litigatrix. How do these two sides get reconciled?"[58]

Anonymity allows people to escape accountability for their words, but this comes at a cost—the loss of authorship credit under one's real name. Lat wanted to have the praise and attention his female alter ego A3G was getting. He increasingly grew frustrated that he was toiling over the blog but getting little recognition for it. He wanted the attention the blog was attracting to be associated with his name. But the irony was that in his quest to get credit for the blog, he risked destroying the blog and even his career.

After revealing his identity, Lat braced himself for the firestorm that would ensue. After his identity was announced, his supervisors in the United States Attorney's office asked him to stop blogging immediately. Lat quickly locked his blog down, making it inaccessible to the public without a special password. Near the end of a stressful week, in which he wondered whether he would be fired, Lat met with his boss. He would be able to keep his job—on the assumption that Underneath Their Robes would be kept underneath its password.

But Lat's story has a happy ending. A few weeks later, he left the U.S. Attorney's office to accept a job blogging full-time at Wonkette, the political gossip blog that had publicized Jessica Cutler's Washingtonienne blog. He later went on to launch a new legal gossip blog, Above the Law. Lat now blogs under his real name.

The Virtues of Anonymity

The saga of Article III Groupie demonstrates how easy it seems to be anonymous on the Internet. A person can readily create a blog under a pseudonym or can post anonymous comments to blogs or online discussion groups. According to a survey, 55 percent of bloggers use pseudonyms rather than their real identities.[59]

Anonymity can be essential to free speech. As the Supreme Court has noted: "Anonymous pamphlets, leaflets, brochures and even books have played an important role in the progress of mankind. Persecuted groups and sects from time to time throughout history have been able to criticize oppressive practices and laws either anonymously or not at all."[60]

Anonymous speech has a long history as an important mode of expression. Between 1789 and 1809, six presidents, fifteen cabinet members, twenty senators, and thirty-four congressmen published anonymous political writings or used pen names. It was common for letters to the editor in local newspapers to be anonymous. Ben Franklin used more than forty pen names during his life.[61] Mark Twain, O. Henry, Voltaire, George Sand, and George Eliot were all pseudonymous authors. Indeed, James Madison, Alexander Hamilton, and John Jay published the Federal Papers under the pseudonym Publius. Their opponents, the Anti-Federalists, also used pseudonyms.[62]

Anonymity allows people to be more experimental and eccentric without risking damage to their reputations.[63] Anonymity can be essential to the presentation of ideas, for it can strip away reader biases and prejudices and add mystique to a text. People might desire to be anonymous because they fear social ostracism or being fired from their jobs. Without anonymity, some people might not be willing to express controversial ideas.[64] Anonymity thus can be critical to preserving people's right to speak freely.

Accountability

Anonymity also has a dark side. As Adam Smith observed in *The Wealth of Nations*: "While [a 'man of low condition,' as opposed to a 'man of rank and fortune'] remains in a country village his conduct may be attended to, and he may be obliged to attend to it himself. In this situation, and in this situation only, he may have what is called a character to lose. But as soon as he comes to a great city, he is sunk in obscurity and darkness. His conduct is observed and attended to by nobody, and he is therefore likely to neglect it himself, and to abandon himself to every low profligacy and vice."[65] According to Smith, people behave differently when they can do so anonymously. People "of rank and fortune" are generally going to be noticed no matter where they are; but ordinary people will be noticed only in the small village. In the large city, a person becomes a face in the crowd and has achieved an anonymity of sorts in daily life. This anonymity, Smith observes, will tempt people to behave badly. When people are less accountable for their conduct, they are more likely to engage in unsavory acts.

When anonymous, people are often much nastier and more uncivil in their speech. It is easier to say harmful things about others when we don't have to take responsibility. When we talk about others, we affect not only their reputation but ours as well. If a person gossips about inappropriate things, betrays confidences, spreads false rumors and lies, then her own reputation is likely to suffer. People will view the person as untrustworthy and malicious. They might no longer share secrets with the person. They might stop believing what the person says. As U.S. Supreme Court Justice Antonin Scalia observed, anonymity can making lying easier; and the identification of speakers can help significantly in deterring them from spreading false rumors and can allow us to locate and punish the source of such rumors.[66]

Anonymity also facilitates deception. People can readily masquerade as other people in creating blogs and profiles. Harriet Miers was the first Supreme Court Justice nominee to have her own blog—Harriet Miers's Blogg!!![67] Her first entry:

> OMG I CAN'T BELIEVE I'M THE NOMINEE ! ! ! This is BIGGEST DAY OF MY LIFE ! ! ! ! *EVER !!!!*
>
> *OMG OMG OMG*

Needless to say, it was fake. Miers is not alone. There was a blog called Luttig's Lair impersonating Judge J. Michael Luttig.[68] In one high school, some students created fake blog entries in another student's name, boasting about sexual adventures that never happened.[69] In another incident, an anonymous person created a fake Myspace profile for a twelve-year-old girl, using her real phone number and saying she was a stripper.[70] Anyone can sign up on a free blogging service and create a blog. In anybody's name. In your name. You might have a blog and not even know about it.

When people can avoid being identified, they can slip away from their bad reputations. In one instance, a woman joined an online chat group for eating disorders. She said she, too, suffered from an eating disorder, but she was eventually revealed to the group to be a fraud. After being booted from the group, she moved over to a group of sexual abuse victims. When revealed as a phony in that group, she reappeared in a group of people suffering from AIDS.[71] As sociologist Robert Putnam observes: "Anonymity and fluidity in the virtual world encourage 'easy in, easy out,' 'drive-by' relationships. The very casualness is the appeal of computer-mediated communication for some denizens of cyberspace, but it discourages the creation of social capital. If entry and exit are too easy, commitment, trustworthiness, and reciprocity will not develop."[72] In other words, anonymity inhibits the process by which reputations are formed, which can have both good and bad consequences. Not having accountability for our speech can be liberating and allow us to speak more candidly; but it can also allow us to harm other people without being accountable for it.

Thus anonymity is a form of privacy protection, yet it can also facilitate privacy violations. Anonymity can preserve privacy by allowing people to speak freely without being publicly identified, yet it can undermine privacy by allowing people to more easily invade the privacy of others. As the tension between anonymity and accountability demonstrates, along with the tension between privacy and free speech, the choice isn't as simple as one between freedom and constraint. Rather, it is a choice that involves freedom on both sides.

Wikipedia: The Power and Peril of Openness

The virtues and vices of anonymity are starkly implicated in Wikipedia, one of the most fascinating creations on the Internet. Created by Jimmy Wales in 2001, Wikipedia is an experiment in the power of collective knowledge.[73] Wikipedia is an online encyclopedia, whose authors collaborate with readers, who can volunteer information and edit entries. This exchange is made possible by "wiki," a Web-based application by which people can add and edit text collaboratively. It is named for the Hawaiian term *wiki wiki*, which means "quick."

By 2004, just a few years after its inception, Wikipedia had surpassed 1 million entries. By 2006 it had grown to 3.5 million entries.[74] Wikipedia is now the largest encyclopedia ever written, and it is available for free. As of late 2006 Wikipedia has become one of the most visited websites in the world.[75]

Unlike a regular encyclopedia, which quickly ages in its leather-bound covers, Wikipedia is dynamic, growing and changing each day. It is constantly updated. Anybody can edit and change a Wikipedia article. It relies on the collective wisdom of the Internet.

Most of us would be quite flattered to find an entry about ourselves on Wikipedia. Not so for John Seigenthaler. Seigenthaler was a lifelong journalist who fought for free speech and civil rights. He was an assistant to Bobby Kennedy when he was serving as attorney general during his brother John Kennedy's presidential administration. In 2005 Seigenthaler was in his late seventies and could look back on a long distinguished career. However, he was shocked to find a very different take on his life in his Wikipedia bio: "John Seigenthaler Sr. was the assistant to Attorney General Robert Kennedy in the early 1960's. For a brief time, he was thought to have been directly involved in the Kennedy assassinations of both John, and his brother, Bobby. Nothing was ever proven."[76]

Seigenthaler was furious. In a *USA Today* editorial, Seigenthaler wrote:

I have no idea whose sick mind conceived the false, malicious "biography" that appeared under my name for 132 days on Wikipedia, the popular, online, free encyclopedia whose authors are unknown and virtually untraceable. . . .

At age 78, I thought I was beyond surprise or hurt at anything negative said about me. I was wrong. One sentence in the biography was true. I was Robert Kennedy's administrative assistant in the early 1960s. I also was his pallbearer. It

was mind-boggling when my son, John Seigenthaler, journalist with NBC News,
phoned later to say he found the same scurrilous text on Reference.com and An-
swers.com.[77]

Ironically, Seigenthaler had previously founded a center to protect the First
Amendment right to free speech. Now he was being burned by it. Seigenthaler
said that he still believed in free speech, but "what I want is accountability."[78]

Seigenthaler tried to track down the person who had posted the information, but to no avail. He located the Internet protocol (IP) address of the author and from that determined that the author's Internet service provider
(ISP) was BellSouth Internet. An IP address is a unique number that is assigned to every computer connected to the Web. An example might look like
this: 210.28.111.120. BellSouth Internet knew the name of the customer with
the IP address but would not reveal it unless ordered by a court. Seigenthaler

would have to file a defamation lawsuit against the person, but he wasn't interested in suing.

Eventually the misinformation was removed from Wikipedia, more than four months after it had been posted. Seigenthaler described the difficulty of cleaning up the stain of the rumor: "When I was a child, my mother lectured me on the evils of 'gossip.' She held a feather pillow and said, 'If I tear this open, the feathers will fly to the four winds, and I could never get them back in the pillow. That's how it is when you spread mean things about people.' For me, that pillow is a metaphor for Wikipedia."[79]

Enter Daniel Brandt, an outspoken critic of Wikipedia who had read about the case and was able to trace the IP address to a Nashville company. He then emailed the company asking for information about its services and got a response with the same IP address. Tipped off that the culprit was nearly in sight, a *New York Times* reporter called the company. This prompted the person to come forward, confess, and apologize to Seigenthaler. He explained that it was just a silly prank to rile a coworker. Because of the publicity, the person resigned from his job.[80]

In response to the Seigenthaler debacle, Wikipedia changed its open policy and required users to register before creating new articles. All users, whether registered or not, could still edit articles except certain ones that were frequently abused. For example, at the top of the Seigenthaler article is the following statement: "Because of recent vandalism, editing of this article by anonymous or newly registered users is currently disabled. Such users may discuss changes, request unprotection, or create an account." The Seigenthaler entry is now corrected, and the offensive information has long been removed.[81] But the cost of protecting the entry from abuse was to sacrifice some anonymity and openness.

One of the problems with anonymity is that it makes it harder to assess an author's reputation. An open system that allows people to edit anonymously is more easily abused because bad-faith authors are not held accountable. For some time, vandals have been attacking Wikipedia, deliberately adding falsehoods to articles.[82] The legal scholar Bruce Boyden observes: "All it takes is one dedicated person with low scruples, a grudge, and a little extra time on their hands, and the harms skyrocket."[83] And it's not just random miscreants who try to manipulate Wikipedia entries anonymously. Several employees of politicians were caught trying to doctor Wikipedia entries anonymously. One intern for U.S. Representative Martin Meehan deleted part of a Wikipedia entry about Meehan's early promises to serve only four terms (he was currently on his seventh term). At one point, the spate of abuses inspired Wikipedia to block federal congressional IP addresses from editing entries.[84] Even Jimmy Wales, the founder of Wikipedia, was caught anonymously editing his own Wikipedia entry. He deleted references to Larry Sanger as a cofounder of the encyclopedia. "I wish I hadn't done it. It's in poor taste," Wales confessed. "People have a lot of information about themselves but staying objective is difficult."[85]

The Seigenthaler case exposed some of the tensions at the heart of Wikipedia. When anybody can spread information online, it becomes harder to know what information to trust and what information not to trust. When we read entries in the *Encyclopaedia Britannica,* we know that they are written by experts and carefully vetted. Wikipedia entries are a collaborative exercise, and they can be written by those in the know as well as any fool stumbling along the information superhighway. People can just as easily introduce false information as true information.

The results can be extremely useful, yet sometimes unreliable. As the law professor Orin Kerr puts it, Wikipedia entries "seem to be a strange mix of accurate statements and egregious errors."[86] Wikipedia is more optimistic: "We assume that the world is full of reasonable people and that collectively they can arrive eventually at a reasonable conclusion, despite the worst efforts of a very few wreckers. It's something akin to optimism."[87] Pimples and all, Wikipedia is an example of the benefits of collective action. What is remarkable about Wikipedia is how often it works. In many cases, it serves as a terrific resource, but it also has a fair amount of dubious data.

Wikipedia entries matter so much because they often appear near the top of Google searches. And Wikipedia has enough good information to make the articles worth looking at. Ironically, it is because the articles have a lot of valid and useful information that their errors become so problematic. Nobody would even pay attention to Wikipedia if it contained mostly false data. Since it contains so much accurate information, Wikipedia encourages users to rely upon its articles and leaves them more readily deceived by the false information.

Wikipedia dispenses with one of the primary features of ordinary encyclopedias. No longer must authors of entries have credentials. On the one hand, we trust a traditional encyclopedia entry because we trust the author. Authors have staked their reputations on their work. In contrast, Wikipedia entries can have dozens of authors, and we know little about them. Wikipedia lists a history of the edits by each author, but authors use pseudonyms like "Gopple" or

"Taco," so we don't know who they are or what their expertise is. How much are we to trust a fact added by someone named "Gopple," about whom we know little else?

The irony, in the end, is that Wikipedia must defend its own reputation. It must ensure that its articles are dependable, for if they contain too much junk information, people might no longer find the site trustworthy. Wikipedia's reputation thus depends upon balancing openness and anonymity against accountability. The Seigenthaler case pushed Wikipedia toward a less anonymous system. But the more Wikipedia limits anonymity, the less free and open the project becomes. It's a difficult trade-off, one that lies at the core of so many of the thorny problems with online speech.

THE LAW OF ANONYMITY

Anonymity also implicates reputation in another way. The more people can spread falsehoods or invade privacy without accountability or fear of repercussions, the more likely they are to do so. Anonymous speech can cause reputational harm to others, and it can undermine the ability of those harmed to seek redress. Anonymity hobbles the pursuit of legal remedies for privacy violations and defamation. How, then, should we balance anonymity with accountability?

One way to strike a balance is to enforce traceable anonymity.[88] In other words, we preserve the right for people to speak anonymously, but in the event that one causes harm to another, we've preserved a way to trace who the culprit is. A harmed individual can get a court order to obtain the identity of an anonymous speaker only after demonstrating genuine harm and the need to know who caused that harm.

Traceable Anonymity

Traceable anonymity is for the most part what currently exists on the Internet. Many people use the term *anonymity* rather imprecisely—to refer to both anonymous speech (no name or identifier attached) and pseudonymous speech (using a pen name). In most cases such conflation is not problematic, and for convenience and readability, I use the term in the same way here.

But there's another dimension to anonymity that is not captured by the language we use—traceability. Traceability involves the extent to which anonymous or pseudonymous postings can be traced to the author's true identity.

Many people assume that when they are anonymous, they are untraceable, but this is often a myth. It is relatively easy to blog anonymously, but it is hard to be nontraceable. The reason has to do with the Internet Protocol, mentioned above. Whenever a user communicates over the Internet, her IP address is logged. For any session of Internet use, the ISP typically has information that links a particular customer with her IP address.

Suppose you write an anonymous comment on my blog saying something bad about me. At a minimum, I will know the IP address of the computer you posted from. I might even have information about the organization that assigned you your IP address. Thus I will know your ISP or the company where you work from and the city you were in when you posted. This is how Brandt traced the Seigenthaler defamer. If you post from work, your employer has information about which specific computer your post came from, and the comment may be traced back to your office computer. If you post from home, your ISP can connect your IP address to your account information. Thus even when you're anonymous, you can be tracked down.

Many people don't realize that their anonymous blogging or comments can be traced back to them. It is indeed possible to make yourself untraceable, but it involves significant care and know-how.[89] For example, anonymizing services are available to cloak your IP address.

But one mistake can leave your identity exposed. Even if you conceal your IP address, it is still possible to be traced. People often leave behind various snippets of personal information that when assembled can identify them. According to one study, "a large portion of the US population can be re-identified using a combination of 5-digit zip code, gender, and date of birth."[90] In 2006 AOL turned over twenty million search queries to researchers. AOL did not perceive a privacy problem because it did not include subscribers' names along with the queries. The *New York Times*, however, demonstrated that some subscribers could still be identified. A reporter analyzed the searches for one anonymous user and was able to zero in on the person.[91]

Most people don't do even a minimal job of avoiding traceability. And perhaps that's not so bad so long as the law provides adequate protection against others finding out their IP addresses or account information. In other words, the key is for the law to allow the unmasking of anonymous people when they engage in harmful speech about others. But people shouldn't be unmasked too readily. The law thus must draw a careful line between when it is appropriate to unmask an anonymous speaker and when it isn't.

Balancing Anonymity and Accountability

The First Amendment to the U.S. Constitution limits restrictions on anonymous speech.[92] According to the Supreme Court: "Despite readers' curiosity and the public's interest in identifying the creator of a work of art, an author generally is free to decide whether or not to disclose his or her true identity."[93] When a person tries to identify anonymous speakers by requesting their records from their ISP, several courts have required heightened standards before ordering the unveiling.[94]

Suppose you invade my privacy or defame me by something you write anonymously on your blog. I can sue you in what has become known as a "John Doe" lawsuit. Since I don't yet know who you are, I sue you under the pseudonym you use or under "John Doe." I then must convince the judge that my case is strong enough to go forward.[95]

"John Doe" lawsuits provide a good compromise between anonymity and accountability, but the solution isn't perfect. Consider the case of Allegheny Energy Service. Yahoo! hosts message boards for all publicly traded companies. One of these companies was Allegheny Energy Service.[96] In 2003 Allegheny company officials discovered a rather unsettling posting on the Yahoo! board:

> I work for this company (non-exempt) and have a lot of years under my belt. Yes, A.N. and his cronies turned his respectable Blue Chip into a POS [Piece of Shit]. He and they ruined a good chunk of my 401K. Now I have to delay retiring. They offered up all sorts of crap on a silver plated tray for us to swallow. . . .
>
> Just like Allegheny Energy's Work Management horse manure which has done nothing more than take the tools out of workers' hands and created a non productive pile of dung. Another STUPID program that Allegheny Energy probably spent millions on for nothing, absolutely nothing. Then we were force fed "love thy n*gger" with Allegheny Energy's DIVERSITY program.

Allegheny's lawyers wanted to find out what employee had posted the racial slur. To find out, they filed a "John Doe" lawsuit against the anonymous poster, claiming a "breach of a duty of loyalty" to the company. The anonymous poster was not aware a lawsuit had been filed. Allegheny's attorneys then filed an "emergency motion" to prevent the poster from posting more messages. They claimed that Doe's posting violated the company's antiharassment policy. They subpoenaed Yahoo! to obtain its records about the poster's account. Yahoo! released the identity of the poster—Clifton, an engineering technician who had been working for Allegheny Energy Service for sixteen years. Clifton had posted to the Yahoo! message board from home, using his wife's Yahoo! account. After establishing Clifton's identity, Allegheny dropped the "John Doe" lawsuit.

Company officials later called Clifton into a conference room and handed him a copy of his Yahoo! message board posting. The director of employee relations told Clifton that his racial slur violated Allegheny's diversity policy. Clifton was later fired for "placing a racially derogatory posting on the Yahoo message board in violation of Allegheny Energy's Positive Work Environment expectations."

This case raises several difficult issues about free speech, anonymity, and accountability. Allegheny Energy used a rather dubious technique to obtain Clifton's identity. Ordinarily, Allegheny Energy has no right to find out the identity of an anonymous speaker. But it obtained a subpoena for the speaker's identity with a legal action that appears to have been brought solely to unmask the speaker. Clifton was speaking outside of work, using his home computer, and trying to be anonymous. Does an employer have any justification for uncovering the identity of an employee who posts anonymously from home? On the other hand, Clifton's racial slur was quite offensive. If one of Allegheny Energy's employees is publicly making such comments, shouldn't an employer have the right to know? Should Clifton be able to make such remarks without being accountable for them?

As odious as Clifton's statements were, it wasn't invading anybody's privacy or defaming anyone. These were his personal views expressed on his own time. Moreover, Allegheny Energy appears to have filed a sham case just to find out Clifton's identity. Thus it is extremely important to establish high thresholds for making anonymity traceable. Otherwise, the promise of anonymity will begin to ring hollow. The law must restrict bad-faith lawsuits designed solely to unmask anonymous speakers.

WHO SHOULD BE RESPONSIBLE FOR HARMFUL SPEECH?

One of the most wonderful features of the Internet is its interactivity. On my blog, for example, anybody can post a comment. People can even do so anonymously if they want. Comments appear below my posts, and sometimes the discussion in the comments is much more interesting than the initial post. I have some power over the commentators. I can edit or delete comments I

find irrelevant, uncivil, or offensive. I can require people to identify themselves rather than grant them anonymity. But I prefer to permit anonymous
comments, as this encourages greater candor and more comments.

But anonymity can make it difficult to track down a commentator. If a person suffers a privacy violation or defamation as a result of a comment, can he
hold me as well as the commentator responsible? This is a very important issue, one with dramatic repercussions for both free speech and the protection
of reputation online.

The Plight of Kenneth Zeran

About a week after the Oklahoma City bombing in 1995, a person with the
username "KenZZo3" posted an advertisement on an AOL bulletin board.[97]
The advertisement was entitled "Naughty Oklahoma T-shirts." People could
order shirts with slogans such as:

> Visit Oklahoma . . . It's a BLAST!!!
> Putting the kids to bed . . . Oklahoma 1995
> McVeigh for President 1996

The message said interested people should call "Ken" at Kenneth Zeran's
home phone number.

Zeran, however, hadn't posted the advertisement. He learned about the
posting when he began receiving phone calls from irate people. Zeran called
AOL and demanded that the posting be removed and that a retraction be
posted. AOL removed the posting the following day but refused to post a retraction. The phone calls continued, and they were nasty and threatening.
Zeran's business consisted of listing apartments on a monthly basis, and he
had given out his phone number on the listings. He felt helpless, since changing his phone number would hurt his business.

Zeran discovered that a second posting had been made using a similar username to the previous one. The posting stated that some of the T-shirts had
sold out, but that new T-shirts were available with additional offensive slogans. The new posting said that callers should ask for "Ken" and to "please
call back if [the phone line was] busy." Zeran kept receiving threatening calls.
He called AOL again to take down the new posting and to block future ones.
The AOL operator told him that AOL was working on terminating the
abuser's account. But the postings kept on coming. New advertisements
touted odious Oklahoma City bombing bumper stickers and key chains. And

the phone calls kept increasing. Within a few days, Zeran was receiving a call about every two minutes. When a copy of the advertisement was discovered by a local radio station, the broadcaster Mark Shannon read some of the T-shirt slogans over the air and urged listeners to call Zeran to express their outrage. A barrage of calls ensued, including death threats. Some of the calls were so menacing that the local police began to monitor Zeran's house.

Finally, the media began to report that the advertisement was a hoax, and the radio station issued an apology. The phone calls slowly began to abate, and about three weeks after the initial advertisement, Zeran was receiving only about fifteen calls per day—a marked improvement. But the ordeal had taken its toll on Zeran, who was so shaken up that his doctor prescribed an antianxiety drug.

Nobody knows who posted the advertisements, but Zeran was determined to get some justice for his plight. He sued AOL for negligently failing to remove the defamatory postings. Zeran was suing AOL not directly for defamation but for taking an unreasonable delay in removing the defamatory postings.

Zeran's case ended when the U.S. Court of Appeals for the Fourth Circuit declared that AOL was immune from suit.[98] AOL could not be sued because Congress, concerned that ISPs and others might be responsible if one of their users made a defamatory statement, had passed a law immunizing the hosts of Internet communication forums from liability for things said by others using these forums.

Suppose a person makes a defamatory comment about you on my blog. You sue me because the statement appears on my blog. But I didn't make the statement—all I did was provide the forum in which another person said it. Why would you want to sue me rather than the person who made the statement? Because I might have a very popular blog with tens of thousands of readers. I might be wealthy and the person making the statement might not be. Or the person might have posted anonymously, and I'm the only one who can be tracked down to sue. This is what happened in Zeran's case. AOL maintained the bulletin board. It had a lot of money, and the person who posted the bogus T-shirt ads was anonymous. So AOL was the natural target.

But ISPs such as AOL have millions of users. Should AOL be responsible if some of its users defame others or invade their privacy? Certainly not initially. After all, AOL is providing a rather open forum on its bulletin boards. All sorts of people can post messages, and AOL cannot possibly monitor every one. AOL is simply providing a place for people to talk—a microphone and soapbox in cyberspace—that's all. It shouldn't be responsible for what they say.

That was the logic Congress followed in 1996, when it passed Section 230 of the Communications Decency Act (CDA), immunizing ISPs and the hosts of online forums from liability for the speech of their users. The statute reads: "No provider or user of an interactive computer service shall be treated as the publisher or speaker of any information provided by another information content provider."[99] According to the court that heard Zeran's suit: "Congress recognized the threat that tort-based lawsuits pose to freedom of speech in the new and burgeoning Internet medium. The imposition of tort liability on service providers for the communications of others represented, for Congress, simply another form of intrusive government regulation of speech. Section 230 was enacted, in part, to maintain the robust nature of Internet communication and, accordingly, to keep government interference in the medium to a minimum."[100]

Section 230 was the law when Zeran sued AOL, so how could he possibly have a case? In defamation law, if I help you spread a defamatory statement, I can be liable under defamation law as a "distributor" if I know or have reason to know that the statement is defamatory. When the statement was first posted, AOL would clearly not be liable. But after Zeran told AOL that it was false and begged them to take it down, then AOL had reason to know it was defamatory. Since AOL didn't take it down until much later, Zeran argued that AOL should be liable for the time during which it knew about the bogus ad yet did nothing.

Does Section 230 immunize AOL even after it knows that somebody has posted a defamatory statement? Based on the way the statute is worded, this is a complicated question. Courts have wrangled over this issue, with most courts holding that Section 230 provides a broad immunity, waiving liability even after an ISP knows that a posting is defamatory. Unfortunately for Zeran, the court concluded that AOL was still immune.[101] Zeran was out of luck. He couldn't track down the anonymous person who posted the T-shirt ads. He couldn't sue AOL. He had no way to fight back.

AOL certainly doesn't have time to monitor every comment posted on its network. There are millions of communications by AOL users, and AOL cannot possibly police them all. But in this case, Zeran had informed AOL about the message. Should that affect the ISP's responsibilities? Despite Zeran's pleas, AOL acted slowly, and Zeran continued to suffer harm. Shouldn't the law provide some incentive to AOL to respond promptly to such a complaint? Under the court's interpretation of Section 230, AOL could ignore Zeran with impunity.

Immunity for Bloggers

Section 230 doesn't immunize bloggers for what they themselves say. At most, it may immunize them for comments to their posts written by others. To what extent should bloggers or websites that allow others to post comments be immune when one of the comments defames or invades a person's privacy?

On my blog, my coauthors and I allow anonymous comments. I had a first-hand experience with a defamatory comment to one of my blog posts. I wrote a post criticizing the bar exam, which all lawyers must pass in order to be licensed. An anonymous person wrote a nasty comment outing the identity of a pseudonymous blogger and stating several falsehoods about her. Here's the relevant part of the comment, in which I have changed her name and the name of her blog to protect her anonymity:

> Does the [bar exam] test legal ability? Debatable. Jane Doe, aka Legal Blogger Girl, aka host of legalbloggergirl.com, would say no because she failed the NY bar 6 times in a row, mainly due to absurdly low [bar exam] scores.
>
> Although Jane Doe is a proven liar and horrid test taker, I agree the [bar exam] should go.

Jane Doe blogged under the pseudonym Legal Blogger Girl. The anonymous commenter to my blog had revealed Jane Doe's actual identity, ruining her ability to be anonymous. And the statement about failing the bar seemed very likely to have been false.

Jane Doe emailed me requesting that I delete the comment. Although I couldn't be certain, I was fairly confident that it was false. It had little relevance to my post and seemed to be merely a nasty potshot. I had no trouble promptly deleting it. A few weeks later, I was surprised when Jane emailed me again to say that the comment was still there. Apparently, the anonymous commentator had reposted the comment. I deleted it again. This time, the commentator finally stopped.

Deleting the comment only took a few seconds, and I could readily see why Jane Doe wanted the comment gone. But what if I weren't sympathetic to her plight? If Section 230 gives me complete immunity, then it says that I could simply ignore her and be completely immune. After all, I didn't post the comment—somebody else did. Why should I be responsible for what some anonymous person said?

Although somebody else made the comment, I provided him with the forum in which to do it. I allowed him to post his comment, and I allowed him to do it anonymously. I can easily shut off comments to my blog, but I like having comments because it creates a dialogue in which people can read and discuss my ideas. My blog has a fairly sizable readership, so it is a forum where people will be heard. I believe, therefore, that I have some responsibility to ensure that the website I control is not causing harm to others. The law should encourage me to take Jane Doe's complaint seriously and do what I can to prevent my website from causing her harm.

Many courts, however, interpret Section 230 as providing bloggers like me with blanket immunity for comments posted by others. That means that I could simply thumb my nose at Jane Doe. But there is an alternative way to interpret Section 230, a way I believe is preferable to blanket immunity. Section 230 might be read to grant immunity only before the operator of a website is alerted that something posted there by another violates somebody's privacy or defames her. If the operator of a website becomes aware of the problematic material on the site, yet doesn't remove it, then the operator could be liable. In other words, I certainly shouldn't be liable to Jane Doe for the comment, but if I refuse to take it down after she asks, then perhaps I should be liable. At that point, I know about the comment, I am on notice that it is causing harm to another, and instead of doing something about it, I'm embracing the comment by leaving it up on the website. As I stated in the previous chapter, however, legal liability must be modified to limit damages and encourage informal ways of resolving disputes.

This is an example of the difference between the libertarian and middle-ground approaches. When it is interpreted as granting broad immunity from lawsuits, Section 230 advances the libertarian approach, valuing free speech above all else. The middle-ground approach, in contrast, seeks to encourage people to work out the problem informally first, by spurring bloggers to remove harmful comments. If this informal process fails, a lawsuit can be brought, but otherwise, the law would function to serve as an impetus to get people to work it out among themselves.

Nude on the Net

In one case, a woman's ex-boyfriend impersonated her in a Yahoo! chat room. Anybody can sign up as a Yahoo! user for free and can use any name. The ex-boyfriend posted naked photos of the woman and included her email address and work phone number. His goal was to get men to start harassing her. When she discovered what happened, the woman was appalled. According to the woman, she wrote to Yahoo!, explaining that she didn't create this profile and wanted the photos removed. A month passed, and Yahoo! did nothing. She wrote to Yahoo! again. No response. Finally, she spoke with a Yahoo! employee, who promised to help her remove the photos. But the woman claims that Yahoo! still didn't get the photos taken down.

The woman sued Yahoo! but the court threw out the case because Yahoo! was immune under Section 230.[102] If Yahoo! or bloggers can be liable if, after being informed, they fail to remove a comment that is defamatory or invasive of privacy, then they might become too cautious and remove comments too quickly. This will have a negative impact on speech, because if a person doesn't like a comment about herself, ISPs or bloggers might be extra careful and remove it in order to avoid a lawsuit. The result would be a kind of heckler's veto, where a person could have a comment removed by complaining about it, whether justifiably or not.

On the other hand, if Yahoo! or bloggers ignore a person's complaints about harmful comments, then that person might be without much recourse. Shouldn't Yahoo! have removed the photos? This seems like an awful situation for the plaintiff—nude photos of herself, as well as her contact information, are placed on the Internet and she is helpless in getting them removed. Is there such a big harm in forcing Yahoo! to remove them? Shouldn't people have some ability to halt the distribution of nude pictures or falsehoods or other personal information about themselves on the Internet? While the plaintiff shouldn't be entitled to obtain large money damages from Yahoo! the law should provide an incentive for Yahoo! to respond to legitimate take-down requests. Copyright law, for example, provides for a such a system when users of Internet service providers like Yahoo! post content that infringes upon copyright. Internet services providers are not liable if they remove copyright-infringing content posted by their users.[103] Notice and take-down systems can certainly be abused by people requesting removal of content that is not defamatory or invasive of privacy, but the law could address this problem by penalizing abusers.

Chase529

Chase Masterson is a well-known actress, having appeared in several television shows. Her real name is Christianne Carafano. One day, a profile with the name Chase529 appeared on Matchmaker.com, an Internet dating service.[104] The profile had four pictures of Carafano, along with her home address and phone number. The profile also had the following exchange:

> Q: Have you had, or would you consider having a homosexual experience?
> A: I might be persuaded to have a homosexual experience.
> Q: What is your main source for current events?
> A: Playboy/Playgirl.
> Q: Finally, why did you call [Matchmaker.com]?
> A: Looking for a one-night stand.

The answers to other questions were even more provocative:

> Q: Try to describe the type of person you might be interested in meeting?
> A: Hard and dominant in more ways than one. Must have strong sexual appetite.
> Q: Describe your personality type?
> A: I like sort of being controlled by a man in and out of bed.
> Q: What's the first thing others notice about you?
> A: My beauty.
> Q: What is sexy?
> A: A strong man with a dominating attitude with a yet controlling touch.[105]

People who responded to the profile received an automatic reply that gave out Carafano's home address and phone number.

Carafano didn't write the profile. It was written by an anonymous person in Berlin. Carafano wasn't even aware that the profile existed. She soon found out when she began to be contacted by people responding to the profile. Some of the responses were sexually explicit and threatening. Fearing for her safety and that of her son, Carafano moved out of her home and spent several months in hotels. An assistant to Carafano contacted Matchmaker and demanded that the profile be removed. Matchmaker blocked the profile from public view and deleted it soon afterward.

Carafano sued Matchmaker for invasion of privacy and defamation. Matchmaker argued that it was immune under Section 230 because it had not created the profile. The court agreed with Matchmaker. Although noting "the serious and utterly deplorable consequences that occurred in this case," the court noted that "Matchmaker did not play a significant role in creating, developing or 'transforming' the relevant information."[106]

The court's decision makes a lot of sense. Internet dating websites host tens of thousands—sometimes millions—of profiles. They are not responsible when a prankster creates a fake profile that invades another's privacy or is defamatory. So they should be immune when this happens. But unlike the broad interpretations of Section 230, once an Internet dating service is notified about a problem, it should respond or be liable. Matchmaker responded and removed the profile. Thus it should not be liable.

The Nazi Art Thief Who Wasn't

Ellen Batzel, an attorney in North Carolina, hired Bob Smith, a handyman, to do some work on her home.[107] Batzel loved to collect art, and she had many paintings in her collection.

The working relationship turned ugly, and Smith sued Batzel in small-claims court for payment for the repairs. Smith also decided to retaliate against Batzel outside the courts. He sent an email to the Museum Security Network about Batzel's art. The network consisted of a website and an email newsletter about stolen art. It had about one thousand readers, mainly those in the art and museum world, as well as law enforcement officials and journalists. It was run by Tom Cremers, who was the director of security at the Rijksmuseum in Amsterdam. Cremers received the following email:

From: Bob Smith [e-mail address omitted]
   To: securma@museum-security.org
   Subject: Stolen Art

Hi there,
I am a building contractor in Asheville, North Carolina, USA. A month ago, I did a remodeling job for a woman, Ellen L. Batzel who bragged to me about being the granddaughter of "one of Adolph Hitler's right-hand men." At the time, I was concentrating on performing my tasks, but upon reflection, I believe she said she was the descendant of Heinrich Himmler.
Ellen Batzel has hundreds of older European paintings on her walls, all with heavy carved wooden frames. She told me she inherited them.
I believe these paintings were looted during WWII and are the rightful legacy of the Jewish people. Her address is [omitted].
I also believe that the descendants of criminals should not be persecuted for the crimes of the fathers, nor should they benefit. I do not know who to contact about this, so I start with your organization. Please contact me via email [. . .] if you would like to discuss this matter.
Bob.

As the sole manager of the Museum Security Network, Cremers determined which of the emails he received would be forwarded to the group. He decided to send the email along to the group, and he added a message along with the email noting that "the FBI has been informed of the contents of [Smith's] original message."

Some of Cremers's readers were upset that he had forwarded Smith's email. One wrote to him:

> Mr. Smith is completely out of line for suggesting that some woman with old paintings in her home has amassed a collection of paintings from Nazi war booty. His claims, evidence and assumptions were ridiculous and he was very disrespectful of this woman's privacy in offering this woman's address. . . . I think it was wrong for you to take this man's story seriously. Please respond.

Cremers replied that he considered Smith's message dubious, but he defended his decision to forward it. "What is worse," Cremers asked, "forwarding messages with strange contents or censor[ing] messages?"

A few months later, Batzel discovered the message. She was appalled. She wasn't descended from Nazis and had acquired her art from legitimate dealers. As a result of Cremers's posting Smith's email, Batzel lost some clients and had to defend herself against a campaign to get her disbarred.

Batzel sued Cremers for defamation. The court, however, dismissed the case against Cremers based on Section 230 immunity. Since Cremers did not write the email himself, he was just the conduit for it so long as he "reasonably believed" it was provided to him for posting on the Network.[108]

If this case hadn't involved the Internet, Cremers would have a much tougher defense. He would no longer be immune under Section 230. He could be liable for spreading the defamatory statement to others. But because he forwarded it over the Internet, he was immune.

The court's interpretation of Section 230 was quite broad. Smith wasn't merely posting a comment to a website or an online discussion group. Instead, he was emailing a tip to Cremers, who decided what was posted and what wasn't. By forwarding the email, Cremers became the speaker, much as he would have been had he heard a rumor and written about it to the group himself.

Judge Gould issued a powerful dissent in the case: "The majority rule licenses professional rumor-mongers and gossip-hounds to spread false and hurtful information with impunity. So long as the defamatory information was written by a person who wanted the information to be spread on the Internet (in other words, a person with an axe to grind), the rumormonger's injurious conduct is beyond legal redress." Judge Gould wrote that Section 230 was not intended to be stretched to immunize people for their "decisions to spread particular communications" and "cause trickles of defamation to swell into rivers of harm." Gould continued: "Congress wanted to ensure that excessive government regulation did not slow America's expansion into the exciting new frontier of the Internet. But Congress did not want this new frontier to be like the Old West: a lawless zone governed by retribution and mob justice."[109]

What Should the Law Do?

Although existing law lacks nimble ways to resolve disputes about speech and privacy on the Internet, completely immunizing operators of websites works as a sledgehammer. It creates the wrong incentive, providing a broad immunity that can foster irresponsibility. Bloggers should have some responsibilities to others, and Section 230 is telling them that they do not. There are certainly problems with existing tort law. Lawsuits are costly to litigate, and being sued can saddle a blogger with massive expenses. Bloggers often don't have deep pockets, and therefore it might be difficult for plaintiffs to find lawyers willing to take their cases. Lawsuits can take years to resolve. People seeking to protect their privacy must risk further publicity in bringing suit.

These are certainly serious problems, but the solution shouldn't be to insulate bloggers from the law. Unfortunately, courts are interpreting Section 230 so broadly as to provide too much immunity, eliminating the incentive to foster a balance between speech and privacy. The way courts are using Section 230 exalts free speech to the detriment of privacy and reputation. As a result, a host of websites have arisen that encourage others to post gossip and rumors as well as to engage in online shaming. These websites thrive under Section 230's broad immunity.

The solution is to create a system for ensuring that people speak responsibly without the law's cumbersome costs. The task of devising such a solution is a difficult one, but giving up on the law is not the answer. Blogging has given amateurs an unprecedented amount of media power, and although we should encourage blogging, we shouldn't scuttle our privacy and defamation laws in the process.

FREEDOM ON BOTH SIDES OF THE SCALE

Words can wound. They can destroy a person's reputation, and in the process distort that person's very identity. Nevertheless, we staunchly protect expression even when it can cause great damage because free speech is essential to our autonomy and to a democratic society. But protecting privacy and reputation is also necessary for autonomy and democracy. There is no easy solution to how to balance free speech with privacy and reputation. This balance isn't like the typical balance of civil liberties against the need for order and social control. Instead, it is a balance with liberty on both sides of the scale—freedom to speak and express oneself pitted against freedom to ensure that our reputations aren't destroyed or our privacy isn't invaded.

As I have tried to demonstrate in this chapter, a delicate balance can be reached, but it is not an easy feat. In many instances, free speech and privacy can both be preserved by shielding the identities of private individuals involved in particular stories. With the Internet, a key issue for the law is who should be responsible for harmful speech when it appears on a website or blog. Much speech online can be posted by anybody who wants to comment to a blog post or speak in an online discussion forum. Commentators can cloak themselves in anonymity and readily spread information on popular blogs and websites. The law currently takes a broadly pro–free speech stance on online expression. As a result, it fails to create any incentive for operators of websites to exercise responsibility with regard to the comments of visitors.

Balancing free speech with privacy and reputation is a complicated and delicate task. Too much weight on either side of the scale will have detrimental consequences. The law still has a distance to go toward establishing a good balance.

Chapter 7 Privacy in an Overexposed World

In our overexposed world, is anything private anymore? Currently, the law recognizes as private only information that is completely secret. Information exposed to others is public. Privacy, however, is far more complicated, as it involves a cluster of nuanced expectations of accessibility, confidentiality, and control. If we are to protect privacy today, we need to rethink our understandings of privacy. This chapter is about how to do so.

PRIVACY IN PUBLIC

The Burning Man Festival is held each year in the barrens of the Nevada desert. Tens of thousands of people converge on a vast dusty area far away from the urban world to engage in a spiritual celebration of "radical self-expression." People dance, frolic, parade, act out skits, paint their bodies, sing, and create art. There is a lot of nudity. The festival is named for its concluding ritual, in which a forty-foot effigy of a man is set on fire. The Burning Man Festival has been an annual event since 1986. At first, it drew fewer than two dozen people, but it has now grown to more than twenty-five thousand.[1]

In 2002 a website called Voyeur Video began to sell a dozen videos of nude participants at the festival. The videos, priced at $29.95, were peddled along with other classics such as *Kinky Nude Beach Day* and *Springbreak Stripoffs*. Voyeur Video fashioned itself not as a pornography company but as "a news company that reports on adult parties where people get naked and naughty."[2]

At the Burning Man festival, participants were allowed to make videos and take pictures, but only with the permission of festival organizers. Voyeur Video sought and was denied permission to videotape the event.[3] The company videotaped the festival anyway. The organizers sued. Among the many causes of actions were the Warren and Brandeis torts of appropriation and public disclosure. Video Voyeur backed down. It agreed to stop selling the videos and to turn them over to the Burning Man organizers.

The Burning Man case, although never fully litigated, raises several important questions about the nature of privacy. If a person is naked at a festival with twenty-five thousand others, how can that person claim privacy? Should the law recognize such claims?

The Law's Binary Understanding of Privacy

A husband and wife were engaged in a romantic embrace near an ice cream stand at a farmer's market. Their photo was snapped, and it appeared in the October 1947 issue of *Harper's Bazaar* in an article celebrating the splendor of love. The photo was also published in the May 1949 issue of *Ladies' Home Journal*. Although the photo depicted the couple in a moment of love, the couple wasn't in love with the fact that their intimacy was displayed in national magazines, and they felt humiliated and embarrassed. They sued the magazines for publicly disclosing private facts.

But the court threw out their case because the couple "had voluntarily exposed themselves to public gaze in a pose open to the view of any persons who might then be at or near their place of business."[4] According to the court, "There can be no privacy in that which is already public." The court reasoned that "the photograph did not disclose anything which until then had been private, but rather only extended knowledge of the particular incident to a somewhat larger public then had actually witnessed it at the time of occurrence."

One judge dissented in the case. He noted that "there is no news or educational value whatsoever in the photograph alone" and that a picture with models could readily have been used to illustrate the story. The judge went on to argue:

By plaintiffs doing what they did in view of a tiny fraction of the public, does not mean that they consented to observation by the millions of readers of the defendant's magazine. In effect, the majority holding means that anything anyone does outside of his own home is with consent to the publication thereof, because, under those circumstances he waives his right of privacy even though there is no news value in the event. If such were the case, the blameless exposure of a portion of the naked body of a man or woman in a public place as the result of inefficient buttons, hooks or other clothes-holding devices could be freely photographed and widely published with complete immunity.

The judge has a point. There is a difference between what is captured in the fading memories of only a few people and what is broadcast to a worldwide audience. The law, however, generally holds that once something is exposed to the public, it can no longer be private. Traditionally privacy is viewed in a binary way, dividing the world into two distinct realms, the public and the private. If a person is in a public place, she cannot expect privacy. If information is exposed to the public in any way, it isn't private. According to the Restatement of Torts, one of the most influential documents for courts applying the tort of public disclosure: "There is no liability when the defendant merely gives further publicity to information about the plaintiff which is already public. Thus there is no liability for giving publicity to facts about the plaintiff's life which are matters of public record."[5] As one court ruled, appearing in public "necessarily involves doffing the cloak of privacy which the law protects."[6]

In one case, a husband and wife were arrested in a bar and taken away in handcuffs. A television film crew filmed the arrest. It turned out that the arrest was based on mistaken identity. The couple called the television station and begged that the footage not be broadcast. No such luck. The footage was aired. The couple sued, but the court dismissed the case because the arrest was filmed in public and was "left open to the public eye."[7]

Thus, according to the prevailing view of the law, if you're in public, you're exposing what you're doing to others, and it can't be private. If you really want privacy, you must take refuge in your home.

The Challenge of New Technology

Modern technology poses a severe challenge to the traditional binary understanding of privacy. Today data is gathered about us at every turn. Surveillance cameras are sprouting up everywhere. There are twenty-four-hour surveillance cameras in public linked to websites for anybody to view. Go to EarthCam and click on one of many major cities, such as Washington, D.C.,

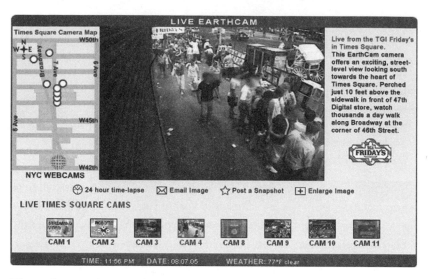

The EarthCam website, displaying a feed from its live Times Square camera. Image courtesy of EarthCam, Inc.

Chicago, New York, or Seattle, among others.[8] In New York, for example, you can watch a camera that captures people walking down the sidewalk at 47th Street in Times Square.

Armed with cell phone cameras, everyday people can snap up images, becoming amateur paparazzi. Websites like Flickr allow people to post their photos and share them with the world.[9] Some people are posting a daily stream of photos, obsessively documenting every aspect of their lives. Beyond pictures, people are posting videos on the Internet for the world to watch. On YouTube, the leading video website, people around the globe are viewing more than one hundred million videos per day. On a daily basis, people add more than sixty-five thousand videos to YouTube.[10] Other variations of blogs are emerging, ones devoted primarily to pictures and video. A "moblog" is short for "mobile weblog."[11] Moblogs consist of postings based on what people capture in their mobile devices, such as cell phone cameras. Video blogs, or "vlogs" for short, consist of video feeds. According to one vlogger, everyone can "create media and have a distribution outlet for it that bypasses television and mainstream media."[12]

Today, privacy goes far beyond whether something is exposed to others. What matters most is the nature of the exposure and what is done with the information. There is a difference between casual observation and the more indelible recording of information and images. As the law professor Andrew McClurg points out, captured images have permanence, something fleeting memories lack. People can scrutinize a photo and notice details that they might not otherwise see when observing the scene as it unfolds.[13]

A second difference involves the degree of anonymity we expect in our everyday activities. As one prescient judge wrote, privacy can be "invaded through extensive or exhaustive monitoring and cataloguing of acts normally disconnected and anonymous."[14] We often engage in our daily activities in public expecting to be just a face in the crowd, another ant in the colony. We run into hundreds of strangers every day and don't expect them to know who we are or to care about what we do. We don't expect the clerk at the store to take an interest in what we buy. In other words, we're relatively anonymous in a large part of our lives in public. Identification dramatically alters the equation.

Suppose somebody followed you around in a drug store. The person assiduously scribbled down an inventory of what you bought. Or the person snapped a photo of the products you had in your basket as you were waiting at the checkout counter. Perhaps you wouldn't want the world to know you had bought hemorrhoid cream. Or perhaps you wouldn't be thrilled that others would know about your diarrhea problem or the kind of birth control you used. You bought all these things in public, and you exposed them to other people. Does this mean that you don't expect privacy in what you bought?

A third component of our expectations involves our understanding of context. Although we do things in public, we do them in a particular context before a particular set of people. As the information technology scholar Helen Nissenbaum points out, "it is crucial to know the context—who is gathering the information, who is analyzing it, who is disseminating it and to whom, the nature of the information, the relationships among the various parties, and even larger institutional and social circumstances."[15] McClurg aptly notes that "a photograph permits dissemination of an image not just to a larger audience, but to different audiences than the subject intended." Moreover, "conduct which would be appropriate for one environment may be inappropriate or embarrassing in another."[16] We tell jokes to our friends we wouldn't tell to our grandmother. We realize that there are different social norms for different situations, and broadcasting matters beyond their original context takes away our ability to judge the situation appropriately.

Fourth, much of our daily lives occurs in realms that are neither purely public nor purely private. Instead, our activities often take place in the twilight between public and private. We used to speak on the phone at home or in closed phone booths, but with cell phones, we now carry out our conversations in a variety of public places. Suppose you're on a train and you have a cell phone conversation with a friend. The person sitting next to you secretly records your conversation and makes the recording available online. Despite the fact you exposed your conversation to people nearby, you didn't expect your conversation to be recorded and made available to the world.

Most of us have moments when we're in public where we would not want a photo taken of us, much less placed on the Internet. Most of us have times when we expose personal information to others but do not expect it to be shared more widely. We frequently have conversations in public that we don't expect to be overheard. When we chat in a restaurant, we don't expect others to be straining to eavesdrop on our discussion above the din of other dinner conversations. At most, we might expect one or two people to hear fragments of what we're saying, but we certainly don't expect to see a transcript of our conversation appear on the Internet.

Thus merely assessing whether information is exposed in public or to others can no longer be adequate to determining whether we should protect it as private. Unless we rethink the binary notion of privacy, new technologies will increasingly invade the enclaves of privacy we enjoy in public. Privacy is a complicated set of norms, expectations, and desires that goes far beyond the simplistic notion that if you're in public, you have no privacy.

Video Voyeurism

In some instances, the law is beginning to advance beyond the simplistic binary view of privacy. The rise of video voyeurism has pushed the law toward a greater recognition of different degrees of privacy. New technology has made video voyeurism easy. Anybody armed with a cell phone camera can quickly snap photos of others in the buff and post them online. In one incident, nude photos of a men's wrestling team at the University of Pennsylvania appeared on a website. One athlete said: "I pulled up the home page and I am looking at myself naked on the Internet. . . . It is terrible because I have no control over it."[17]

Another practice is the taking of "upskirt" photos—pictures taken up women's skirts. More than one hundred websites are devoted to providing upskirt photos or pictures of people showering or undressing.[18] To take these photos, all a person needs is a cell phone camera.

Several states have responded by passing laws with criminal penalties for video voyeurism.[19] Some initial attempts at creating these laws, however, failed because of the binary view of privacy. In one case, two men took upskirt photos of unsuspecting women in a mall. Both were convicted under a Washington video voyeurism statute. The Washington law defined the crime as taking photos "for the purpose of arousing or gratifying the sexual desire of any person" when the photo was taken "in a place where [the victim] would have a reasonable expectation of privacy."[20] The Washington Supreme Court, however, overturned the conviction because "although the Legislature may have intended to cover intrusions of privacy in public places, the plain language of the statute does not accomplish this goal." The court reasoned that "casual surveillance frequently occurs in public. Therefore, public places could not logically constitute locations where a person could reasonably expect to be safe from casual or hostile intrusion or surveillance."[21] The law was later amended to include both public and private places.

In 2004 Congress enacted the Video Voyeurism Prevention Act.[22] Congress criminalized video voyeurism, and it heeded the lesson from the Washington law, explicitly providing that the act would apply "regardless of whether [the victim] is in a public or private area." Unfortunately, Congress's act applies only on federal property, so you're safe from upskirt photos if you're walking in the Capitol Building or on other federal property. But if you're in the local mall, then you better hope that your state has a video voyeurism law, and if it does, that it has made clear that you can expect some level of privacy in public. The example of video voyeurism demonstrates that privacy expectations do not turn solely on place.

Many places aren't purely private or purely public. Suppose you're in a gym locker room and somebody snaps a photo of you undressing and posts it online. Is the locker room a public or a private place? It isn't entirely private, since it is open to other people, and you're undressing in front of many others. But although you're not in seclusion, you can expect that others won't take photos of you. Restrooms, stores, bars, and other places are open to the public, but this doesn't eliminate your expectations of privacy in those places. Expectations of privacy turn on norms. You expect privacy in the gym locker room because the norms are clear that it is inappropriate for others to snap your photo in this context. And in the Nevada desert, the participants of Burning Man have established a set of norms about how others are to use photos.

So we're back to the Burning Man festival. The Burning Man case illustrates that a claim of privacy is not the same as a claim of absolute secrecy. The participants of Burning Man obviously didn't mind being seen nude by other participants. They didn't even mind having their photos taken by others. What they didn't want was their images being exploited by pornographers. All-or-nothing notions of privacy fail to grasp the central difference between fellow festival goers and commercial exploiters for porn. There's a mutual camaraderie among festival goers that isn't shared with the pornographers. The Burning Man participants thus had nuanced expectations of privacy—about how their information would be used within a limited circle of people.

The Difficulties of Recognizing Privacy in Public

The law should begin to recognize some degree of privacy in public. But there are difficulties with doing so. Suppose you witness an interesting event on the subway and you want to capture it on your cell phone camera to post on your blog. If the people you were photographing on the subway had privacy rights in public, you might need their permission to post the photo. And if they are engaging in a social taboo, they might not be eager to give you permission. Should you be allowed to post the picture anyway?

The abstract hypothetical I suggest above can apply to a number of situations already discussed in this book—the dog poop girl and the New York City subway flasher. One might ask incredulously: So the dog poop girl engages in a nasty transgression and the law will stop people from taking her picture and exposing her misbehavior? Should the law give the creep who flashes on the subway a right to sue a person who took a photo of him in the act? These are potential implications of a robust recognition of privacy in public. The law need not go this far, but is there a logical stopping point? I've discussed some of the problems with online shaming, so perhaps protecting the dog poop girl or the subway flasher has significant benefits in curtailing the abuse of shaming. One might argue that only people engaged in illegal activities or severe norm violations lack privacy, but who is to judge this? The average person with a cell phone camera? It is difficult to stop shaming unless we protect privacy in public. Doing so doesn't mean absolute protection, just a limit on certain kinds of uses and disclosures. People can still snap pictures and turn them over to the police. People should be deterred, however, from taking matters into their own hands by placing the photos online.

When the law begins to recognize privacy in public, the tricky question is:

How much? Would streakers in Times Square still have the right to claim privacy if people posted their photos on the Internet? At some point, what is done in public is indeed public. There are no easy answers, and the resolution will depend upon the norms and expectations in each circumstance. The virtue of the binary view of privacy is clarity. It is an easy rule to apply. Yet the simplicity of this view is its downfall—it seems far too outmoded given new technology. Therefore, although it will be difficult, it is better to develop and protect a more nuanced notion of privacy.

Accessibility of Information

In 2006 Facebook (a social network website consisting of millions of high school and college students) launched a feature called News Feed that instantly alerted users whenever their friends added information or photos to their profiles. Facebook users constantly update their profiles, adding new text and new images. They might update their roster of friends. The News Feed feature immediately notified all of a person's friends about each new change in that person's profile.

News Feed was met by an enormous outcry from users, who vociferously objected to the extensiveness of the exposure. According to one of the users, "Facebook is becoming the Big Brother of the Internet recording every single move."[23] "It's just so unnecessary," another user complained. "You don't have to know everything your friends do and the changes they make. . . . It's kind of creepy."[24] As one user expounded: "Before News Feed, yes, you could see the profile, and you could see the pictures, and you could see the comments, and you could see the relationship status, but the users felt that it was just for people who cared, and who wanted to know. But now, all of this information was thrown down the throats of everyone, and it was very strange."[25] Shortly after the change, a protest group called "Students Against Facebook News Feeds" emerged on Facebook.[26] People joined the group in droves. Within days, the number of protesters had swelled to more than seven hundred thousand.[27]

Facebook quickly responded. Mark Zuckerberg, the creator of Facebook, wrote an open letter to Facebook users: "We really messed this one up. When we launched News Feed and Mini-Feed we were trying to provide you with a stream of information about your social world. Instead, we did a bad job of explaining what the news features were and an even worse job of giving you control of them. I'd like to try to correct those errors now."[28]

The Facebook privacy debacle is especially interesting because it had nothing to do with the exposure of new information. No new secrets about Facebook users were being revealed. The information that the users complained about was already available on their profiles—posted voluntarily by themselves. Instead, all the new system did was alert users to that new information. In other words, the Facebook system was merely making existing information more accessible. Perhaps this explains why Facebook officials were so surprised by the backlash. After all, Facebook users are not a bunch who seem very concerned about their privacy. Why, then, was there such a vehement reaction?

The Facebook change brought users an increased awareness of the privacy dangers of the Internet. Although Facebook users might think it is too quaint to expect all of their secrets to remain in the bag, this doesn't mean that they don't care about privacy. They just see privacy differently. What many of the Facebook users objected to was the increased accessibility of their personal data—the fact that others would be alerted to every new update to their profiles immediately. Privacy can be violated not just by revealing previously concealed secrets, but by increasing the accessibility to information already available. The desire for privacy is thus much more granular than the current binary model recognizes. Privacy involves degrees, not absolutes. It involves establishing control over personal information, not merely keeping it completely secret. As the computer security expert Bruce Schneier argues: "People are willing to share all sorts of information as long as they are in control. When Facebook unilaterally changed the rules about how personal information was revealed, it reminded people that they weren't in control."[29]

For example, suppose you had a spat with a friend and wanted to eliminate that person from your circle of friends on Facebook. You might not want this change to be announced prominently to all your other friends. You might want the change to be made quietly, where it might be noticed by a few friends, or by no one besides you and the former friend. In other words, you might want some changes to fly under the radar. The binary view of privacy doesn't recognize the wide swath of middle ground between the realms of absolutely public and absolutely private. Increasingly, however, our lives occupy this middle ground. That's why I believe we must abandon the binary view of privacy and develop a more nuanced view.

CONFIDENTIALITY

Aleksey was an ambitious twenty-three-year-old student at Yale University. Desiring to be an investment banker, he applied to UBS, a global financial company. His application, however, was rather unusual. First of all, his résumé was rather long—eleven pages in all. Even more peculiarly, he sent along a seven-minute video of himself entitled "Impossible Is Nothing."

The video begins with Aleksey being interviewed as if he were a famous individual. The interviewer calls Aleksey a "model of personal development and inspiration to many around you," then asks, "How do some people like yourself become very proficient in their fields faster than most?" "Well, thank you," Aleksey replies. "I guess the first thing people need to understand is that success is a mental transformation; it is not an external event."

Throughout the video, with an aloof and serious tone, Aleksey pontificates about his philosophy of success. "Ignore the losers," Aleksey says, "bring your A-game, your determination and your drive to the field, and success will follow you." In other pearls of advice, Aleksey declares that "failure cannot be considered an option," and that "luck doesn't jump into anyone's lap."

The video frequently cuts to scenes demonstrating Aleksey's athletic prowess. He performs a series of rather unusual skills for an investment banker position. Aleksey lifts massive dumbbells, bench presses 495 pounds, serves a 140-mph tennis ball, does an acrobatic ski jump, and concludes by breaking a stack of bricks with a karate chop.

"If you're going to work, work," Aleksey declares. "If you're going to train, train. If you're going to dance, then dance, but do it with passion." The video then cuts to Aleksey dancing with a scantily clad woman to Chayanne's "Solamente Tu Amor." The video concludes with Hans Zimmer's "The Way of the Sword" playing over end credits.

Needless to say, Aleksey wasn't hired by UBS. But his video was forwarded around Wall Street, and it soon wound up on YouTube. In a short time, hundreds of thousands of people had downloaded it. Aleksey sent requests to websites to take the video down, but in vain.[30] Aleksey had become an Internet sensation. One media website in the United Kingdom declared Aleksey's video the "greatest CV ever filmed."[31] The mainstream media pounced on the story. The *New York Post* called his video a "six-minute ego-mercial."[32] An article in the *New York Times* declared that Aleksey "may be the most famous investment-banking job applicant in recent memory."[33] Throughout the blogosphere, people accused Aleksey of being a pathological liar, of faking the feats in the video, and of plagiarizing in a book he had self-published. At DealBook, a blog sponsored by the *New York Times*,[34] commentators to a post by journalist Andrew Sorkin declared:

That kid should be stripped of his degree. It seems reasonably clear that he has lived a life of lies.

Another victim of a self-absorbed, dishonest and Idol-worshipping American culture.

What an insufferable, self-absorbed, arrogant and self-aggrandizing jerk. In other words, a perfect fit for Wall Street.

Aleksey appeared on television media shows to respond to his worldwide mockery. On MSNBC, Aleksey stated in an interview that he was shocked to see his video and résumé spread across the Internet. His résumé contained his phone number and email address, and he was receiving harassing cell phone calls and thousands of nasty emails.[35] At Harvard students threw an Aleksey theme party, with people dressing up in karate uniforms and dancing attire.[36] The blog Gawker anointed Aleksey with the title of "pioneer Douchebag."[37] In an interview on ABC's *20/20*, Aleksey stated that he thought he had no chance now for a career on Wall Street. "So far," he said, "it's been like going through hell."[38]

Did Aleksey get what he deserved? Perhaps such a pompous person should be put in his place. But at what cost? On Sorkin's DealBook post, other commentators questioned whether it was appropriate for Aleksey's résumé and video to be leaked on the Internet:

> I am deeply disturbed [that] a resume sent in confidence to a highly respected firm had been made public and that confidence [was] broken. Should we all worry about where [our resumes] end up once sent to the firm of our choice?

> Although the kid is obviously a ridiculous egomaniac and not a particularly good liar, the real guilty party here is UBS.

> This fellow is being subjected (in Clarence Thomas' immortal words) to a "high-tech lynching." Whether or not he embellished or misrepresented anything in his job app or his resume or anything else in his life, it's beyond the pale to have the entire snarky Internet . . . pile on him in public.

In all fairness to UBS, the precise story of how the video and resume got leaked is unclear. UBS issued a statement about the matter: "As a firm, UBS obviously respects the privacy of applicants' correspondence and does not circulate job applications and resumes to the public. To the extent that any policy was breached, it will be dealt with appropriately."[39]

Assuming Aleksey's application was leaked by somebody at UBS, is the application really private? One could argue that Aleksey's application was no longer private after he sent it to UBS. However, there is a significant difference between a few employees at UBS having a chuckle over Aleksey's application and the entire world making Aleksey the butt of their jokes. Although the video wasn't completely secret since Aleksey exposed it to some people at UBS, the general public wasn't Aleksey's intended audience. Should the law respect Aleksey's desire to expose his personal information selectively? Or since he revealed his information to others, can he continue to claim that it is private?

Should We Assume the Risk of Betrayal?

Suppose your spurned ex-lover decides to post the intimate details of your relationship online. Or imagine that a trusted friend reveals your deepest secrets on her blog. This is increasingly happening online. Jessica Cutler's Washingtonienne blog is a prime example. The private information about people on the Internet often doesn't come from strangers but from friends, family members, coworkers, and others.

If you tell something to your doctor, you expect her to keep it confidential. It's an unwritten expectation, something that is rarely explicitly said but that is generally understood. Indeed, doctors are under ethical obligations to keep patient information confidential. People don't expect their doctor to be blogging about them on the sly.

Confidentiality differs substantially from secrecy. Secrecy involves hiding information, concealing it from others. Secrecy entails expectations that the skeletons in one's closet will remain shut away in the darkness. In contrast, confidentiality involves sharing one's secrets with select others. Confidentiality is an expectation within a relationship. When we tell others intimate information, we expect them to keep it confidential. Sharing personal data with others makes us vulnerable. We must trust others not to betray us by leaking our information.

The importance of confidentiality has been recognized since antiquity. Ethical rules have long existed for physicians to maintain the confidentiality of their patients' information. The Hippocratic Oath, circa 400 B.C., provides that doctors "will keep silence" about what their patients tell them.[40] Confidentiality is essential for certain communications to take place. Mark Twain explained most vividly why confidentiality is so important: "The frankest and freest and privatest product of the human mind and heart is a love letter; the writer gets his limitless freedom of statement and expression from his sense that no stranger is going to see what he is writing. Sometimes there is a breach-of-promise case by and by; and when he sees his letter in print it makes him cruelly uncomfortable and he perceives that he never would have unbosomed himself to that large and honest degree if he had known that he was writing for the public."[41]

American law currently plays Jekyll and Hyde with regard to protecting confidentiality. Sometimes, the law strongly protects confidentiality. For example, the law provides potent protections for patient-physician confidentiality. As one court put it: "There can be no reticence, no reservation, no reluctance when patients discuss their problems with their doctors."[42] The law protects the confidentiality of people's discussions with their attorneys to "encourage full and frank communication."[43] The law also protects marital communications between spouses, a protection that dates as far back as ancient Jewish and Roman law.[44]

But in many cases, the law turns a blind eye to breaches of confidentiality, holding that we must assume the risk that we'll be betrayed. Most courts have not protected communications between parents and children.[45] As a result, parents and children can be forced to testify against each other in court.[46] In criticizing this doctrine, one court declared: "Forcing a mother and father to reveal their child's alleged misdeeds . . . is shocking to our sense of decency, fairness, or propriety."[47]

The law often holds that if you share a secret with others, you assume the risk that they will betray you.[48] In one case from 1970, for example, General Motors began a campaign to dig up dirt on Ralph Nader, who had been criticizing the safety of GM's cars. Among other things, GM sent people to find out Nader's secrets by talking with his friends and acquaintances. GM also made harassing phone calls, wiretapped his telephone, and kept him under extensive surveillance when in public. Although the court held that some of GM's tactics were improper, it concluded that there was nothing wrong with trying to get Nader's friends to betray his secrets. If a person shares information with another, the court declared, "he would necessarily assume the risk that a friend or acquaintance in whom he had confided might breach the confidence."[49] Although the law protects spouses from having to testify against each other, it often does not provide a remedy when one spouse (or ex-spouse) writes a tell-all book about the other.

In contrast, the law in England strongly protects against betrayal of confidence. People can be liable for disclosing secrets that are entrusted to them in confidence.[50] In one English case, a man who had a homosexual affair with the actor Michael Barrymore told the details to a reporter for the paper *The Sun*. The court protected Barrymore: "When people enter into a personal relationship of this nature, they do not do so for the purpose of it subsequently being published in *The Sun*, or any other newspaper. The information about the relationship is for the relationship and not for a wider purpose."[51] According to the court: "The fact is that when people kiss and later one of them tells, that second person is almost certainly breaking a confidential arrangement."[52]

In another English case, the actors Michael Douglas and Catherine Zeta-Jones made an exclusive deal with *OK!* magazine to publish the photos of their wedding. Guests were told that they weren't allowed to take photos. But not to be outdone, *Hello!* magazine had a photographer masquerade as a guest and secretly snap pictures. The court ruled that *Hello!* had engaged in a breach of confidence.[53]

The United States has a breach-of-confidentiality tort, although it is much weaker than the tort in England.[54] In the United States, the number of relationships understood to be confidential is small. Beyond doctors, lawyers, clergy, and a few others, the information you tell others is often not legally protected. You might trust a best friend with your secrets, but your friend can betray you without breaking the law. Boyfriends, girlfriends, family members, colleagues, and others are under little obligation to keep your information private.

Beyond those you trust the most with your information, you also routinely put your trust in people you barely know. For example, you expect the store clerk not to broadcast your purchases to the world. Day in, day out, we depend upon people keeping our information confidential. And yet these people are generally not understood to have a legal duty to do so.

The companies you share information with are also frequently not understood to owe you a legal duty of confidentiality. Unless you live in a shack in the woods, a significant amount of your most intimate information is shared in some way with others. Your ISP knows what websites you are visiting. Your phone company knows whom you're calling. Your credit card company knows how you're spending your money. Although we trust these companies with our personal information, the law only sometimes imposes upon them an obligation to keep it confidential.

Why is the American breach-of-confidentiality tort so much weaker than the English version? One reason is that the breach-of-confidentiality tort became overshadowed by the other privacy torts. In their 1890 article that inspired the privacy torts, Warren and Brandeis were skeptical of the ability of confidentiality law to protect privacy. At the time, there was a rather robust law protecting confidential relationships. But Warren and Brandeis steered the law in a new direction. As we have seen, Warren and Brandeis had in mind the taking of candid photographs by strangers. In this situation, they noted, there was no confidential relationship. The law thus had to recognize a new protection of privacy, one that would provide remedies against strangers. Although Warren and Brandeis never explicitly rejected confidentiality, it was often overlooked by lawyers and judges who focused only on the other privacy torts instead.

The law should more expansively recognize duties of confidentiality. A large amount of the information about us that finds its way online isn't put there by strangers. It is spread by people's spurned lovers, their ex-spouses, their enemies, and in some cases, their friends. Perhaps we should recognize implicit promises of confidentiality when we share intimate information with others. You don't sign a confidentiality agreement with your doctor or lawyer before you start talking about your symptoms or your legal case. It's implied. We frequently expect confidentiality when we share intimate information. We place our trust in others to keep our secrets. So why not establish that when you tell somebody a secret, there's an implied promise that it's confidential? Although the tort of breach of confidentiality is not nearly as well developed as the tort in England, there is no reason why it can't evolve to provide stronger privacy protection.

Of course, there must be limits to how broadly the law should reach. People gossip all the time. As Benjamin Franklin once quipped, "Three may keep a secret if two are dead."[55] If the law became involved every time people gossiped, it would become far too entangled in our lives. Gossip is so frequent that we'd be constantly litigating. But the law should provide a remedy for gossip when it is spread widely or made permanent. As discussed earlier, Internet gossip is especially damaging. So the law can try to keep gossip off the Internet and confined to whispering tongues.

Social Network Theory

Not all information is confidential. Often the cat is already out of the bag. At that point, there are no obligations of confidentiality. But how do we know when the cat has escaped?

Rarely do we keep complete secrets. Indeed, when we tell someone a secret, we still call it a "secret" even though another person now knows it. Courts have a difficult time determining when a secret is no longer a secret. Suppose I tell it to one thousand people. Can I really claim it is a secret anymore? At some point, it's too late—my secret becomes public information.

In one case, Jane Doe came back to her apartment and saw the corpse of her murdered roommate lying on the floor. She also caught a glimpse of her roommate's killer as he fled.[56] Since the killer was still at large—and since Jane was an eyewitness, the police withheld her identity from the public. But somehow it got leaked to a journalist, who named her in a newspaper article about the murder. Jane sued under the public-disclosure tort. The newspaper argued that Jane's identity wasn't private because she told some of her neighbors, friends, and family members about witnessing the murder. Thus the secret was known to a few people. But the court wisely disagreed with the newspaper, concluding that Jane had not "rendered otherwise private information public by cooperating in the criminal investigation and seeking solace from friends and relatives."

In another case, a couple conceived using in vitro fertilization. Artificial means of conception were against the teachings of their religion, so the couple kept the information confidential from members of their congregation and local community. But employees at the hospital knew about their in vitro fertilization and so did other couples at the hospital undergoing similar procedures. On one occasion, a party was thrown for the in vitro couples. A television crew filmed the event, and despite the couple's best efforts to avoid being filmed, their images were nevertheless broadcast on television. The couple sued under the public-disclosure tort. The court held that the couple retained an expectation of privacy because "attending this limited gathering . . . did not waive their right to keep their condition and the process of in vitro private, in respect to the general public."[57]

In another incident, an HIV-positive individual told nearly sixty other people about his condition. They included family, friends, doctors, and members of an HIV support group. At one point, the person agreed to appear on a television show, but only with his face obscured. Unfortunately, the obscuring process was botched, and the individual was identifiable. He sued. The television company argued that he lost any expectation of privacy by telling so many people. But the court concluded that the individual still expected privacy because the people he told weren't likely to spread the information since they "cared about him . . . or because they also had AIDS."[58]

In all these cases, courts concluded that although people exposed their secrets to several others, they still could claim that the information was private.
But many other courts have concluded otherwise. In one case a Colombian
judge indicted Pablo Escobar, the infamous drug lord of Colombia. Escobar
put a million dollar bounty on the judge's head. After receiving numerous
death threats, she fled to Detroit. She told a few people there about her
identity, but otherwise, she kept it quiet. The media, however, reported her
story and revealed her address. She sued for public disclosure. The court threw
out her case because she had exposed her identity "to the public eye."[59]

In another case, a woman told four coworkers about encounters with her
child that had "sexual overtones." The court concluded that she no longer expected privacy in the information because she had shared it with four others in
the office.[60]

How many people must know before the cat's out of the bag? Simply doing
a head count of how many people know the information is the wrong approach. If something can remain private despite being known by four other
people, why not five? Or ten? Or fifty? When is the exposure so great that we
should say that the information is public and no longer private?

There is no magic number. Instead, as the law professor Lior Strahilevitz
suggests, we should look to social networks.[61] As we have seen, people relate
to each other in various groups or cliques. It is generally likely that our information will stay within the groups we associate with and not leave these
boundaries. Instead of counting how many other people know certain information, we should focus on the social circles in which information travels. We
all associate in various social circles. We have our groups of friends, the people
where we work, our families. We share information within these groups.
Rarely does gossip leap from one group to another. People in one social circle
will often not know or care about a person in a completely different circle.

We're all separated by only a few links, but a degree of separation can be a
chasm when it comes to the flow of gossip. As Strahilevitz notes, a "rural
farmer in Omaha and a banker in Boston may be separated by only a few
links, and yet they will live their entire lives oblivious to each other's exis-
tence." Suppose the farmer has a friend (Bob) who has a friend (Jane) who
knows the banker. The farmer tells Bob about their mutual friend Jack's adulterous affair. Bob may tell Jane about it, but probably only if Jane knows Jack.
Otherwise, why would Jane care? Strahilevitz observes that the information
won't spread beyond the farmer's immediate social circle. Indeed, it probably
won't even spread to the farmer's friends who don't know Jack, let alone

friends of friends. Only if the information is "particularly sordid, humorous, or memorable" will it spread further. If it does spread, those who don't know Jack will care only about the salacious details, not about his identity. Thus as the story radiates beyond those who know Jack, his name is likely to be dropped.

Social network theory often focuses primarily on connections, but networks involve more than nodes and links. There are norms about information sharing that are held within certain groups, such as norms of confidentiality. My colleagues at the law school where I teach constitute a social circle. Gossip travels quickly throughout the faculty, in part because we all work in the same building and encounter each other throughout the year. But while we might not be very careful about keeping secrets about our colleagues from our fellow colleagues, we're less likely to share gossip with students. Our relationships with students are more formal than our relationships with other colleagues, so gossip is not to be a likely topic of conversation. Many faculty might be wary of embarrassing a colleague by spreading rumors among the students. So despite close proximity between professors and students, despite many links between nodes, information might not spread evenly throughout a network because of norms.

In other words, certain groups guard secrets more tightly. Other times, secrets will not leave the group simply because outsiders won't be interested. The adage "What happens in Vegas stays in Vegas" aptly describes the phenomenon. What is gossiped about in certain groups often stays within those groups.

As Strahilevitz argues, we should examine how information is likely to travel. Information should be considered private if it remains within a confined group—even if that group is rather large. Once it has traversed too many social circles, then it is no longer private. But if the information is confined in a particular social circle, and a person takes it beyond these boundaries, that's when the law should assign liability—to the person who crossed the boundary.

According to Strahilevitz, the case in which the person's HIV status was still private despite being known to sixty others was correctly decided because the circles in which the person spread the information would readily respect the privacy of HIV-positive individuals. This isn't the kind of information that people typically spread about others, especially those who also suffer from the disease. Given these facts, Strahilevitz contends that the information was not likely to spread beyond the particular circle.

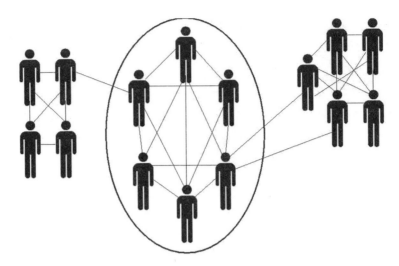

This diagram depicts three social groups in a network. The circle around the group in the center represents a boundary of information flow. Information circulating in the center group will rarely jump beyond that group even though some people in the group are linked to others in different groups.

Strahilevitz argues that the court was wrong, however, in the case involving the judge whose life was threatened by Pablo Escobar: "According to the court, [the woman] used her real name when shopping in stores or eating in restaurants, which waived an expectation of privacy in her identity. Under a network theory approach, these acts, combined with her notoriety in Colombia, would not have eliminated her reasonable expectation of privacy in her identity." The people she used her real name with were a few individuals she had "fleeting contact" with, such as people she encountered when shopping and at restaurants. These individuals were unlikely to care enough about who she was to spread news of her identity. Nor were they likely to "put two and two together" and realize that she was the woman with the bounty on her head. Her "general obscurity in Detroit properly engendered a reasonable expectation of privacy with respect to her shopping and visiting restaurants."[62]

Applying social network theory to the law of privacy doesn't require special expertise in sociology. We all have pretty good intuitions about how gossip travels. We readily understand that information can traverse quickly within certain groups but not spread beyond. It is this key intuition, one we know from experience and that is confirmed by social network theory, that privacy law needs to better understand and incorporate. When information is contained within a particular group and a person causes it to leap the boundary, then this is a privacy violation even if the original group is large. So a big group of people can know a secret, and it can still be deemed private because it is not expected to circulate beyond that group.

From Realspace to the Internet

Even if information is already circulating orally as gossip among a few people, putting it online should still be understood as a violation of privacy—even if it is read only by people within one's social circle. In other words, a person might expose your secrets in her blog but defend herself by saying: "But only a few of my friends read my blog." The difficulty is that putting the information online increases dramatically the risk of exposure beyond one's social circle. Placing information on the Internet is not just an extension of water cooler gossip; it is a profoundly different kind of exposure, one that transforms gossip into a widespread and permanent stain on people's reputations.

There has been a long-standing recognition that written gossip can be more pernicious than oral gossip. In the late eighteenth century, for example, politicians frequently circulated gossip about each other. President Thomas Jefferson was a master at spreading gossip about his foes. Despite the crudeness of the practice, there was an "etiquette of gossip."[63] One of the primary rules was that gossip should never be put to pen, since letters and papers often found their way into the wrong hands, and even worse, could become exposed to the public. As the historian Joanne Freeman observes, written gossip was particularly dangerous because it could transform "one man's gossip into fodder for someone else's gossip."[64] Elites were careful about gossip; they understood its power and they tried to keep it in check as much as possible.

Today the line in the sand is the Internet. When gossip spreads to the Internet, it can spiral out of control. Even if it is posted on an obscure blog, information can still appear in a Google search under a person's name. Therefore the law should view the placing of information online as a violation of privacy—even gossip that had previously been circulating orally in one particular social circle.

How Far Should Liability Be Extended?

Social network theory explains why placing gossip on the Internet changes it so dramatically. The Internet allows information to traverse boundaries more rapidly and spread much farther. But when should liability end? Suppose that Jack posts private details about Jill's love life on his blog. Jack's blog has a small readership. Marty, a blogger from a popular blog, with hundreds of thousands of readers, thinks that the story is interesting and posts excerpts of Jack's post. Who should be liable—Jack, Marty, or both?

Only Jack should be liable for damages. He's the one who breached the gossip boundary and spread the information to the Internet. Once the information is on the Internet, however, it would be impractical and problematic to hold liable others beyond the person who initially placed it there. A line must be drawn at cyberspace; once information is out on the Internet, those subsequently discussing and disseminating it should not be liable. To conclude otherwise would seriously chill the freewheeling and lively discussion that rapidly erupts across the blogosphere.

While this rule has its difficulties, it is the most practical approach. How is Marty to know how many others have read Jack's blog? At some point, liability must stop. When information is on the Internet, many people may readily link to it, talk about it, copy it, repost it, and so on. Putting gossip on the Internet is like throwing meat to alligators. People snap it up in a frenzy. Without protection from liability, people would be severely chilled in their blogging. They would never know when the information they have found on the Internet is really safe to blog about. Therefore only the person who first posts the gossip should be liable for damages. Those repeating the information should not be liable for damages—but they should be required to remove at least the last names of the harmed individuals if asked. If a reasonable request for suppression of personal information is denied, a victim should be able to seek legal recourse against bloggers and others who continue to broadcast identifiable information they find elsewhere on the Net.

The Danger of Too Much Confidentiality

One of the problems with confidentiality—and with privacy more generally—is that it impedes the spread of true information. If we protect confidentiality, we take away information that might be helpful in assessing people's reputations. In one example, a nurse was fired by a hospital for making serious errors. The nurse negotiated for the hospital to agree not to disclose any information about his performance on the job. The nurse then applied for a job at another hospital. That hospital sought a reference from the nurse's former place of employment. Despite promising confidentiality, the former hospital told the other one the reasons for firing the nurse. After a legal challenge, the court upheld the agreement as valid.[65] Was the former hospital in the wrong? Should it be liable for giving out an honest evaluation of the nurse's performance? After all, it served the public interest by accurately providing information about a bad nurse whose errors could harm or kill future patients. It provided correct information that was helpful in assessing the nurse's qualifications. Confidentiality would have allowed the nurse to escape from his past. Should the law permit the withholding of such important information?

This case reveals the cost of confidentiality—sometimes the restriction of truth can cause harm to others. Hard cases exist, but most information on the Internet does not rise to this level. The law protects confidentiality even in some difficult cases because of the larger value of ensuring trust between people and encouraging candid conversations.

CONTROL

Dr. Laura Schlessinger hosted a popular national radio call-in show. She had conservative views, sternly espousing her moral judgments about sex, marriage, parenting, and abortion. She once declared that the best mothers are ones who stay at home, that being gay is a "biological error," and that women having sex outside marriage are "presenting themselves virtually as unpaid whores."[66] Dr. Laura, as she often has been called, published many books, including *Ten Stupid Things Women Do to Mess Up Their Lives, The Proper Care and Feeding of Husbands,* and *How Could You Do That?! The Abdication of Character, Courage, and Conscience,* among others.

In 1998 a website called Club Love posted about twelve photos of Schlessinger in the nude, taken about twenty-five years earlier when she was in her twenties. The website was run by Internet Entertainment Group, the same porn company that attempted to distribute a video of Pamela Anderson and Brett Michaels having sex.[67] The photos had been taken by Bill Ballance, who had introduced Schlessinger to radio back in 1974. Ballance had begun a brief affair with Schlessinger after she separated from her first husband, whom she later divorced. He kept the photos tucked away for years, then suddenly decided to sell them to Internet Entertainment Group.

One of the photos included a shot with Schlessinger in a spreadeagle pose. The website enabled people to click on any part of Schlessinger's anatomy and enlarge it for closer viewing. Internet Entertainment Group called the photos "The Dirty Dozen."[68] Soon after the photos were publicized, more than seventy other websites posted copies.[69]

Dr. Laura was distraught. She had strong words for Ballance: "I am mystified as to why, 23 years later, this 80-year-old man would do such a morally reprehensible thing."[70] She immediately sued and obtained a temporary restraining order against Internet Entertainment Group from posting the photos. But shortly afterward, the judge lifted the order on free-speech grounds. Before the case went any further, Dr. Laura dropped it.

Dr. Laura wasn't the only one upset. Internet Entertainment Group was also up in arms—against the other websites that it claimed were copying its photos. Copyright in a photo is owned initially by the person who takes the photo, not by the person whose photo is taken. When Ballance sold the photos, Internet Entertainment Group acquired the copyright. Seth Warshavsky, the head of Internet Entertainment Group, said: "We shut those sites down. We own the copyright to those photos and we intend to protect that copyright. If anyone, including Dr. Laura herself, tries to print those pix, we will shut them down."[71] That's right—Internet Entertainment Group's copyright even gives it the ability to control how Dr. Laura herself uses the photos.

While some might cheer this comeuppance of the harsh champion of family values, Internet Entertainment Group obtained the photos through Ballance's breach of confidentiality. It seems fairly clear that Schlessinger believed that the photos were to be kept by Ballance in confidence and not sold for profit. Copyright law gives Internet Entertainment Group a vigorous set of legal protections to control the use of the photos. The law gives Schlessinger much less control. Should the law be this way?

A System of Controlling Information

A problem with the binary view of privacy is that it is an all-or-nothing proposition. We often don't want absolute secrecy. Instead, we want to control how our information is used, to whom it is revealed, and how it is spread. We want to limit the flow of information, not stop it completely. Moreover, different people have different entitlements to know information about others. We might want to keep a person's HIV-positive status from her employer, but what about that person's spouse? Or people with whom the person had unprotected sex? In some cases, the law could say that some people should be entitled to know information but others shouldn't be.

But is control over information really feasible? If we expose information to others, isn't it too difficult for the law to allow us still to control it? Perhaps the law is reticent about granting control because of the practical difficulties. Information spreads rapidly, sometimes like a virus, and it is not easily contained. But in other contexts, the law has developed a robust system of controlling information. For example, copyright law recognizes strong rights of control even though information is public. The Copyright Act protects "original works of authorship fixed in any tangible medium of expression."[72] Copyright law protects a wide range of works: movies, books, music, software, art, and photographs, among other things. To obtain copyright protection, one need not lock one's work behind closed doors. I expose copyrighted material to the public all the time. You're reading this book, which is copyrighted. My exposing the book to you doesn't eliminate my protection. You can't do whatever you want to with my book, such as photocopy it cover to cover and start selling bootleg copies in the streets of New York. But you can do some things with it. You can copy it for your own use. You can lend the book to others. You can quote from it. The copyright system focuses on the use of information—it allows certain uses and prohibits others. And it does so regardless of whether the information has been publicly exposed.

Moreover, copyright law provides protection even when a work can be readily copied. I don't have to take any steps to protect my work. Even if you can easily make copies and sell it, the law doesn't allow you to. In fact, the law even creates liability when others facilitate your violating my copyright protection. If you infringe upon my copyright, the law provides me with a powerful set of remedies. I can obtain a court order to forbid you from continuing to use my material improperly. I can sue for damages. Under certain circumstances you might also be subject to criminal penalties.

Copyright and privacy are both ways of controlling information. As the law professor Jonathan Zittrain notes, "there is a profound relationship between those who wish to protect intellectual property and those who wish to protect privacy."[73] The legal scholar Lawrence Lessig observes, "Just as the individual concerned about privacy wants to control who gets access to what and when, the copyright holder wants to control who gets access to what and when."[74] In privacy discussions, however, there seems to be a much lesser recognition of control. Control in the privacy context is seen as outlandish or impossible. Copyright law demonstrates otherwise. It reveals that the law is willing and able to control information.

Of course, copyright law isn't always effective at keeping information under control. People routinely violate copyright law, and as Zittrain notes, it is hard to control intellectual property when it can be so readily copied and transferred.[75] Despite these limitations, however, copyright law still has significant effects on the way information is disseminated and used.

I invoke copyright law not as a means to regulate privacy but merely to demonstrate that the law can and does afford a vigorous system of control over information. With regard to privacy, the law needs better ways to allow people to exercise control over their personal data. I have discussed a few dimensions of such control already—a greater recognition of privacy in public and of duties to keep people's information confidential. The key question, of course, is how much control. Too much control over personal information can be just as bad as too little.

Copyright law's balance of freedom and control has been the subject of considerable debate and controversy. Several scholars, including Lessig, have criticized copyright law for providing too much control.[76] Copyright protections, for example, can impede me from creating works that use parts of others' works. For example, I might want to create my own *Star Wars* books and movies, using the characters George Lucas created, such as Darth Vader and Luke Skywalker. Copyright law bars me from doing this without Lucas's permission. Copyright's protections are so strong that even the First Amendment right to freedom of expression yields before them.[77] Copyright law's zealous protection of control over information can stifle creativity and free speech. In the context of privacy protection, the law need not foster the same level of control that copyright law affords. The key point is that the law is capable of providing a system for controlling information—even when information is not concealed from public view.

Refurbishing the Appropriation Tort

The closest privacy law comes to copyright is the appropriation tort. This tort, as described earlier, prevents the use of someone else's name or likeness for financial benefit.[78] Unfortunately, the tort has developed in a way that is often ineffective in protecting against the privacy threats we are facing today. Although the original rationale of the tort was to protect a person's privacy, the tort has in many cases been transformed into a kind of property right. Many of the successful cases involve celebrities whose identities have been used to endorse particular products without their consent. According to Jonathan Kahn, the "early association of appropriation claims with such intangible, non-commensurable attributes of the self as dignity and the integrity of one's persona seems to have been lost, or at least misplaced, as property-based conceptions of the legal status of identity have come to the fore."[79] An early 1905 case—the first state court to recognize the tort—explained the tort as protecting a person's freedom: "The body of a person cannot be put on exhibition at any time or at any place without his consent. The right of one to exhibit him-

self to the public at all proper times, in all proper places, and in a proper manner is embraced within the right of personal liberty. The right to withdraw
from the public gaze at such times as a person may see fit, when his presence
in public is not demanded by any rule of law, is also embraced within the right
of personal liberty."[80] The court declared that the use of a person's identity
against his will was akin to seizing his liberty, making him temporarily "under
the control of another," with the effect "that he is no longer free, and that he
is in reality a slave."[81]

But this meaning of the tort gradually became lost over the years. By 1960
the renowned torts scholar William Prosser explained that the injury redressed by the appropriation tort was "not so much a mental one as a propri-
etary one."[82] Thus appropriation used to focus primarily on protecting
people's dignity, but now it centers around the profit-value of one's identity.
We want to control information, however, not just to profit from it.

The appropriation tort is often limited to instances in which a person's
identity is exploited for commercial gain. The tort doesn't apply when
people's names or likenesses are used in news, art, literature, and so on. As one
court noted, the tort doesn't apply to "factual, educational and historical data,
or even entertainment and amusement concerning interesting phases of human activity."[83] The appropriation tort thus protects against my using your
name or picture to advertise my products, but it allows me to use your name
and picture when writing about you. I can write your unauthorized biography,
for example, and you will not be able to sue me for appropriation.[84] I can use
your picture in a news story about you. This limitation is a fairly big one. The
appropriation tort would rarely apply to the discussion on the Internet of
people's private lives or the posting of their photos.

The appropriation tort might be expanded to encompass a broader set of
problematic uses of information about a person, but such an expansion would
have to address some difficult issues. How much control do we want to give
people over their images? An approach consistent with the newsworthiness
test of the public disclosure tort would counsel that the appropriation tort apply when people's photos are used in ways that are not of public concern.

IS PRIVACY LAW UP TO THE TASK?

In this chapter, I've proposed that American privacy law adopt more nuanced
understandings of privacy. Privacy law should recognize privacy in public;
and it should better protect confidentiality. More generally, the law should al-

low individuals to exercise greater control over their personal information, even after it has been exposed to the public or to other people.

But are my recommendations too radical for our law? After all, law develops rather conservatively. It wears a bow tie, and it doesn't like change. Nevertheless, little by little, the law does evolve. The concepts discussed in this chapter—privacy in public, confidentiality, and control—are already present in American law, as well as in the law of many other countries. The law is beginning to recognize privacy in public places. A tort for breach of confidentiality exists in many countries—England, Australia, New Zealand, Canada, and others.[85] The tort exists in America, too, but it has not yet blossomed to its fullest potential. And the law recognizes the concept of control over information rather robustly in other contexts—perhaps too much in the copyright context. Thus there is plenty of legal precedent for privacy law to recognize more nuanced understandings of privacy. The seed certainly exists; the question is whether we'll let privacy law grow to respond to the new challenges we face.

Chapter 8 Conclusion:

The Future of Reputation

What will the future hold for our reputation? I have explored in this book the ways our reputations are shaped by the exposure of personal information. We love to talk about each other, and the information we circulate has profound consequences for how people are judged. In many instances, revealing another's personal information can be beneficial to society. It enables communities to enforce norms. It educates us about the lives of others. It allows us to better assess others' reputations. But it also can be problematic. Gossip can unfairly stain a person's reputation; it often exists as a bundle of half-truths and incomplete tales. False rumors can wreak havoc on reputations. And shaming can spin out of control. We cling to only a limited degree of control over our reputation, but this control can make a world of difference. By concealing information about our private lives and our violations of social taboos, and by preventing damaging falsehoods about us from circulating, we can make ourselves less vulnerable to misunderstanding, misjudgment, or unfair condemnation.

The problems escalate when anybody can spread information far and wide over the Internet. Whispering voices and babbling tongues become permanent records readily found in an online search. Increasingly, people are gossiping and shaming others online, as well as exposing their own tawdry secrets. And increasingly, people are googling one another, including employers who are using the information they find online for hiring decisions.

We are witnessing a clash between privacy and free speech, a conflict between two important values that are essential for our autonomy, self-development, freedom, and democracy. We must do something to address the problem, but if we err too much in one direction or the other, the situation could become much worse. In this book, I have attempted to provide a framework for how we can rework the law to make it a useful instrument in balancing privacy and free speech. I have suggested delicate compromises that involve making some modest sacrifices on both sides.

WHAT THE LAW CAN DO, AND WHAT IT CAN'T

Throughout history, most societies have devised ways for people to protect their reputations from gossip and rumor. We have progressed from brawls to duels to law. In the nineteenth century, in response to new technologies posing new threats to privacy, Samuel Warren and Louis Brandeis proposed a way that the law could help provide protection. Their approach, which allowed people to sue others for invading privacy, was a modest middle-ground approach, one that I argued we should continue to use today.

The alternatives are unworkable or unpalatable. A libertarian approach would leave the law out of it, but such an approach would do little to address the problem. And the threat to privacy by the increasing spread of personal information online is too significant to ignore. An authoritarian approach, which involves direct restrictions on Internet expression, would be too oppressive and stifling of free speech. Lawsuits are a middle-ground solution, one that is far from flawless, yet the best among a set of imperfect choices.

But improvements are needed in the existing law for this approach to work effectively. In the framework I have sketched in the previous few chapters, the law should encourage informal attempts at resolving privacy disputes. To do so, law must function as a credible threat yet lawsuits must be a last resort, a measure that provides redress only in egregious cases or when informal ways to resolve disputes don't exist or have failed.

We should expand the law's recognition of privacy so that it covers more situations. We must abandon the binary view of privacy, which is based on the archaic notion that if you're in public, you have no claim to privacy. Instead, we must recognize that privacy involves accessibility, confidentiality, and control. We often expose information to many others, but we nevertheless expect that it has only a certain level of accessibility. The law should also increase its recognition of duties of confidentiality. When we share information with friends, family, and even with strangers, an implicit expectation often exists that they will keep it to themselves. The law should protect and reinforce these expectations. More broadly, the law should afford people greater control over their personal information. Too often, the law clings to restrictive notions of privacy that render it impotent to address contemporary problems. For example, victims of privacy invasions must suffer further injury when pursuing legal redress when their names enter the public record; this undermines their right to pursue a remedy. People should be permitted to keep their names confidential in privacy cases. Updating and expanding the legal understandings of privacy will assuage the law's current handicaps in grappling with privacy issues.

Another part of the equation is reconciliation of the rights of free speech and of privacy. Free speech isn't absolute, and privacy can further the same goals as free speech. In many instances, we can protect both privacy and speech by allowing people to tell their stories anonymously. And a blogger who knows about a statement on his site that is defamatory or invasive of privacy should be obliged to take it down. Unfortunately, the law currently immunizes people for comments on their blogs, even when they know about the harmfulness of the information and ignore pleas to do anything about it.

Thus the law must expand in its recognition of privacy interests and reach a more careful balance between privacy and free speech, one that doesn't give free speech an undue advantage. With these changes, the law can serve to encourage people to be more aware of the consequences of their speech, and it can force people to work out disputes over defamation and invasion of privacy informally. Redefining the limits on the law's reach—expanding the understanding of privacy, for example, and cutting back on overly broad immunities in the name of free speech—is necessary for the law to achieve this goal.

Taking these steps, however, must be accompanied by limitations on some of the troubling costs that the law produces. Law involves many interlocking parts, and tinkering with one part can throw another part out of line. Since lawsuits can be costly and chilling of speech, we must counterbalance any expansion in the law's reach. Plaintiffs should first be required to pursue informal solutions with the spreaders of the information. A case should proceed to lawsuit only if the speaker doesn't take reasonable steps to address the harm or if the damage is irreparable. Perhaps parties should even be required to seek alternative dispute resolution before going to court. Mediation and arbitration might serve as cheaper ways to determine the merits of a person's complaint and what measures, if any, a speaker should take to rectify the situation.

My proposals for addressing the problem rectify it primarily through informal nonmonetary means. In many instances, people sue primarily for vindication and to stop the dissemination of the harmful information. Money damages are often not the primary goal. The virtue of the Internet, unlike print media, is that online content can readily be edited and names can be removed. As discussed before, in some cases, all it will take is for a person's name to be edited out of the story.[1] In other cases, the information will have spread too far for there to be a plausible way to clear it from the Internet. Where possible, the law can encourage people to work out their problems among themselves, which will often provide quick and inexpensive results. In some cases money damages might still be appropriate, but for quite a large number of situations, the pursuit of financial redress will be neither practical nor effective.

Other steps can be taken to improve the protection of privacy online. The creators of websites should be encouraged to build in mechanisms for dispute resolution and to establish meaningful ways for people to protect their privacy. For example, social network websites could require people to promise confidentiality as one of the terms of membership. The websites could have users agree to a basic set of rules for respecting others' information. In other words, people should be given choices over how to control the dissemination of their personal information, and those reading people's profiles should be aware of (and bound to) those preferences. When people take efforts to keep information limited in one domain or network, the law should strive to protect those efforts.

Another promising development is the rise of services like ReputationDefender, a company that helps people find and remove harmful information about themselves online. According to the company's website:

> We will find the unwelcome online content about you or your loved ones, even if it is buried in websites that are not easily examined with standard online search engines. And if you tell us to do so, we will work around the clock to get that unwelcome content removed or corrected.[2]

Such services can help make informal ways of resolving the problem more effective and efficient.

On social network websites, people share information with a network of friends. Users can make their profiles available within certain networks (their school, their friends, and so on) but not generally available to all users. The law can protect a user's ability to keep information within her social network and prevent others from betraying confidence and revealing that information to others outside the network. For example, the law could bar a prospective employer from trying to gain access to an applicant's profile uninvited.

With the appropriate improvements, the law can help us make significant headway by encouraging the development of ways to resolve disputes over privacy, rumor mongering, and shaming online. We can reach a reasonable balance between privacy and free speech. The task is complicated, as it requires a combination of legal reforms and considerable fine-tuning of the law. But with the framework I'm proposing in this book, the law can play an effective role.

The Limits of Law

There is, of course, a limit to how much the law can do. The law is an instrument capable of subtle notes, but it is not quite a violin. Part of the solution depends upon how social norms develop with regard to privacy. The law's function is to lurk in the background, to ensure that people know that they must respect confidentiality or the privacy even of people in public. In the foreground, however, norms will largely determine how privacy shall be protected in the brave new online world. In a fascinating study, the law professor Robert Ellickson went to Shasta County, a rural area in California, to study the behavior of ranchers. He discovered that many disputes arose because of stray cattle, and that although there were laws to address the issue, the ranchers had adopted their own set of norms to deal with it. For example, Ellickson noted, "Ranchers who suffer trespasses [by wayward cattle] virtually never file claims against others' insurance companies. An adjuster for the company that insures most Shasta County ranchers stated that he could not recall, in his twenty years of adjusting, a single claim by a rancher for compensation for trespass damage." A rancher would often take care of another rancher's cows that strayed onto his land until his neighbor picked them up. During that time the rancher would feed and house the cow. Although the law permitted ranchers to recover the costs for taking care of the stray cow, the ranchers never did. The norm was that you should take care of your neighbor's cow if it strayed onto your land. According to Ellickson: "People may supplement, and indeed preempt, the state's rules with rules of their own."[3] The ranchers had a well-developed system of norms, and they didn't need to resort to the law.

What do ranchers and cattle disputes have to do with the Internet? Ellickson's study illustrates a more general insight about the law and norms. The law is a puny instrument compared with norms. As the law professor Tracey Meares observes, "Social norms are better and more effective constraints on behavior than law could ever be."[4] Although the law can't supplant norms, it can sometimes help to shape them. With the ranchers, the law was something they could have resorted to if they were unhappy with the norms. But the norms worked, and the law was rarely needed.

Blogosphere Norms vs. Mainstream Media Norms

Currently, bloggers are much less restrained than the mainstream media in what they write about. The mainstream media have established ethical guidelines (albeit loose ones) to protect people's privacy, but the norms of the blogosphere are still in their infancy. In the nineteenth century, the media routinely focused on the sex scandals of politicians, but reporters and editors became much more restrained during the first half of the twentieth century.[5] As the historian John Summers observes: "Partisan rivals and 'paul pry' journalists continued to gossip uncharitably about [President Grover] Cleveland, yet both averted their gaze from his successor, Benjamin Harrison, whose moral worthiness suffered no significant assaults. The aloof William McKinley also enjoyed a gossip-free administration. So, too, did William Howard Taft and Woodrow Wilson escape from the discomfort of entering public debate about their sexual peccadilloes."[6]

Ethical codes for journalists sprang up in the early twentieth century. These codes urged that gossip about the private lives of public figures should not get front page attention, that reputations should not "be torn down lightly," that attacks on a person's reputation should not be published before the person had the opportunity to be heard, and that "a newspaper should not invade private rights or feelings without sure warrant of public right as distinguished from public curiosity."[7] President John F. Kennedy benefited greatly from the media's reluctance to report on people's private lives, as the media avoided reporting on his many sexual infidelities.[8]

Today this norm has changed, as was emphatically demonstrated by the extensive reporting on President Clinton's affairs. Although the media readily plunder the private lives of politicians, they continue to exercise great restraint with politicians' children. President Clinton actively worked to keep his daughter, Chelsea, away from the media, and the media generally cooperated.[9] When Chelsea attended Stanford University, the editors of the *Stanford Daily* even resolved to fire any member of its staff who disclosed information about Chelsea to the public.[10] The press has also exercised restraint for President Bush's daughters, and when one daughter was arrested for underage drinking, the media was deeply divided about the extent of coverage to give to the story.[11] These norms exist in spite of great public interest in the children's lives.

Another long-standing media norm is extending anonymity to rape victims. For example, in August 2002, two teenage girls were kidnapped and raped. While they were captive, their names and photographs were widely broadcast to assist in the search. Once they were found alive, most of the media ceased displaying their names and photographs.[12] Although this norm is widely followed, there are occasional violators, a recent example being the radio commentator who disclosed the identity of National Basketball Association star Kobe Bryant's alleged sexual assault victim.[13]

Media self-restraint is difficult to achieve because the media are far from a monolithic entity. There are many different styles of journalism, and a vast number of media entities cater to different tastes. If the *New York Times* will not report it, the *National Enquirer* will. As a result, certain segments of the media—such as tabloids—may routinely run stories that a majority of the media does not consider newsworthy. The media also have a tendency to follow the crowd. If one media entity begins reporting on a story, others often quickly follow suit.[14]

But the mainstream media have developed at least some norms of restraint in order to protect privacy. While the norms need shaping and strengthening, they are at least partially developed. The blogosphere has less-well-developed norms, and it needs to establish a code of ethics. People should delete offensive comments quickly if asked. People should ask permission before speaking about others' private lives. Someone who speaks about another person's private life without her consent should take steps to conceal her identity. People should avoid posting pictures of other people without getting their consent. People should avoid Internet shaming.

These rules are easier stated in theory than developed or enforced in practice. The blogosphere is growing rapidly, with people entering the online media community daily. With so many different bloggers, and with so many new ones joining the ranks each day, the norms of the blogosphere are not stable.

The law can help shape norms in the blogosphere, however, by threatening to become involved if such norms don't evolve.

One of the key contributions the law can make is to foster greater awareness of the difference between the offline and online spread of information. People are viewing the Internet as a mere extension of their offline world. Many people who enter the blogosphere are using it to gossip just as they do in realspace. The boundary between online and offline is blurring, but it is an important line to keep clear. Online, information is permanent and more easily spread. The law must make the boundary between online and offline more salient in people's minds.

Establishing norms, of course, is a difficult task, and the law can do only so much. The norms of those speaking online are quite varied, and the law is unlikely to create unanimity in attitudes and behavior. We must be realistic in our expectations about what the law can do. At best, the law will be able to provide modest guidance and direction. It can nudge norms in the right direction. But the law is far from a magic elixir.

THE SELF-EXPOSURE PROBLEM

Although gossip and rumors are spread without the targets' knowledge or consent, an increasingly large number of people are putting their own personal information online. I have argued that it is justified for the law to try to stop people from gossiping about others, but how ought the law to respond to people's gossip about themselves?

The great nineteenth-century philosopher John Stuart Mill articulated a key principle that still resonates today: "The only part of the conduct of any one for which he is amenable to society, is that which concerns others. In the part which merely concerns himself, his independence is, of right, absolute."[15] In other words, if your conduct hurts others, the law should regulate it to rectify or prevent the harm. But if your conduct affects only yourself, then the law should leave you alone.

Applied to the issues discussed in this book, the law should be most involved when people are violating the privacy of other people. But it should be less involved when people are merely self-disclosing personal information. The law becomes too authoritarian if it prevents people from voluntarily revealing their own personal information.

Mill's principle, of course, isn't perfect, as our actions are rarely entirely self-contained. When teenagers expose too much of their own personal information online, it can affect their friends and families. Children's public indiscretions can embarrass their parents and siblings, and parental public indiscretions can cause humiliation to children. But by and large, although no person is an island, the law should respect people's wishes to expose themselves online if they desire.

Should anything be done about the children and teenagers who are discussing their private lives on blogs and social network sites? Children and teens are not fully mature; they might not understand the long-term consequences of what they are doing. If the law can't stop them from exposing their lives online, then is there any way to address the problem?

Do People Want Privacy Anymore?

Perhaps there isn't a problem. What if a teen's decision to expose her intimate secrets on the Web isn't the product of lack of maturity but instead is a manifestation of generational differences?

In today's world of reality television, the law professor Anita Allen wonders whether people expect privacy anymore: "Our parents may appear on the televisions shows of Oprah Winfrey or Jerry Springer to discuss incest, homosexuality, miscegenation, adultery, transvestitism, and cruelty in the family. Our adopted children may go on television to be reunited with their birth parents. Our law students may compete with their peers for a spot on the MTV program *The Real World,* and a chance to live with television cameras for months on end and be viewed by mass audiences."[16]

Beyond television, people, especially high school and college students, are rushing to post a treasure trove of data about themselves online. Perhaps the emerging generation is just not that concerned about privacy. In a survey of the users of the social network site Facebook, almost 90 percent said that they had never read Facebook's privacy policy.[17] Nearly 60 percent of Facebook users said that they weren't very concerned about privacy, with a little more than 30 percent saying that they were somewhat concerned, and only 9.7 percent saying that they were very concerned.[18] One researcher even created an automatic script that asked hundreds of thousands of Facebook users to be added as a friend, thus allowing full access to their profile information. About 30 percent said yes. As the professors Ralph Gross and Alessandro Acquisti note, these 30 percent "are willing to make all of their profile information available to a random stranger and his network of friends."[19] Studies like these suggest that although people express some concern over privacy, it is not always reflected in their behavior.

A Nuanced View of Privacy

People's views about privacy, however, are much more complicated than the rather simplistic notions of privacy in existing law and policy. If we see people exhibiting themselves before the public without inhibition, our natural reaction is to think that they obviously don't want privacy. But the reality is more nuanced. Recall the Facebook incident discussed in the previous chapter. Facebook added the News Feed feature alerting people's friends about the up-to-the-minute changes made in their profiles. And users got quite upset over this change, viewing it as invasive of privacy.

I think that two lessons can be gleaned from the Facebook incident. First, Facebook users didn't want absolute secrecy for their information; they were concerned about the extensiveness of the exposure. They wanted a certain level of exposure and were angry when the News Feed feature upset their established balance. Second, the Facebook incident may also reflect the fact that many people just don't appreciate the extensiveness of their exposure online. Although they may understand that what they put online is widely exposed, they might not really grasp the consequences.

Part of the problem is that the Internet makes it hard to visualize the breadth of our exposure. Placing information on a website and writing blog posts and comments feels more akin to chatting with friends, writing a diary, or talking on the telephone than like broadcasting live on television, publishing a novel, or addressing a crowded auditorium. This difficulty is compounded by the often ambivalent desire we have for concealment and exposure. Some teenagers have contradictory ambitions for their posts. One teenager interviewed for a story in the *New York Times Magazine* explained that "he wanted his posts to be read, and feared that people would read them, and hoped that people would read them, and didn't care if people read them."[20] Although at first blush the teenager's statement doesn't make much sense, its self-contradictions actually capture the ambivalent attitudes of many bloggers. Writing blog posts is exciting in many ways. It can be cathartic. It can be fun to express oneself openly. People enjoy venturing their deepest secrets, hoping for a sense of acceptance or understanding or even just a bit of attention. One blogger wrote: "Maintaining a blog with no one visiting or commenting would be [as] sad as a clown doing a show with no one watching."[21]

Blogging can be like writing a diary, only with the hope that others might read it. By blogging, you're putting yourself out there, often unfiltered and unedited. And because you can't see or touch your audience, because you blog in the solitude of your room, in front of your computer late at night, it doesn't seem like exhibitionism. There's no bright spotlight. It's just you and your computer. Blogging has an uncanny way of encouraging you to doff your inhibitions. Most of the time you wonder: Is anybody listening? Often, the answer is no. People feel as though they're exposing themselves on a stage before an empty auditorium. But with the Internet, in an instant, the spotlights could come on and the auditorium could be overflowing with people. The Electronic Frontier Foundation, in a guide to blogging safely, notes: "If you blog, there are no guarantees you'll attract a readership of thousands. But at least a few readers will find your blog, and they may be the people you'd least want or expect. These include potential or current employers, coworkers, and professional colleagues; your neighbors; your spouse or partner; your family; and anyone else curious enough to type your name, email address or screen name into Google or Feedster and click a few links."[22] A top law school recently provided blogging advice to its students: "We urge you to take the long view and the adult view of what you write. THINK about the words you send out into the world, and imagine what they would make you look like when you—and surely some of you will—find yourself under review at a confirmation hearing for a professional position you dearly desire."[23]

Get Me an Editor . . . or Not

One of the main differences between blogs and mainstream media publications is style. Blog posts are edgy, not polished and buffed into the typical prefabricated write-by-the-numbers stock that often gets produced by the mainstream media. Discourse on the Internet is pungent. In many respects, this is a virtue. Just as the key to robust free speech is battling attempts at censorship, the key to robust blogging is, I think, battling internal censors. I often fire off posts about whatever half-baked (even quarter-baked) idea happens to be buzzing in my head at a particular moment.

But blog posts are created with no editors and published with no time delays. There's little time to cool down before sounding off. Just click the Publish button and unleash it to the world . . . then think about the consequences later. It goes without saying that this is a recipe for some problems. That nude picture a teenager puts up in a moment of indiscretion—it can be forever present, forever regretted. One girl chronicled her mental breakdown on her blog, describing her self-mutilation, sexual experiences, and family turmoil. When she thought the better of it, she removed the posts from her blog.[24]

Another part of the problem is that blogs and social network websites are the "in" technology that children have integrated into their lives. They are a means of socialization and communication. Just as conversations migrated to the telephone and then to email and instant messaging, now they are migrating to social network websites. The problem is that these sites are not designed in ways to emphasize the potential harms to privacy and other consequences. Cyberspace is the new place to hang out, the perils of exposure notwithstanding. The pressure to fit in, to do what everybody else is doing, overrides concerns about privacy.

In the end, I believe that people still want privacy, but privacy in the digital age is much more complicated than its old-fashioned equivalent. Rarely can we completely conceal information about our lives, but that doesn't mean that we don't expect to limit its accessibility, ensure that it stays within a particular social circle, or exercise some degree of control over it. Moreover, although it would be too authoritarian for the law to stop people from expressing themselves online, there are things that can be done to provide them with more protection.

THE POWER OF ARCHITECTURE

The technological design of the websites has an enormous impact on people's privacy. Lawrence Lessig and Joel Reidenberg emphasize the importance of Internet "architecture"—the code used to structure our choices on the Web.[25] Architecture can shape people's behavior.[26] Physical architecture, such as buildings, can affect the way we live and interact with our peers. Spaces can be designed to encourage people to be more open, to communicate with each other more frequently. Or spaces can be designed to encourage solitude. Like physical spaces, virtual spaces on the Internet are also designed environments. Social network websites are a structured form of interaction, created according to rules set up by those who create the site. The design choices social network websites make will have profound effects on the way their users interact with each other.

Changing the Defaults

One of the primary problems with social network websites is that they are designed to encourage people to expose a lot of information with very little thought about the consequences. The default privacy setting on MySpace, for example, is that anybody in the public can view one's profile.

Who Can View My Full Profile

- ○ My Friends Only
- ◉ Public

Privacy Settings

- ☐ Friend Requests - Require email or last name
- ☐ Comments - approve before posting
- ☐ Hide Online Now
- ☑ Show My Birthday to my Friends
- ☐ Photos - No Forwarding
- ☐ Blog Comments - Friends Only
- ☐ Friend Requests - No Bands

Group Invite Privacy Settings

Block Group Invites From:

- ☐ Everyone (including my friends)
- ☐ Users who are not added to my friends
- ☐ Bands (who are not added to my friends)
- ☐ Filmmakers (who are not added to my friends)
- ☐ Comedians (who are not added to my friends)

A section of the Myspace privacy settings. Under "Who Can View My Full Profile," the option selected by default is "Public."

Likewise, although Facebook allows users to restrict who can see their information, the default setting allows everybody to see it.[27] Unless a user changes the default settings, her profile will be accessible to millions of people. The default settings on many social network websites privilege openness over privacy. According to one study, although Facebook "provides users with a very granular and relatively sophisticated interface to control the searchability and visibility of their profiles," the users "tend to not change default settings."[28] In another study, two researchers concluded: "As a whole, users are familiar with the privacy features Facebook offers, and choose not to use them."[29]

Simply changing default settings might protect a lot of people. The settings or preferences screen on various websites may constitute one of the most important influences on the shape of privacy in the future. The law should not force companies to set specific defaults, but the companies should be encouraged to think about how the design of their websites affects privacy.

The Concept of "Friend"

As discussed earlier in this book, social network sites often have a very loose concept of "friend." The sites divide a person's social universe into "friends" and everybody else. Of course, a person's social network is far more complex, but it must be translated into the terms established by the social network websites. Because social network websites lack a more granular set of categories for social relationships, they encourage users to share information with others who otherwise would not be privy to it. Two scholars who study social network websites, Judith Donath and danah boyd, astutely observe: "By making all of one's connections visible to all the others, social network sites remove the privacy barriers that people keep between different aspects of their lives." To illustrate this phenomenon, they tell the story of a high school teacher who joined Friendster. To protect her privacy, she allowed her profile to be viewed only by "friends." But then one of her students found out she was on Friendster and asked to be added as a friend. This put her in an awkward position for several reasons. Her only choices were to acknowledge the student as a friend or to completely rebuff the student. No intermediate category existed for their relationship. Donath and boyd observe: "She had originally joined with some friends, many of whom had created 'crazy, fun' profiles, including suggestive testimonials, risqué photographs, and references to wild times at the Burning Man festival. . . . Although she could edit her own profile to be quite sedate, her friends' profiles were not. Accepting her student's friendship request would reveal her full network to her class, while saying 'no' felt rude and distancing."

We live complex lives, and we often inhabit many very different social circles. Donath and boyd note that "sometimes simply encountering people from different aspects of someone's life can be quite revealing. The discomfort can be felt both by the performer caught in two roles and the observer."[30] The difficulty with social network websites is that they view a person's relationships as one unified social network, when in fact people have a rather elaborate set of connections. Each connection involves different levels of exposure and different ways of sharing information. And while we may share information freely among one social circle, we may not want information to bleed between the different social circles we occupy simultaneously. But social network websites tear down these boundaries. They present a simplified picture of people's social network that eliminates the many nuanced barriers to information flow.

To participate, people must often share information beyond the limits they would ordinarily establish in the real world.

The law shouldn't force websites to alter their design. This would be too authoritarian. But it is important for websites to consider the consequences that their architectural choices will have on the lives of millions of people.

Employer Responsibilities

Although there isn't a lot the law can do to address the self-exposure problem, the law can operate to help protect people in some limited contexts. Chris Hoofnagle, a researcher at Berkeley Law School, proposes the regulation of employers who would google prospective employees.[31] Under federal law, if an employer asks a credit-reporting agency to conduct a background check on a prospective employee, the employer has certain obligations to the applicant. For example, if information in the report dissuades the employer from making a job offer, he must reveal that to the applicant.[32] The purpose of this require-ment is to allow the applicant a chance to explain. Perhaps the report was in error. Perhaps there's a reasonable explanation. With the use of search engines like Google, employers can conduct amateur background checks without any legal protections. There is no requirement that employers tell applicants that they were googled. What often happens is that an applicant is simply not called in for an interview, or if interviewed, is simply not invited back for fur-ther consideration. As we have seen, employers are increasingly using Google as well as searching social network websites to find out about applicants. But a lot of the information online isn't accurate. Another problem is that informa-tion about a different person with the same name can be mixed in. A require-ment that employers who conduct online searches of applicants notify them about the search will at least give applicants a chance to be heard.

Of course, such a requirement could readily be violated. It would be diffi-cult to prove that an employer had googled an applicant. But even if enforce-ment was problematic, many employers would probably respect a requirement to notify applicants. Moreover, such a rule would help establish a norm. And in such a difficult area to navigate, creating a norm would be a significant step forward.

Education

At the end of the day, if people want to expose themselves to the world, there's only so much that can be done to stop them. Self-disclosure is nevertheless a problem, as teenagers and college students are often revealing too much information and later regretting that they cannot take it back. Education is the most viable way to shape people's choices in this regard. For example, one study indicated that people have a lot of misunderstandings about who is able to search their Facebook profiles. Although most Facebook users are "aware of the true visibility of their profile . . . a significant minority is vastly underestimating the reach and openness of their own profile."[33] We need to spend a lot more time educating people about the consequences of posting information online. In a survey conducted in 2006, "two thirds of parents had never talked with their teen about their MySpace use, and 38 percent of them had never seen their child's MySpace profile."[34] Teenagers and children need to be taught about privacy just like they are taught rules of etiquette and civility.

TO THE END OF THE INTERNET

A television commercial that I find immensely amusing opens with a guy surfing the Internet on his computer. He clicks the mouse, and all of a sudden, a computerized voice from his PC says: "You have reached the end of the Internet. You have seen all that there is to see." It's a commercial for high-speed broadband. The message is that the advertised broadband service is so fast that you can see the entire Internet.

Of course, the humor in this is that you can't exhaust the Internet. It's too big. Every day it grows by millions of new Web pages and blog posts. The Internet is akin to the endless library imagined by the writer Jorge Luis Borges. In his story "The Library of Babel," Borges wrote of a library with an "infinite number of hexagonal galleries." Initially, "when it was announced that the library contained all books, the first reaction was unbounded joy." But then people discovered the rub: finding the right book could take centuries, and many books were totally incomprehensible.[35] And so it is with the Internet. Unlike the hapless users of Borges's library, we Internet users have what has become known as "the search"—the ability to use search engines like Google to help us find the information we're looking for. Google's great innovation has been not only to comb the Internet to bring back as many relevant pieces of information as possible but also to rank them in an order calculated to reflect their relative usefulness.[36]

But "the search" is just in its infancy. John Battelle, the author of a popular book on Internet searching, observes: "As every engineer in the search field loves to tell you, search is at best 5 percent solved—we're not even in the double digits of its potential."[37] For example, a large part of the Internet has not been combed or cataloged by Google. The so-called invisible Web remains, which "comprises everything that is available via the Web, but has yet to be found by search engines."[38] Google searches the epidermis of the Web, but lots of content still remains undiscovered.[39] What will happen when the search improves?

The Internet is still quite young. In the first chapter of this book, I likened the Internet to a teenager, beginning to test out its new freedom and powers yet still in the early days of its development. The Internet is growing up rapidly, and no end is in sight. Nor is there any end to the issues in this book. Right now, the next great innovations are probably being created in somebody's dorm room or garage. After all, that's where Facebook and Google began.[40] What's ahead will be amazing. It makes me giddy with excitement to think about it—but also a bit frightened.

Will people be blogging and using social network websites a decade from now? Who knows? But people will almost certainly be spending a lot of time online. And it is a safe bet that people will be exposing details about their lives, as well as gossiping, shaming, and spreading rumors. The technologies may change, but human nature will remain the same.

Although the Internet poses new and difficult issues, they are variations on some timeless problems: the tension between privacy and free speech, the nature of privacy, the virtues and vices of gossip and shaming, the effect of new technologies on the spread of information, and the ways in which law, technology, and norms interact. New technologies do not just enhance freedom but also alter the matrix of freedom and control in new and challenging ways.

The questions are immensely complex, and there are no easy answers. Just when we think we're smoothing problems out, new technology adds another wrinkle. But we can take steps to protect privacy if we make an effort. We must. After all, it's just the beginning.

Notes

CHAPTER 1. INTRODUCTION

1. Don Park, *Korean Netizens Attack Dog-Shit-Girl,* Don Park's Daily Habit, June 8, 2005, http://www.docuverse.com/blog/donpark/EntryViewPage .aspx?guid=e5e366f9-050f-4901-98d2-b4d26bedc3e1.

2. Jonathan Krim, *Subway Fracas Escalates into Test of Internet's Power to Shame,* Wash. Post, July 7, 2005, at D1.

3. Park, *Korean Netizens Attack, supra.*

4. As of May 2006, the newspaper with the largest circulation in the United States is USA Today, with a circulation of 2,272,815. Other circulation figures: New York Times, 1,142,464; Chicago Tribune, 579,079; Boston Globe, 397,288. *See* Katharine Q. Steele, *U.S. Newspaper Circulation Fell 2.5% in Latest Period,* N.Y. Times, May 9, 2006. These are among the largest newspapers. Most have considerably smaller circulations. About half of the top hundred newspapers have circulations under 200,000, and papers close to the bottom of the top hundred list have circulations not much above 100,000. For a useful chart of newspaper circulation figures, see NYU School of Journalism, *The State of Blogging at America's 100 Largest Newspapers,* March 1, 2006, http://journalism.nyu.edu/pubzone/blueplate/issue1/ top100.html.

5. LAWRENCE LESSIG, CODE AND OTHER LAWS OF CYBERSPACE 58 (1999).

6. Steve Johnson, *Dog Poop Girl Gets Online Whiplashing*, DoggieNews.com, July 11, 2005, http://www.doggienews.com/2005/07/dog-poop-girl-gets-online-whiplashing.htm.

7. http://www.blogdogs.com/.

8. http://www.poopreport.com/.

9. *Subway Turd Terrorist Gets Dubbed "Dog-Shit-Girl,"* PoopReport.com, June 30, 2005, http://www.poopreport.com/BMnewswire/1353.html.

10. Cass R. Sunstein, *Social Norms and Social Roles,* 96 Colum. L. Rev. 903, 914 (1996).

11. *See* comments to Don Park, *Korean Netizens Attack Dog-Shit-Girl,* Don Park's Daily Habit, June 8, 2005, http://www.docuverse.com/blog/donpark/EntryViewPage.aspx ?guid=e5e366f9-050f-4901-98d2-b4d26bedc3e1.

12. Quoted in Jonathan Krim, *Subway Fracas Escalates into Test of Internet's Power to Shame,* Wash. Post, July 7, 2005, at D1.

13. Samantha Henig, *The Tale of Dog Poop Girl Is Not So Funny After All,* Columbia Journalism Review, July 7, 2005, http://www.cjrdaily.org/archives/001660.asp.

14. John Battelle, The Search 73–86 (2005). The technology behind Google was developed in 1996, but the company wasn't created until 1998.

15. Neil Swidey, *A Nation of Voyeurs: How the Internet Search Engine Google Is Changing What We Can Find Out About Each Other and Raising Questions About Whether We Should,* Boston Globe Magazine, Feb. 2, 2003, at 10.

CHAPTER 2. HOW THE FREE FLOW OF INFORMATION LIBERATES AND CONSTRAINS US

1. An early version of the printing press was invented in China in A.D. 600. *See* Paul Levinson, The Soft Edge: A Natural History of the Future of the Information Revolution 22 (1997). Gutenberg's invention sparked mass production of manuscripts in the West.

2. Gini Graham Scott, Mind Your Own Business: The Battle for Personal Privacy 37–38 (1995); Robert Ellis Smith, Ben Franklin's Web Site: Privacy and Curiosity from Plymouth Rock to the Internet 102–20 (2000).

3. For a discussion of how blogs are transforming journalism, see Dan Gillmor, We the Media (2004).

4. Daniel W. Drezner & Henry Farrell, *The Power and Politics of Blogs,* Aug. 2004, at 4, http://www.danieldrezner.com/research/blogpaperfinal.pdf.

5. Hugh Hewitt, Blog 37–42 (2005).

6. Drezner & Farrell, *The Power and Politics of Blogs, supra,* at 14, 15–16.

7. Jennifer Vogelsong, *For Better or for Worse, Teens Are Leading the Way When It Comes to Journaling Online,* York Daily Record, July 17, 2005.

8. Drezner & Farrell, *The Power and Politics of Blogs, supra* (over 10 million blogs in 2004); Carl Bailik, *Measuring the Impact of Blogs Requires More than Counting,* Wall St. Journal Online, May 26, 2005, http://online.wsj.com/public/article/0,,SB111685593 903640572-lZIyf_FU605JAeIW46oycF3f TH4_20060526,00.html?mod-tff _main_tff_top (31.6 million blogs in 2005).

9. David Sifry, *The State of the Blogosphere: August 2006,* Sifry's Alerts, Aug. 7, 2006, http://www.sifry.com/alerts/archives/000436.html.

10. *Id.*

11. http://www.dailyrotten.com/.

12. http://www.wonkette.com/.

13. http://gawker.com/.

14. http://overheardinnewyork.com.

15. http://www.thesuperficial.com.

16. http://www/thesneeze.com/mt-archives/cat_steve_dont_eat_it.php.

17. http://www.cryingwhileeating.com.

18. http://www.wibsite.com/wiblog/dull/.

19. http://belledejour-uk.blogspot.com. For a discussion of the blog, see Jason Deans, *Channel 4 to Dramatise "Call-Girl" Web Diaries,* The Guardian, Jan. 20, 2005, http://www.guardian.co.uk/print/0,3858,5107415-111748,00.html.

20. *Web Therapy,* The Guardian, Feb. 8, 2005, http://www.guardian.co.uk/print/0,3858,5121805-111748,00.html.

21. http://roughdraft.typepad.com/dotmoms.

22. Jeffrey Rosen, *Your Blog or Mine?* N.Y. Times Magazine, Dec. 19, 2004.

23. Todd Eastham, *Internet Is Bulletin Board for Katrina Victims,* Reuters, Sept. 4, 2005.

24. http://www.xanga.com/item.aspx?user=ToTo247&tab=weblogs&uid=261268578.

25. Kerry Burke, Scott Shifrel & Melissa Grace, *Victim's E-Journal Led to Slay Suspect,* N.Y. Daily News, May 17, 2005, http://www.nydailynews.com/front/story/310320p-265498c.html.

26. Glenn Reynolds, An Army of Davids 44, 92, 95 (2006).

27. *Beantown Becomes Blogtown: At the Democratic Convention, Online Journalism Arrives,* Wall St. Journal, July 26, 2004.

28. Donna Smith, *Blogs Seen as Powerful New Tool in U.S. Court Fight,* Reuters, July 8, 2005.

29. Reynolds, Army of Davids, *supra,* at 9.

30. G. Jeffrey MacDonald, *Teens: It's a Diary. Adults: It's Unsafe,* Christian Science Monitor, May 25, 2005.

31. *Id.*

32. Robert J. Samuelson, *A Web of Exhibitionists,* Newsweek, Sept. 20, 2006.

33. Giles Turnbull, *The Seven-Year-Old Bloggers,* BBC News, June 14, 2004, http://news.bbc.co.uk/1/hi/magazine/3804773.stm.

34. *Social Network,* Wikipedia, Feb. 8, 2007, http://en.wikipedia.org/wiki/Social_network.

35. For a general introduction to social networks, see Duncan J. Watts, Six Degrees: The Science of a Connected Age (2002); Albert-László Barabási, Linked (2002); Malcolm Gladwell, The Tipping Point (2000).

36. Watts, Six Degrees, *supra,* at 38–40.

37. John Guare, Six Degrees of Separation: A Play (1990).

38. Quoted in Anick Jesdanun, *MySpace Rises as New Online Star,* Associated Press, Feb. 12, 2006.

39. Reuters, *Myspace, Seventeen Launch Parents Education Program,* Sept. 24, 2006.

40. Michelle Andrews, *Decoding Myspace,* U.S. News & World Report, Sept. 18, 2006.

41. Samuelson, *Web of Exhibitionists,* supra.

42. Andrews, *Decoding Myspace, supra.*

43. Ralph Gross & Alessandro Acquisti, *Information Revelation and Privacy in Online Social Networks (The Facebook Case),* ACM Workshop on Privacy in the Electronic Society, Nov. 7, 2005, at §2.1.

44. Judith Donath & danah boyd, *Public Displays of Connection,* 22 BT Technology Journal 71, 72 (2004).

45. *Id.*

46. Gross & Acquisti, *Information Revelation, supra,* at §2.1.

47. Libby Copeland, *Click Clique: Facebook's Online College Community,* Wash. Post, Dec. 28, 2004.

48. *Id.*

49. Harvey Jones & José Hiram Soltren, *Facebook: Threats to Privacy,* Dec. 14, 2005, at 4, http://ocw.mit.edu/NR/rdonlyres/Electrical-Engineering-and-Computer-Science/6-805Fall-2005/8EE6D1CB-A269-434E-BEF9-D5C4B4C67895/0/facebook.pdf.

50. *Id.* at 14.

51. Gross & Acquisti, *Information Revelation, supra,* at §3.3.

52. *Id.*

53. Fred Stutzman, *Student Life on the Facebook,* Jan. 8, 2006, http://chimprawk.blogspot.com/2006/01/student-life-on-facebook.html.

54. Seth Kugel, *A Web Site Born in U.S. Finds Fans in Brazil,* N.Y. Times, Apr. 10, 2006, at C1.

55. Anthony Hempell, *Orkut at Eleven Weeks: An Exploration of a New Online Social Network Community,* Apr. 16, 2004, http://www.anthonyhempell.com/papers/orkut/.

56. http://www.orkut.com/About.aspx.

57. Nandini Vaish, *Netting New Friends: Online Social Networking Is Catching on in India in a Big Way with Some Unusual Results,* India Today, Dec. 4, 2006, at 74.

58. Savita V, *India-Specific e-communities on the Rise,* The Economic Times, Dec. 7, 2006, http://economictimes.indiatimes.com/articleshow/733381.cms.

59. http://www.nexopia.com; http://www.piczo.com.

60. http://www.adoos.com.

61. http://www.passado.com; Reuters, *Networking Site Passado Plans to Expand,* Dec. 11, 2006.

62. http://www.bebo.com; Mark Ward, *Teen Craze Over Networking Sites,* BBC News, Dec. 20, 2006.

63. Sara Kehaulani Goo, *A Search for Ourselves,* Wash. Post, Dec. 20, 2006, at D01.

64. Leo Lewis, *Mixi Prepares to Cater for Flood of Baby Boomers,* Financial Times, Dec. 6, 2006, at 28; Tim Kelly, *Mixi Mixes It Up in Asia,* Forbes, Oct. 16, 2006. Mixi is located at http://mixi.jp/.

65. http://mop.com/; http://www.cuspace.com/.

66. Barbara Grady, *Cyworld Enters MySpace Territory,* San Mateo County Times, Aug. 15, 2006.

67. http://us.cyworld.com/.

68. Grady, *Cyworld, supra.*

69. Hwang Si-young, *Cyworld Faces Challenges in Overseas Expansion,* Korea Herald, Dec. 10, 2006.

70. *Id.*

71. http://www.dogster.com/; http://www.catster.com/.

72. http://www.hamsterster.com/.

73. Ben McGrath, *Oops,* New Yorker (June 30, 2003).

74. Steven L. Nock, The Costs of Privacy: Surveillance and Reputation in America 2 (1993).

75. Proverbs 22:1.

76. William Shakespeare, Othello, act II, sc. iii.

77. Arthur Miller, The Crucible 133 (Penguin ed. 2003) (originally published in 1953).

78. John Adams, *Discourses on Davila: A Series of Papers on Political History, in* 6 The Works of John Adams 234 (Charles Francis Adams, ed. 1854).

79. C. H. Cooley, Human Nature and the Social Order (1902); *see also* J. Sidney Shrauger & Thomas J. Schoeneman, *Symbolic Interactionist View of Self-Concept: Through the Looking Glass Darkly, in* The Self In Social Psychology 25, 25 (Roy F. Baumeister, ed. 1999); Arnold M. Ludwig, How Do We Know Who We Are? A Biography of the Self 54 (1997). Dianne M. Tice observes: "In 1902, Cooley proposed the 'looking glass self' as a metaphor for how the self-concept is determined by the views of others, and many subsequent theorists and researchers have reconfirmed that other people's perceptions constitute an important part of the self and exert a strong influence on individuals' conceptions of themselves." Diane M. Tice, *Self-Concept Change and Self-Presentation: The Looking Glass Self Is Also a Magnifying Glass, in* The Self in Social Psychology, *supra,* at 195, 215.

80. Nock, Costs of Privacy, *supra,* at 124.

81. Francis Fukuyama, Trust: The Social Virtues and the Creation of Prosperity 26 (1995). For more about trust, see Trust and Reciprocity (Elinor Ostrom & James Walker, eds. 2003); Eric M. Uslaner, The Moral Foundations of Trust (2002); Russel Hardin, Trust and Trustworthiness (2002); Trust in Society (Karen S. Cook, ed. 2001); Trust: Making and Breaking Cooperative Relations (Diego Gambetta, ed. 1988); Adam B. Seligman, The Problem of Trust (1997); Helen Nissenbaum, *Securing Trust Online: Wisdom or Oxymoron?,* 81 B.U. L. Rev. 635 (2001).

82. Nock, Costs of Privacy, *supra,* at 124.

83. Avner Greif, Institutions and the Path to the Modern Economy: Lessons from Medieval Trade 58–89 (2006).

84. Robert D. Putnam, Bowling Alone: The Collapse and Revival of American Community (2000).

85. Associated Press, *The Decline of Manners in the U.S.,* Oct. 14, 2005.

86. Fukuyama, Trust, *supra,* at 310; Pamela Paxton, *Trust In Decline?* Contexts (Winter 2005).

87. Carol A. Heimer, *Solving the Problem of Trust, in* Trust in Society 40, 65 (Karen S. Cook, ed. 2001).

88. Nock, Costs of Privacy, *supra,* at 3.

89. Marshall McLuhan, The Gutenberg Galaxy 31 (1962) ("The new electronic interdependence recreates the world in the image of a global village."); *see also* Marshall McLuhan & Bruce R. Powers, The Global Village: Transformations in World Life and Media in the 21st Century (1989).

90. Ostrowe v. Lee, 175 N.E. 505, 506 (N.Y. Ct. App. 1931).

91. The quotation is from Theodore Tilton, husband of Elizabeth Tilton, who had a scandalous extramarital affair with the famous preacher Henry Ward Beecher during the late nineteenth century. Tilton is quoted in RICHARD WIGHTMAN FOX, TRIALS OF INTIMACY: LOVE AND LOSS IN THE BEECHER-TILTON SCANDAL 35 (1999).

92. Rosenblatt v. Baer, 383 U.S. 75, 86 (1966).

93. Robert C. Post, *The Social Foundations of Defamation Law: Reputation and the Constitution,* 74 Calif. L. Rev. 691, 694 (1986) (quoting J. HAWES, LECTURES ADDRESSED TO THE YOUNG MEN OF HARTFORD AND NEW HAVEN 95 (1828)); *see also* THOMAS STARKIE, A TREATISE ON THE LAW OF SLANDER, LIBEL, SCANDALUM MAGNATUM, AND FALSE RUMOURS (1826).

94. *See id.* at 707–8.

95. *Id.* at 711.

96. Nicholas Emler, *Gossip, Reputation, and Social Adaptation, in* GOOD GOSSIP 117, 119 (Robert F. Goodman & Aaron Ben-Ze'ev, eds. 1994)

97. SHAKESPEARE, OTHELLO, *supra,* act II, sc. iii, ll. 261–66.

98. RICHARD A. POSNER, THE ECONOMICS OF JUSTICE 271 (1983).

99. Richard A. Epstein, *The Legal Regulation of Genetic Discrimination: Old Responses to New Technology,* 74 B.U. L. Rev. 1, 12 (1994).

100. Barbara Mikkelson & David P. Mikkelson, *Tommy Rot,* Urban Legends Reference Pages, May 6, 2006, http://www.snopes.com/racial/business/Hilfiger.asp; *Tommy Hilfiger "Racist" Rumor Is Fashionable Again,* About.com, http://urbanlegends.about.com/library/weekly/aa121698.htm.

101. ABC News, *Misidentified Bryant Accuser Fires Back,* ABCNews.com, Sept. 30, 2004, http://abcnews.go.com/GMA/print?id=124910; Jill Lieber & Richard Willing, *Teen Misidentified as Bryant's Accuser Fights Back,* USA Today, July 28, 2003.

102. ABC News, *Misidentified Bryant Accuser, supra.*

103. Lieber & Willing, *Teen Misidentified,* supra.

104. Jennifer 8. Lee, *Net Users Try to Elude the Google Grasp,* N.Y. Times, July 25, 2002.

105. Richard A. Posner, *Bad News,* N.Y. Times, July 31, 2005.

106. David Linhardt, *Employers Screen Applicants With Facebook,* University Daily Kansan, Jan. 30, 2006.

107. Alan Finder, *For Some, Online Persona Undermines a Resume,* N.Y. Times, June 11, 2006.

108. *Id.*

109. *Id.*

110. O. Kharif, *Big Brother Is Reading Your Blog,* Business Week Online, Feb. 28, 2006.

111. Bree Sposato, *MySpace Invaders,* N.Y. Magazine, Nov. 21, 2005.

112. Ivan Tribble, *Bloggers Need Not Apply,* Chronicle of Higher Education, July 8, 2005.

113. Associated Press, *Official Sues Students Over MySpace Page,* Sept. 22, 2006.

114. *Heather Armstrong: Bloggers on Blogging,* Rebecca's Pocket (Aug. 2005), http://www.rebeccablood.net/bloggerson/heatherarmstrong.html.

115. http://www.dooce.com.

116. Heather Armstrong, *I Have Something to Say,* Dooce.com, Feb. 12, 2002, http://www.dooce.com/archives/daily/02_12_2002.html.

117. Heather Armstrong, *Collecting Unemployment,* Dooce.com, Feb. 26, 2002, http://www.dooce.com/archives/daily/02_26_2002.html.

118. Scott Jaschik, *You May Have Been YouTubed,* Inside Higher Ed, Sept. 6, 2006, http://insidehighered.com/news/2006/09/06/youtube.

119. Sara Kehaulani Goo, *YouTubers Ponder Google,* Wash. Post, Oct 11, 2006.

120. http://www.icann-ncc.org/pipermail/discuss/2003-April/006826.html. The website at this URL has been removed from the Internet.

121. Alan Feuer & Jason George, *Internet Fame Is Cruel Mistress for Dancer of the Numa Numa,* N.Y. Times, Feb. 26, 2005, at A1.

122. *Id.*

123. http://www.newnuma.com.

124. The facts about the Little Fatty incident are from Raymond Zhou, *Fatty—The Face That Launched 1,000 Clicks,* China Daily, Dec. 11, 2006, http://www.chinadaily.com.cn/cndy/2006-11/15/content_733158.htm; Clifford Coonan, *The New Cultural Revolution: How Little Fatty Made It Big,* The Independent, Dec. 27, 2006; Jane Macartney, *Face of "Little Fatty" Finds Fame Among China's Web Users,* The Times, Nov. 21, 2006; Reuters, *"Little Fatty" an Instant Internet Phenomenon in China,* Dec. 8, 2006. To see more of the images, visit http://www.slideshare.net/debasish/little-fatty-chinas-internet-hero.

125. The video was posted at http://www.waxy.org/archive/2003/05/13/finding_.shtml.

126. Tu Thanh Ha, *"Star Wars Kid" Cuts a Deal With His Tormentors,* Globe and Mail, April 7, 2006.

127. For more background about the story, see Amy Harmon, *Fame Is No Laughing Matter for the "Star Wars Kid,"* N.Y. Times, May 19, 2003, at C3.

128. *Daily Log: Star Wars Kid,* Waxy.org, Apr. 29, 2003, http://www.waxy.org/archive/2003/04/29/star_war.shtml.

129. Quoted in Stewart Kirkpatrick, *Shame and Misfortune,* The Scotsman, Apr. 29, 2004.

130. Harmon, *Fame Is No Laughing Matter, supra.*

131. Amanda Paulson, *Internet Bullying,* Christian Science Monitor, Dec. 30, 2003; Jan Wong, *15 Minutes of Shame,* Globe & Mail, May 7, 2005.

132. Ha, *"Star Wars Kid" Cuts a Deal, supra;* Tu Thanh Ha, *Parents File Lawsuit Over Star Wars Kid Video,* Globe and Mail, July 23, 2003.

133. Ghyslain Raza, Wikipedia, http://en.wikipedia.org/wiki/Ghyslain_Raza.

134. Carl Bailik, *How Big an Internet Star Was the "Star Wars" Kid?* Wall St. Journal Online, Dec. 14, 2006, http://online.wsj.com/public/article/SB116602807064149031-HC7A4Ifkyv8bz__bUCj6CT8PHus_20071215.html. According to one estimate by a U.K. firm, the Star Wars Kid video has been viewed about 900 million times. Bailik casts considerable doubt on these statistics. But it is probably safe to say that the video has been viewed more than 100 million times. On video websites such as YouTube, numerous versions of the video are posted, and the views of them amount to about 100 million. *Id.* Several years ago, Ghyslain's "lawyer said in a court filing that the video

was so widely circulated that one Internet site solely dedicated to the two-minute clip recorded 76 million visits by October, 2004." Ha, *"Star Wars Kid" Cuts a Deal, supra.*

135. *Only the Very Best Videos of . . . The Star Wars Kid,* Screaming Pickle, http://screaming pickle.com/humor/legends/StarWarsKid/.

136. *Put the Star Wars Kid in Episode III,* http://www.petitiononline.com/Ghyslain/petition .html.

137. http://www.petitiononline.com/mod_perl/signed.cgi?Ghyslain.

138. *Daily Log: Star Wars Kid TV Tribute Roundup,* Waxy.org, Mar. 20, 2005, http://www .waxy.org/archive/2005/03/20/star_war.shtml.

139. Marie-Chantale Turgeon, *10 Reasons to Blog,* http://www.meidia.ca/archives/2005/06/ 10_reasons_to_b.php?l=en.

140. Eve Fairbanks, *The Porn Identity,* New Republic, Feb. 6, 2006.

CHAPTER 3. GOSSIP AND THE VIRTUES OF KNOWING LESS

1. April Witt, *Blog Interrupted,* Wash. Post Magazine, Aug. 15, 2004, at W12.

2. *Id.*

3. Jessica Cutler's blog, Washingtonienne, has been taken off the Internet. Archived copies of the blog are still available online. The blog Wonkette has posted an archived copy. *See The Lost Washingtonienne,* Wonkette, http://www.wonkette.com/archives/the -lost-washingtonienne-wonkette-exclusive-etc-etc-004162.php. The blog is also reproduced in its entirety in Robert's legal complaint against Jessica.

4. Julie Bosman, *First With the Scoop, if Not the Truth,* N.Y. Times, Apr. 18, 2004.

5. Wonkette is located at http://www.wonkette.com. At the time Wonkette linked to Jessica's blog, it had fewer daily visitors. Although it was already quite popular at the time, its coverage of Jessica's blog helped to catapult Wonkette to higher levels of popularity.

6. Witt, *Blog Interrupted, supra.*

7. Quoted in Wonkette, *Washingtonienne: Eliminated by Process,* May 21, 2004, http:// www.wonkette.com/archives/washingtonienne-eliminated-by-process-009677.php.

8. Witt, *Blog Interrupted, supra.*

9. Ana Marie Cox, *Washingtonienne Speaks!! Wonkette Exclusive!! Must Credit Wonkette!! The Washingtonienne Interview!!* Wonkette, May 21, 2004, http://www.wonkette.com/ politics/media/washingtonienne-speaks-wonkette-exclusive-must-credit-wonkette-the -washingtonienne-interview-9693.php.

10. http://www.jessicacutleronline.com/.

11. Witt, *Blog Interrupted, supra.*

12. Ana Marie Cox, *Biography Page,* Ana Marie Cox Website, http://www.anamariecox .com/bio.html.

13. In the interest of full disclosure, I have provided advice to Robert's counsel subsequent to his filing of the lawsuit. Before providing advice, I made it clear that I would continue to publicly express my opinions about the case regardless of whether they were critical of Robert's positions in the case. The opinions expressed about the case in this book are solely my own.

14. *Internal Affairs: Playboy.com Poses Questions to the Infamous Washington, D.C., Sex Blogger,* Playboy.com, Aug. 31, 2004, http://www.playboy.com/commerce/email/cyber club/08_31_04/story/dcintern_pop.html.

15. Witt, *Blog Interrupted, supra.*

16. Orin Kerr, *When Professors Read Pseudonymous Student Blogs,* Volokh Conspiracy, Apr. 26, 2005, http://volokh.com/archives/archive_2005_04_24-2005_04_30.shtml#111454088o.

17. Anonymous George Washington University Law School Student, *Hoist By My Own Petard,* Idlegrasshopper, Apr. 20, 2005, http://idlegrasshopper.blogspot.com/2005/04/ hoist-by-my-own-petard.html.

18. *Former Boston Herald Columnist Fired from Teaching Job,* Associated Press, July 19, 2005.

19. *More Midterm Meltdowns,* The Phantom Professor, Feb. 25, 2005, at http://phantom prof.blogspot.com/2005_05_01_phantomprof_archive.html. This post has been removed from the website.

20. *Office Hours,* The Phantom Professor, May 3, 2005, http://phantomprof.blogspot.com/ 2005_05_01_phantomprof_archive.html.

21. Scott Jaschik, *The Phantom Professor,* Inside Higher Education, May 11, 2005, http://www.insidehighered.com/news/2005/05/11/phantom.

22. *Id.*

23. Colleen McCain Nelson, *SMU Blogger Unmasked, Unemployed,* Dallas Morning News, May 15, 2005.

24. *Id.*

25. Jaschik, *Phantom Professor, supra.*

26. *Id.*

27. *Id.*

28. *Id.*

29. Daniel J. Solove, *The Virtues of Knowing Less: Justifying Privacy Protections Against Disclosure,* 53 Duke L.J. 967, 1005–6 (2003); *see also* David Bauder, *Identifying Rape Victims Troubles Media,* Ft. Lauderdale Sun-Sentinel, Aug. 3, 2002, at 3A.

30. Fernanda B. Viegas, *Bloggers' Expectations of Privacy and Accountability: An Initial Survey,* Journal of Computer-Mediated Communication, vol. 10, issue 3 (2005), http:// jcmc.Indiana.edu/vol10/issue3/viegas.html.

31. Quoted in *id.*

32. Eric Hsu, *Students' Web Sites Put Schools in Quandary,* Bergen (N.J.) Record, July 24, 2005.

33. H. J. Cummins, *When Blogs and Jobs Collide,* Minneapolis Star Tribune, Aug. 14, 2005.

34. Bob Sullivan, *Kids, Blogs, and Too Much Information,* MSNBC.com, Apr. 29, 2005, http://www.msnbc.msn.com/id/7668788/.

35. MALCOLM GLADWELL, THE TIPPING POINT 7, 9, 30–33, 35, 58–59 (2000).

36. *Id.* at 25.

37. ALBERT-LÁSZLÓ BARABÁSI, LINKED 31, 34 (2002).

38. Aaron Ben Ze'ev, *The Vindication of Gossip, in* GOOD GOSSIP 1, 22, 24 (Robert F. Goodman & Aaron Ben-Ze'ev, eds. 1994)

39. JÖRG R. BERGMANN, DISCREET INDISCRETIONS: THE SOCIAL ORGANIZATION OF GOSSIP 21–22 (1993).

40. KEITH DEVLIN, THE MATH GENE 255 (2000).

41. Sally Engle Merry, *Rethinking Gossip and Scandal, in* REPUTATION: STUDIES IN THE VOLUNTARY ELICITATION OF GOOD CONDUCT 47 (Daniel B. Klein, ed. 1997).

42. Nicholas Emler, *Gossip, Reputation, and Social Adaptation, in* GOOD GOSSIP, *supra*, at 117, 135.

43. KAREN J. BRISON, JUST TALK: GOSSIP, MEETINGS, AND POWER IN A PAPUA NEW GUINEA VILLAGE 11 (1992). When gossip occurs behind people's backs, rumors often "circulate unchecked" and are hard to combat if "diffuse and hidden." *Id.* at 12.

44. Diane L. Zimmerman, *Requiem for a Heavyweight: A Farewell to Warren and Brandeis's Privacy Tort*, 68 Cornell L. Rev. 291, 333–34 (1983).

45. This argument is frequently raised in support of outing gays. *See, e.g.*, Kathleen Guzman, *About Outing: Public Discourse, Private Lives*, 73 Wash. U. L.Q. 1531, 1568 (1995) ("Outers offer up the victim as a 'sacrificial lamb' to portray themselves as purifying redeemers, able to solve the problems of discrimination."). Outing gays, the argument goes, will help alter society's perception of gays by demonstrating that mainstream people or role models are gay. For more background on outing, see John P. Elwood, Note, *Outing, Privacy, and the First Amendment*, 102 Yale L.J. 747, 776 (1992) (arguing that outing to establish a person as a gay role model should be outweighed by privacy rights, whereas outing to point out the hypocrisy of public officials should be permitted).

46. BRISON, JUST TALK, *supra*, at 112.

47. MARTIN HEIDEGGER, BEING AND TIME 158 (Joan Stambaugh, trans. 1996) (originally published in 1953).

48. PATRICIA MEYER SPACKS, GOSSIP 4 (1985).

49. BRISON, JUST TALK, *supra*, at 12. Professor Cynthia Kierner observes that gossiping was a way to "jockey for social position" in postrevolutionary America. CYNTHIA A. KIERNER, SCANDAL AT BIZARRE: RUMOR AND REPUTATION IN JEFFERSON'S AMERICA 64 (2004).

50. Robert Post, *The Legal Regulation of Gossip: Backyard Chatter and the Mass Media, in* GOOD GOSSIP, *supra*, at 65, 65.

51. Paul M. Schwartz, *Internet Privacy and the State*, 32 Conn. L. Rev. 815, 843 (2000).

52. *Id.* at 842–43.

53. RICHARD A. POSNER, THE ECONOMICS OF JUSTICE 232–34 (1981).

54. STEVEN L. NOCK, THE COSTS OF PRIVACY: SURVEILLANCE AND REPUTATION IN AMER-ICA 11–12 (1993).

55. *Id.* at 124.

56. JEFFREY ROSEN, THE UNWANTED GAZE: THE DESTRUCTION OF PRIVACY IN AMERICA 8 (2000); *see also* Lawrence Lessig, *Privacy and Attention Span*, 89 Geo. L.J. 2063, 2065 (2001).

57. KAREL ČAPEK, *The Last Judgment, in* TALES FROM TWO POCKETS 159–60 (Norma Comrada, trans. 1994) (1929).

58. WILLIAM H. GASS, FICTION AND THE FIGURES OF LIFE 45 (1979); *see also* Georg Simmel, *The Sociology of Secrecy and of Secret Societies*, 11 American Journal of Sociology 441, 442 (1906) (we "never can absolutely know another" but form our conception of others based on "fragments").

59. WILLIAM JAMES, THE PRINCIPLES OF PSYCHOLOGY 282 (Harvard U. Press edition 1983) (originally published in 1890). Virginia Woolf embraced this pluralistic conception of selfhood in her novel *Orlando:* "Biography is considered complete if it merely accounts for six or seven selves, whereas a person may well have as many as a thousand." VIRGINIA WOOLF, ORLANDO: A BIOGRAPHY (1928).

60. ERVING GOFFMAN, THE PRESENTATION OF SELF IN EVERYDAY LIFE (1959); *see also* ALAN WESTIN, PRIVACY AND FREEDOM 33 (1967).

61. Roy F. Baumeister, *An Overview, in* THE SELF IN SOCIAL PSYCHOLOGY 1, 8 (Roy F. Baumeister, ed. 1999).

62. Quoted in Philip Roth, *In Defense of Intimacy: Milan Kundera's Private Lives,* Village Voice, June 26, 1984, at 42.

63. JOSEPH BENSMAN & ROBERT LILIENFELD, BETWEEN PUBLIC AND PRIVATE: LOST BOUNDARIES OF THE SELF 174 (1979).

64. *Id.* at 49.

65. MILAN KUNDERA, TESTAMENTS BETRAYED 260–61 (1995).

66. HANNAH ARENDT, THE HUMAN CONDITION 22–24 (1958).

67. ARNOLD M. LUDWIG, HOW DO WE KNOW WHO WE ARE? A BIOGRAPHY OF THE SELF 49 (1997).

68. ERVING GOFFMAN, STIGMA: NOTES ON THE MANAGEMENT OF SPOILED IDENTITY 96 (1963).

69. *Id.*

70. LUDWIG, HOW DO WE KNOW WHO WE ARE? *supra,* at 117.

71. THOMAS NAGEL, CONCEALMENT AND EXPOSURE & OTHER ESSAYS 7 (2002).

72. GOFFMAN, STIGMA, *supra,* at 3, 7–9, 30.

73. SUSAN SONTAG, ILLNESS AS METAPHOR AND AIDS AND ITS METAPHORS 38, 143, 6, 58 (1990).

74. Stan Karas, *Privacy, Identity, Databases,* 52 Am. U. L. Rev. 393, 427 (2002).

75. Paul M. Schwartz, *Privacy and the Economics of Personal Health Care Information,* 76 Tex. L. Rev. 1, 29 (1997).

76. *See, e.g.,* Richard H. McAdams, *Cooperation and Conflict: The Economics of Group Status Production and Race Discrimination,* 108 Harv. L. Rev. 1003 (1995) (reviewing market-based theories of racial discrimination).

77. Pauline T. Kim, *Genetic Discrimination, Genetic Privacy: Rethinking Employee Protections for a Brave New Workplace,* 96 Nw. U. L. Rev. 1497, 1500, 1538 (2002).

78. *R.I.P. Jennicam,* BBC, Jan. 1, 2004, http://news.bbc.co.uk/2/hi/uk_news/magazine/3360063.stm.

79. ALAN F. WESTIN, PRIVACY AND FREEDOM 35 (1967).

80. AMITAI ETZIONI, THE LIMITS OF PRIVACY 196 (1999).

81. FRED CATE, PRIVACY IN THE INFORMATION AGE 30 (1997).

82. Robert C. Post, *The Social Foundations of Privacy: Community and Self in the Common Law Tort,* 77 Calif. L. Rev. 957, 968 (1989).

83. Robert C. Post, *Three Concepts of Privacy,* 89 Geo. L.J. 2087, 2092 (2001).

84. PETER GAY, SCHNITZLER'S CENTURY: THE MAKING OF MIDDLE-CLASS CULTURE, 1815–1914, at 273 (2002).

85. ARNOLD H. MODELL, THE PRIVATE SELF 95 (1993).

86. Lawrence M. Friedman, *Name Robbers: Privacy, Blackmail, and Assorted Matters in Legal History*, 30 Hofstra L. Rev. 1093, 1112 (2002).

87. JOHN DEWEY, EXPERIENCE AND NATURE 167 (Jo Ann Boydston, ed. 1987) (originally published in 1925); *see also* JOHN DEWEY, HUMAN NATURE AND CONDUCT 97 (Jo Ann Boydston, ed. 1988) (originally published in 1922) (discussing "the difference between a self taken as something already made and a self still making through action"). As the psychologist Carl Schneider notes, protection against disclosure is similar to the skin of a fruit or the shell of an egg. CARL D. SCHNEIDER, SHAME, EXPOSURE, AND PRIVACY 37 (1992); *see also* David L. Bazelon, *Probing Privacy*, 12 Gonz. L. Rev. 587, 590 (1977) ("[P]rivacy shelters the emerging individual's thoughts from public disclosure and control so that the fear of being watched, exposed, ridiculed, or penalized does not crush the seeds of independent thinking before they can mature.").

88. FRIEDRICH DÜRRENMATT, THE ASSIGNMENT 24 (Joel Agee, trans., Random House 1988).

89. SECRETARY'S ADVISORY COMMITTEE ON AUTOMATED PERSONAL DATA SYSTEMS, U.S. DEP'T OF HEALTH, EDUCATION & WELFARE, RECORDS, COMPUTERS, AND THE RIGHTS OF CITIZENS (1973), http://aspe.os.dhhs.gov/datacncl/1973privacy/tocprefacemembers .htm.

90. *See generally* T. Markus Funk, *The Dangers of Hiding Criminal Pasts*, 66 Tenn. L. Rev. 287 (1998) (arguing that expunging certain juvenile crimes from a person's record is a mistake).

91. Sarah Bilder, *The Struggle over Immigration: Indentured Servants, Slaves, and Articles of Commerce*, 61 Mo. L. Rev. 743, 756–57 (1996).

92. *See* Funk, *Hiding Criminal Pasts*, at 288 (suggesting that state laws permitting the expunging of juvenile criminal records are "grounded on a belief that juveniles will outgrow their reckless youthful behavior").

93. People v. Price, 431 N.W.2d 524, 526 (Mich. Ct. App. 1988).

94. Merry, *Rethinking Gossip and Scandal, supra*, at 47.

95. LEORA TANENBAUM, SLUT! GROWING UP FEMALE WITH A BAD REPUTATION xvi, xv (2000).

96. ANITA L. ALLEN, WHY PRIVACY ISN'T EVERYTHING: FEMINIST REFLECTIONS ON PERSONAL ACCOUNTABILITY 2 (2003).

CHAPTER 4. SHAMING AND THE DIGITAL SCARLET LETTER

1. Nate Kushner, *Laura K. Krishna Is Just a Dumb Kid With a Nice Mom*, A Week of Kindness, March 30, 2005, http://www.aweekofkindness.com/blog/archives/2005/ 03/laura_k_krishna_1.html. Kushner changed Laura's real last name to Krishna after pleas from Laura and her mother to take the information offline.

2. PZ Myers, *A Plagiarist Gets Her Comeuppance*, Pharyngula, Mar. 29, 2005, http:// pharyngula.org/index/weblog/comments/a_plagiarist_gets_her_comeuppance/. Myers's blog is now located at http://scienceblogs.com/pharyngula/.

3. http://peoriacrackhouse.blogspot.com.

4. Post of July 22, 2005 by Anonymous, Peoria Crack House, http://peoriacrack-house.blogspot.com/2005_07_01_peoriacrackhouse_archive.html.

5. Tracy Connor, *Hunt Perv Caught in a Flash,* N.Y. Daily News, Aug. 26, 2005.

6. *Photo Finish for Flashers,* N.Y. Daily News, Aug. 28, 2005.

7. *Man Caught on Camera Phone Flashing Subway Rider,* Associated Press, Sept. 1, 2005.

8. Kevin Poulsen, *Camera Phone Has Life After Theft,* Wired, Aug. 29, 2005, http://www.wired.com/news/privacy/0,1848,68668,00.html.

9. *Id.*

10. JohnsGoat, *Long Island Trash . . . ,* Long Island Press Electronic Bulletin Board, Aug. 21, 2005, http://www.longislandpress.com/bb/viewtopic.php?p=2037. The post and comments have been removed and can no longer be found on the Internet. I have an archive copy of the post and comments on file.

11. Poulsen, *Camera Phone Theft, supra.*

12. JohnsGoat, *Long Island Trash, supra.*

13. Michael B. Conforti, *To Catch a Thief: Cell Phone Theft Spawns E-Harassment,* Long Island Press, Sept. 1, 2005, http://longislandpress.com/?cp=162&show=article&a_id=5538.

14. JohnsGoat, *Long Island Trash, supra.*

15. *Id.*

16. *Id.*

17. Jim Heid, *The Apple Store Squatter Saga Continues,* Jim Heid's Macintosh Digital Hub, July 11, 2005, http://www.macilife.com/2005/07/apple-store-squatter-saga-continues.html.

18. Steve Rubel, *Is Anyone's Privacy Safe from the Bloggers,* MicroPersuasion, Aug. 3, 2005, http://www.micropersuasion.com/2005/08/is_anyones_priv.html.

19. For background about norms, see ROBERT ELLICKSON, ORDER WITHOUT LAW (1991); Lawrence Lessig, *The Regulation of Social Meaning,* 62 U. Chi. L. Rev. 943 (1995); Richard McAdams, *Cooperation and Conflict: The Economics of Group Status Production and Race Discrimination,* 108 Harv. L. Rev. 1003 (1997); Richard McAdams, *The Origin, Development, and Regulation of Norms,* 96 Mich. L. Rev. 338 (1997); Cass Sunstein, *Social Norms and Social Roles,* 96 Colum. L. Rev. 903 (1996); Lior Strahilevitz, *How Changes in Property Regimes Influence Social Norms: Commodifying California's Carpool Lanes,* 17 Ind. L.J. 1231 (2000); Robert C. Ellickson, *The Evolution of Social Norms: A Perspective from the Legal Academy, in* SOCIAL NORMS 35, 35 (Michael Hechter & Karl-Dieter Opp, eds. 2001).

20. Richard Weste, *The Booke of Demeanor and the Allowance and Disallowance of Certaine Misdemeanors in Companie* (c. 1619). Quoted in NORBERT ELIAS, THE CIVILIZING PROCESS 112 (1994).

21. Rachel Metz, *Cell-Phone Shushing Gets Creative,* Wired.com, Jan. 18, 2005, http://www.wired.com/news/wireless/0,1382,66310,00.html.

22. Christine Rosen, *Our Cell Phones, Ourselves,* New Atlantis (Summer 2004).

23. *Id.*

24. The commercials are available at http://icpm.8m.com/.

25. Henry David Thoreau, Walden and Other Writings 113 (Barnes & Noble, Inc. 1993) (originally published in 1854).

26. Alain Corbin, *Intimate Relations, in* A History of the Private Life, vol. 4, From the Fires of Revolution to the Great War 605 (Michelle Perrot, ed., Arthur Goldhammer, trans. 1990); Michelle Perrot, *The Family Triumphant, id.* at 143.

27. Anita L. Allen, *Lying to Protect Privacy,* 44 Vill. L. Rev. 161, 162 (1991).

28. Metz, *Cell-Phone Shushing, supra.* The cards are available at http://www.coudal.com/shhh.php.

29. Carl D. Schneider, Shame, Exposure, and Privacy 22–26 (1992).

30. http://rudepeople.com.

31. http://platewire.com.

32. Jennifer Saranow, *The Snoop Next Door,* Wall St. Journal, Jan. 12, 2007, at W1.

33. http://flickr.com/photos/uno4300/345254682/; http://flickr.com/photos/nojja/205062960/; http://flickr.com/photos/caterina/59500/.

34. *See, e.g.,* Orn B. Bodvarsson & William A. Gibson, *An Economic Approach to Tips and Service Quality: Results of a Survey,* 36 Social Science Journal 137–47 (1999); Orn B. Bodvarsson & William A. Gibson, *Economics and Restaurant Gratuities: Determining Tip Rates,* 56 Amer. J. Econ. Sociology, 187–204 (1997); April H. Crusco & Christopher G. Wetzel, *The Midas Touch: The Effects of Interpersonal Touch on Restaurant Tipping,* 10 Personality & Social Psychology Bulletin 512–17 (1984); Mary B. Harris, *Waiters, Customers, and Service: Some Tips About Tipping,* 25 Journal of Applied Social Psychology 725–44 (1995).

35. Ofer H. Azar, *The Social Norm of Tipping: A Review,* Journal of Economics, at 3 (2005) http://econwpa.wustl.edu:80/eps/othr/papers/0503/0503013.pdf.

36. http://www.bitterwaitress.com.

37. http://www.bitterwaitress.com/std/index.html?detail=1&id=2135.

38. http://www.bitterwaitress.com/std/index.html?detail=1&id=2120.

39. Katherine Rosman, *Leak Chic: Everybody's an Anonymous Source These Days,* Wall St. Journal, Dec. 15, 2005.

40. http://www.hollabacknyc.blogspot.com.

41. http://dontdatehimgirl.com/.

42. http://dontdatehimgirl.com/about_us/index.html.

43. http://dontdatehimgirl.com/faqs/.

44. Edwin Powers, Crime and Punishment in Early Massachusetts, 1620–1692, at 200 (1966).

45. Mark Spatz, Comment, *Shame's Revival: An Unconstitutional Regression,* 4 U. Pa. J. Const. L. 827, 831 (2002).

46. Powers, Crime and Punishment, *supra,* at 270 (1966); Raphael Semmes, Crime and Punishment in Early Maryland 70 (1938).

47. Lawrence M. Friedman, Crime and Punishment in American History 40 (1993).

48. Francis Watt, The Law's Lumber Room 48, 56 (1898).

49. William Andrews, Punishments in Oldentime: Being an Historical Account of the Ducking Stool, Brank, Pillory, Stocks, Drunkard's Cloak, Whipping Post, Riding the Stang, etc. 5 (Research Publications 1990 on microfiche) (originally published in 1881).

50. Dan Markel, *Are Shaming Punishments Beautifully Retributive? Retributivism and the Implications for the Alternative Sanctions Debate,* 54 Vand. L. Rev. 2157, 2169 (2001).

51. NATHANIEL HAWTHORNE, THE SCARLET LETTER 46, 47 (Barnes & Noble edition, 1998) (originally published in 1850).

52. Barbara Clare Morton, *Bringing Skeletons Out of the Closet and Into the Light: "Scarlet Letter" Sentencing Can Meet the Goals of Probation in Modern America Because It Deprives Offenders of Privacy,* 35 Suffolk U. L. Rev. 97, 102–4 (2001); Toni M. Massaro, *Shame, Culture, and American Criminal Law,* 89 Mich. L. Rev. 1880, 1912–15 (1991).

53. Morton, *Skeletons, supra,* at 102–4.

54. Markel, *Shaming Punishments, supra,* at 2169.

55. MICHEL FOUCAULT, DISCIPLINE AND PUNISH: THE BIRTH OF THE PRISON (Alan Sheridan, trans., Pantheon edition 1977).

56. Jeff Stryker, *Using Shame as Punishment: Have Sex, Get Infamous,* S.F. Chronicle, Mar. 13, 2005.

57. Dan M. Kahan, *What Do Alternative Sanctions Mean?* 63 U. Chi. L. Rev. 591, 632 (1996).

58. John Borland, *Privacy Jam on California Highway,* CNET, May 13, 2004, http://news .com.com/Privacy+jam+on+California+highway/2100-1038_3-5212280.html.

59. Eugene Volokh, *Appalling Service from Dell,* Volokh Conspiracy, Nov. 23, 2005, http://volokh.com/posts/1132781578.shtml.

60. Matthew Fordahl, *Sony to Release Patch to Reveal Hidden Copy-Protection Software,* Associated Press, Nov. 2, 2005.

61. Mark Russinovich, *Sony Rootkits and Digital Rights Management Gone Too Far,* Mark's Sysinternals Blog, Oct. 31, 2005, http://blogs.technet.com/markrussinovich/archive/2005/10/31/sony-rootkits-and-digital-rights-management-gone-too-far.aspx.

62. Kim Hart, *Angry Customers Use Web to Shame Firms,* Wash. Post, July 5, 2006, at D1.

63. Lior Jacob Strahilevitz, *"How's My Driving?" for Everyone (and Everything?),* 81 N.Y.U. L. Rev. 1699, 1708–09 (2006).

64. The programs Strahilevitz recommends are a lot more controlled than much of the online shaming currently taking place.

65. MARTHA C. NUSSBAUM, HIDING FROM HUMANITY: DISGUST, SHAME, AND THE LAW 230, 235 (2004).

66. *Id.* at 235. For more on shame, see WILLIAM IAN MILLER, HUMILIATION (1993); *Shame,* Social Research, vol. 70, issue 4 (Winter 2003).

67. BERNARD WILLIAMS, SHAME AND NECESSITY 78 (1993) ("The basic experience connected with shame is that of being seen, inappropriately, by the wrong people, in the wrong condition. It is straightforwardly connected with nakedness.").

68. See Richard H. McAdams, *The Origin, Development, and Regulation of Norms,* 96 Mich. L. Rev. 338, 412 (1997).

69. NUSSBAUM, HIDING FROM HUMANITY, *supra,* at 234.

70. Ivan Moreno, *Pot Smokers on the Web,* Rocky Mountain News, Apr. 28, 2006, http:// www.rockymountainnews.com/drmn/local/article/0,1299,DRMN_15_4658379,00.html.

71. http://www.colorado.edu/police/420_Photo_Album/index.htm. The website has been removed from the Internet. I have a copy of the website in my files.

72. H. G. Reza, *When Blame Knocks on the Wrong Door*, L.A. Times, Aug. 25, 2005.

73. http://www.revengeworld.com.

74. http://www.revengeworld.com/About.cfm.

75. Rebecca Riddick, *Website Encourages Blacklist of Med-Mal Plaintiffs*, Law.com, July 25, 2006, http://www.law.com/jsp/article.jsp?id=1153744532499.

76. Robert D. Cooter, *Decentralized Law for a Complex Economy: The Structural Approach to Adjudicating the New Law Merchant*, 144 U. Pa. L. Rev. 1643 (1996).

77. Ofer H. Azar, *The Social Norm of Tipping: Does It Improve Social Welfare?* Journal of Economics, at 4 (2005), http://econwpa.wustl.edu:80/eps/othr/papers/0503/0503013.pdf.

78. Lawrence E. Mitchell, *Understanding Norms*, 49 U. Toronto L.J. 177, 243 (1999).

79. Borland, *Privacy Jam, supra.*

80. http://www.carpoolcheats.org/. The website is now completely removed from the Internet. Quotations from the website can be found at Borland, *Privacy Jam, supra.*

81. http://www.christiangallery.com/atrocity/.

82. Frederick Clarkson, *Journalists or Terrorists?*, Salon.com, May 31, 2001, http://archive.salon.com/news/feature/2001/05/31/nuremberg/index.html.

83. Rene Sanchez, *Abortion Foes' Internet Site on Trial*, Wash. Post, Jan. 15, 1999, at A3.

84. Sharon Lerner, *The Nuremberg Menace*, Village Voice, Apr. 4–10, 2001, http://www.villagevoice.com/news/0114,lerner,23570,1.html.

85. *Doctor Says Anti-Abortion Web Site Endangered Her Life*, Associated Press, Jan. 8, 1999, http://www.cnn.com/US/9901/08/abortion.trial.03/.

86. Planned Parenthood v. American Coalition of Life Activists, 290 F.3d 1058 (9th Cir. 2002) (en banc).

87. Strahilevitz, *"How's My Driving?" supra*, at 1708.

88. Gustave Le Bon, The Crowd: A Study of the Popular Mind 1 (1896).

89. Cass R. Sunstein, *Group Judgments: Statistical Means, Deliberation, and Information Markets*, 80 N.Y.U. L. Rev. 962, 1004 (2005).

90. Howard W. French, *Online Throngs Impose a Stern Morality in China*, N.Y. Times, June 3, 2006.

CHAPTER 5. THE ROLE OF LAW

1. David Brin, The Transparent Society 8–9 (1998).

2. Quoted in Daniel J. Solove, Marc Rotenberg & Paul M. Schwartz, Information Privacy Law 635 (2d ed. 2006).

3. Robert Ellis Smith, Ben Franklin's Web Site: Privacy and Curiosity from Plymouth Rock to the Internet 108–9 (2000).

4. *Id.* at 108–10.

5. Charles Dickens, Martin Chuzzlewit 318 (Penguin edition 1975) (originally published in 1843–44).

6. Gini Graham Scott, Mind Your Own Business: The Battle for Personal Privacy 37–38 (1995).

7. Henry James, The Reverberator 62 (1888).

8. Quoted in SMITH, BEN FRANKLIN'S WEBSITE, *supra,* at 117. For an extensive and interesting account of gossip about U.S. presidents and politicians, see GAIL COLLINS, SCORPION TONGUES: GOSSIP, CELEBRITY, AND AMERICAN POLITICS (1998).

9. JANNA MALAMUD SMITH, PRIVATE MATTERS 81 (1997).

10. RICHARD WIGHTMAN FOX, TRIALS OF INTIMACY: LOVE AND LOSS IN THE BEECHER-TILTON SCANDAL 20–21 (1999).

11. JOHN D'EMILIO & ESTELLE B. FREEDMAN, INTIMATE MATTERS: A HISTORY OF SEXUALITY IN AMERICA 162–63 (2d ed. 1997). Other accounts state that Woodhull was motivated by more personal reasons. One commentator concludes that "Woodhull published the story because she was angry at one of Beecher's sisters, who opposed including her in the suffrage leadership." COLLINS, SCORPION TONGUES, *supra,* at 68.

12. SMITH, PRIVATE MATTERS, *supra,* at 73–94.

13. FOX, TRIALS OF INTIMACY, *supra,* at 33.

14. Daniel J. Solove, *Reconstructing Electronic Surveillance Law,* 72 Geo. Wash. L. Rev. 1264, 1272 (2004).

15. SMITH, BEN FRANKLIN'S WEBSITE, *supra,* at 124.

16. E. L. Godkin, *The Rights of the Citizen: IV. To His Own Reputation,* Scribner's Magazine (1890); *see also* E. L. Godkin, *The Right to Privacy,* The Nation, Dec. 25, 1890. For more background about Godkin, see Elbridge L. Adams, *The Right to Privacy and Its Relation to the Law of Libel,* 39 Am. L. Rev. 37 (1905); Dorothy J. Glancy, *The Invention of the Right to Privacy,* 21 Ariz. L. Rev. 1 (1979).

17. DON R. PEMBER: PRIVACY AND THE PRESS 21 (1972).

18. *See* Samuel D. Warren & Louis D. Brandeis, *The Watuppa Pond Cases,* 2 Harv. L. Rev. 195 (1888); Samuel D. Warren & Louis D. Brandeis, *The Law of Ponds,* 3 Harv. L. Rev. 1 (1889).

19. Samuel D. Warren & Louis D. Brandeis, *The Right to Privacy,* 4 Harv. L. Rev. 193 (1890).

20. William L. Prosser, *Privacy,* 48 Cal. L. Rev. 383, 383, 423 (1960).

21. James Barron, *Warren and Brandeis, The Right to Privacy, 4 Harv. L. Rev. 193 (1890): Demystifying a Landmark Citation,* 13 Suffolk U. L. Rev. 875, 893 (1979).

22. SMITH, BEN FRANKLIN'S WEB SITE, *supra,* at 118–19.

23. Warren & Brandeis, *The Right to Privacy, supra,* at 196, 195.

24. SMITH, PRIVATE MATTERS, *supra,* at 76 (1997).

25. *Id.* at 196–97.

26. See Neil M. Richards & Daniel J. Solove, *Privacy's Other Path: Recovering the Law of Confidentiality,* 96 Geo. L.J. (forthcoming Nov. 2007). The article is available online at http://ssrn.com/abstract=969495.

27. *See* Lake v. Wal-Mart Stores, Inc., 582 N.W.2d 231, 235 (Minn. 1998) (noting that Minnesota was one of the few states that had not recognized the privacy torts, but reversing course and embracing the torts). The only states not recognizing any of the privacy torts are North Dakota and Wyoming. ROBERT M. O'NEIL, THE FIRST AMENDMENT AND CIVIL LIABILITY 77 (2001).

28. Harry Kalven, Jr., *Privacy in Tort Law: Were Warren and Brandeis Wrong?* 31 L. & Contemp. Probs. 326, 327 (1966).

29. Alfred C. Yen, *Western Frontier or Feudal Society?: Metaphors and Perceptions of Cyberspace,* 17 Berkeley Tech. L.J. 1207 (2002).

30. John Perry Barlow, *Declaration of the Independence of Cyberspace,* Feb. 18, 1996, http://homes.eff.org/~barlow/Declaration-Final.html.

31. David R. Johnson & David Post, *Law and Borders: The Rise of Law in Cyberspace,* 48 Stan. L. Rev. 1367 (1996).

32. James Grimmelman, *Accidental Privacy Spills: Musings on Privacy, Democracy, and the Internet,* LawMeme, Feb. 19, 2003, http://research.yale.edu/lawmeme/modules.php ?name=News&file=article&sid=938.

33. Letter of Laurie Garrett, Feb. 17, 2003, in comments to *Could This Be True?* MetaFilter, Feb. 11, 2003, http://www.metafilter.com/mefi/23493.

34. Grimmelman, *Accidental Privacy Spills, supra.*

35. Michelle Andrews, *Decoding Myspace,* U.S. News & World Report, Sept. 18, 2006.

36. ACLU v. Miller, 977 F. Supp. 1228 (N.D. Ga. 1997).

37. Jennie C. Meade, *The Duel,* http://www.law.gwu.edu/Burns/rarebooks/exhibits/duel .htm.

38. Barbara Holland, Gentlemen's Blood: A History of Dueling 22 (2003).

39. Cynthia A. Kierner, Scandal at Bizarre: Rumor and Reputation in Jefferson's America 40 (2004).

40. Quoted in Alison L. LaCroix, *To Gain the Whole World and Lose His Own Soul: Nineteenth-Century American Dueling as Public Law and Private Code,* 33 Hofstra L. Rev. 501, 517 (2004).

41. Quoted in Douglas H. Yarn, *The Attorney as Duelist's Friend: Lessons from the Code Duello,* 51 Case W. Res. L. Rev. 69, 113 (2000).

42. Meade, *The Duel, supra.*

43. William Blackstone, Commentaries on the Laws of England, vol. IV, at *199 (1768).

44. C. A. Harwell Wells, Note, *The End of the Affair? Anti-Dueling Laws and Social Norms in Antebellum America,* 54 Vand. L. Rev. 1805, 1807, 1831–32 (2001).

45. Kierner, Scandal at Bizarre, *supra,* at 39.

46. Quoted in Holland, Gentlemen's Blood, *supra,* at 3.

47. As Hamilton explained: "The ability to be in the future useful, whether in resisting mischief or effecting good, in those crises of our public affairs which seem likely to happen, would probably be inseparable from a conformity with public prejudice in this particular." Alexander Hamilton, quoted in Meade, *The Duel, supra.*

48. Van Vechten Veeder, *The History and Theory of Defamation,* 3 Colum. L. Rev. 546, 548 (1903).

49. Kierner, Scandal at Bizarre, *supra,* at 40.

50. Wells, *Anti-Dueling Laws, supra,* at 1823.

51. Holland, Gentlemen's Blood, *supra,* at 3.

52. Kierner, Scandal at Bizarre, *supra,* at 39, 41.

53. *Id.* at 45.

54. *Id.* at 44, 42, 61.

55. LaCroix, *Dueling, supra,* at 511–12, 454, 547–50, 552. Lawrence Lessig notes that al-

though legal prohibitions on dueling were ineffective, another type of legal sanction "might actually have been more effective." People engaging in duels were restricted from holding public office. Since holding public office was "a duty of the elite," the restriction gave gentlemen a reason for "escaping the duel" without "appealing to self-interest or the rules of commoners." Lessig, however, concedes that "even this sanction was ineffective for much of the history of the old South" because legislatures "would grandfather all duels up to the time of the legislation and would repass the grandfather legislation every few years." Lawrence Lessig, *The Regulation of Social Meaning*, 62 U. Chi. L. Rev. 943, 971–72 (1995).

56. Wells, *Anti-Dueling Laws, supra,* at 1839.
57. David S. Parker, *Law, Honor, and Impunity in Spanish America: The Debate Over Dueling, 1870–1920,* 19 Law & Hist. Rev. 311, 319, 325 (2001).
58. LaCroix, *Dueling, supra,* at 515.
59. JOHN LYDE WILSON, THE CODE OF HONOR, OR RULES FOR THE GOVERNMENT OF PRINCIPALS AND SECONDS IN DUELLING 6 (1858), quoted in LaCroix, *Dueling, supra,* at 559.
60. LaCroix, *Dueling, supra,* at 565.
61. Madison v. Yunter, 589 P.2d 126, 130 (Mont. 1978).
62. Quoted in Joanne B. Freeman, *Slander, Poison, Whispers, and Fame: Jefferson's "Anas" and Political Gossip in the Early Republic,* 15 Journal of the Early Republic 25, 31 (1995).
63. Quoted in *id.* at 30.
64. Veeder, *History, supra,* at 563.
65. RODNEY A. SMOLLA, THE LAW OF DEFAMATION §1:2, at 1–4 (2d ed. 2000).
66. Veeder, *Defamation, supra,* at 548.
67. Restatement (Second) of Torts §559.
68. *Id.* at §578.
69. ZECHARIAH CHAFEE, GOVERNMENT AND MASS COMMUNICATION 106–7 (1947).
70. Rodney A. Smolla, *Dun & Bradstreet, Hepps, and Liberty Lobby: A New Analytic Primer on the Future Course of Defamation,* 75 Geo. L.J. 1519 (1987).
71. *See* Lake v. Wal-Mart Stores, Inc., 582 N.W.2d 231, 235 (Minn. 1998) (finally recognizing a common-law tort action for invasion of privacy, noting that Minnesota remained one of the few holdouts).
72. Restatement (Second) of Torts §652B.
73. Id. at §652E.
74. Id. at §652C.
75. Id. at §652C comment (c).
76. Id. at §652D.
77. Rodney A. Smolla, *Accounting for the Slow Growth of American Privacy Law,* 27 Nova L. Rev. 289, 289 (2002).
78. RICHARD A. POSNER, OVERCOMING LAW 545 (1995).
79. Doe v. Blue Cross & Blue Shield United of Wisconsin, 112 F.3d 869, 872 (7th Cir. 1997).
80. Mike, *Todd Hollis and Defamation Suits,* Crime & Federalism, June 8, 2006, http://federalism.typepad.com/crime_federalism/2006/06/todd_hollis_and.html.

81. Comment of mtneergal to Robert J. Ambrogi, *Don'tSueHerBoy,* Law.com Inside Opinions: Legal Blogs, June 30, 2006, http://legalblogwatch.typepad.com/legal_blog_watch/2006/06/dontsueherboy.html.

82. Comment of Big Larry to Robert J. Ambrogi, *id.*

83. Laura Parker, *Jury Awards $11.3M Over Defamatory Internet Posts,* USA Today, Oct. 11, 2006.

84. Jacob A. Stein, *Defamation,* Washington Lawyer (Nov. 2001).

85. Lyrissa Barnett Lidsky, *Silencing John Doe: Defamation and Discourse in Cyberspace,* 49 Duke L.J. 855, 857 (2000).

86. Robert N. Bellah, *The Meaning of Reputation in American Society,* 74 Cal. L. Rev. 743, 744 (1986).

87. Jerome A. Barron, *The Search for Media Accountability,* 19 Suffolk U. L. Rev. 789, 789–90 (1985).

88. Lyrissa Barnett Lidsky, *Defamation, Reputation, and the Myth of Community,* 71 Wash. L. Rev. 1, 14 (1996).

CHAPTER 6. FREE SPEECH, ANONYMITY, AND ACCOUNTABILITY

1. JOHN MILTON, AREOPAGITICA (George H. Sabine, ed. 1954) (originally published in 1644).

2. U.S. CONST. amend. I.

3. Cohen v. California, 403 U.S. 15, 24–25 (1971).

4. New York Times Co. v. Sullivan, 376 U.S. 254, 279–80 (1964).

5. Chaplinksy v. New Hampshire, 315 U.S. 568, 572 (1942).

6. New York Times Co. v. Sullivan, 376 U.S. 254, 271–72 (1964).

7. Gertz v. Robert Welch, Inc., 418 U.S. 323 (1974).

8. *Id.* at 342.

9. New York Times Co. v. Sullivan, 376 U.S. 254, 280 (1964).

10. Randall P. Bezanson, *The Developing Law of Editorial Judgment,* 78 Neb. L. Rev. 754, 774–75, 763–64 (1999).

11. Gertz v. Robert Welch, Inc., 418 U.S. 323, 340–41 (1974).

12. *Id.* at 341 (quoting Rosenblatt v. Baer, 383 U.S. 75, 92 (1966) (Stewart, J. concurring)).

13. William L. Prosser, *Privacy,* 48 Cal. L. Rev. 383, 423 (1960).

14. THOMAS I. EMERSON, THE SYSTEM OF FREEDOM OF EXPRESSION 556 (1970).

15. Eugene Volokh, *Freedom of Speech and Information Privacy: The Troubling Implications of a Right to Stop People from Speaking About You,* 52 Stan. L. Rev. 1049, 1050–51 (2000).

16. Laurent B. Frantz, *The First Amendment in the Balance,* 71 Yale L.J. 1424, 1424 (1962); Alexander Meiklejohn, *The First Amendment Is an Absolute,* 1961 Sup. Ct. Rev. 245, 246.

17. Konigsberg v. State Bar of Cal., 366 U.S. 36, 61, 63 (1961) (Black, J., dissenting).

18. Hugo L. Black, *The Bill of Rights,* 35 N.Y.U. L. Rev. 865, 867 (1960).

19. Elizabeth S. Black, *Hugo Black: A Memorial Portrait,* The Supreme Court Historical Society (1982), http://www.supremecourthistory.org/04_library/subs_volumes/04_c17_j.html.

20. T. Alexander Aleinikoff, *Constitutional Law in the Age of Balancing,* 96 Yale L.J. 943, 943 (1987).

21. *See, e.g.,* Sable Communications, Inc. v. FCC, 492 U.S. 115, 126 (1989) (striking down a ban on indecent dial-a-porn services under strict scrutiny).

22. Gerald Gunther, *The Supreme Court, 1971 Term—Foreword: In Search of Evolving Doctrine on a Changing Court: A Model for a Newer Equal Protection,* 86 Harv. L. Rev. 1, 8 (1972).

23. Volokh, *Freedom of Speech, supra,* at 1083–84.

24. *See, e.g.,* Dun & Bradstreet, Inc. v. Greenmoss Builders, Inc., 472 U.S. 749, 758 (1985) ("We have long recognized that not all speech is of equal First Amendment importance."). Cass Sunstein has argued that a workable system of free speech depends upon "making distinctions between low and high value speech, however difficult and unpleasant that task may be." Cass R. Sunstein, *Low Value Speech Revisited,* 83 Nw. U. L. Rev. 555, 557 (1989).

25. Ohralik v. Ohio State Bar Ass'n, 436 U.S. 447, 456 (1978).

26. Dun & Bradstreet, Inc. v. Greenmoss Builders, Inc., 472 U.S. 749, 758–59 (1985) (quoting First Nat'l Bank of Boston v. Bellotti, 435 U.S. 765, 776 (1978)).

27. Although the Supreme Court has applied strict scrutiny to restrictions on speech of public concern, it has not done so to restrictions on speech of private concern. *See, e.g.,* Florida Star v. B.J.F., 491 U.S. 524, 532 (1989) (refusing "to hold broadly that truthful publication may never be punished consistent with the First Amendment. Our cases have carefully eschewed reaching this ultimate question."); Bartnicki v. Vopper, 532 U.S. 514, 529 (2001) (noting that the Court has "repeated refusal to answer categorically whether truthful publication may ever be punished consistent with the First Amendment.").

28. Diane L. Zimmerman, *Requiem for a Heavyweight: A Farewell to Warren and Brandeis's Privacy Tort,* 68 Cornell L. Rev. 291, 294, 362 (1983).

29. *See, e.g.,* C. Edwin Baker, *Scope of the First Amendment Freedom of Speech,* 25 UCLA L. Rev. 964, 990–1009 (1978) (explaining three theoretical models addressing the scope of First Amendment speech protection); Richard H. Fallon, Jr., *Two Senses of Autonomy,* 46 Stan. L. Rev. 875 (1994) (asserting and applying two theories relating to the autonomy-based First Amendment doctrine); Martin H. Redish, *The Value of Free Speech,* 130 U. Pa. L. Rev. 591, 593 (1982) ("[F]ree speech ultimately serves only one true value, which I have labeled 'individual self-realization.' ").

30. Sean M. Scott, *The Hidden First Amendment Values of Privacy,* 71 Wash. L. Rev. 683, 723 (1996).

31. *See* Paul M. Schwartz, *Privacy and Democracy in Cyberspace,* 52 Vand. L. Rev. 1609, 1665 (1999) (noting that privacy shapes "the extent to which certain actions or expressions of identity are encouraged or discouraged").

32. Julie E. Cohen, *Examined Lives: Informational Privacy and the Subject as Object,* 52 Stan. L. Rev. 1373, 1426 (2000); *see also* Anita L. Allen, Uneasy Access: Privacy for Women in a Free Society 44 (1988) ("The value of privacy is, in part, that it can enable moral persons to be self-determining individuals."); Ruth Gavison, *Privacy and the Limits of Law,* 89 Yale L.J. 421, 455 (1980) ("Privacy is also essential to democratic gov-

ernment because it fosters and encourages the moral autonomy of the citizen, a central requirement of a democracy.").

33. Richard S. Murphy, *Property Rights in Personal Information: An Economic Defense of Privacy,* 84 Geo. L.J. 2381, 2397 (1996).

34. ALAN F. WESTIN, PRIVACY AND FREEDOM 37 (1967).

35. *See* ALEXANDER MEIKLEJOHN, POLITICAL FREEDOM: THE CONSTITUTIONAL POWERS OF THE PEOPLE 26, 154–55 (1960).

36. Owen M. Fiss, *Free Speech and Social Structure,* 71 Iowa L. Rev. 1405, 1411 (1986).

37. Quoted in John H. Summers, *What Happened to Sex Scandals? Politics and Peccadilloes, Jefferson to Kennedy,* 87 Journal of American History 825, 826 (2000).

38. As Keith Boone contends: "Privacy seems vital to a democratic society [because] it underwrites the freedom to vote, to hold political discussions, and to associate freely away from the glare of the public eye and without fear of reprisal." C. Keith Boone, *Privacy and Community,* 9 Soc. Theory & Prac. 1, 8 (1983).

39. JOHN STUART MILL, ON LIBERTY 18 (David Spitz, ed. 1975) (originally published in 1859).

40. Abrams v. United States, 250 U.S. 616, 630 (1919) (Holmes, J., dissenting).

41. Frederick Schauer, *Reflections on the Value of Truth,* 41 Case W. Res. L. Rev. 699, 706 (1991); *see also* Anita L. Allen, *The Power of Private Facts,* 41 Case W. Res. L. Rev. 757, 766 (1991) (arguing that allocations of power can sometimes be more valuable than the protection of true speech); Julie E. Cohen, *Privacy, Ideology, and Technology: A Response to Jeffrey Rosen,* 89 Geo. L.J. 2029, 2036 (2001) ("The belief that more personal information always reveals more truth is ideology, not fact, and must be recognized as such for informational privacy to have a chance."). For a critique of Schauer's position, see Erwin Chemerinsky, *In Defense of Truth,* 41 Case W. Res. L. Rev. 745 (1991).

42. Pearse v. Pearse, 63 Eng. Rep. 950, 957 (Ch. 1846) (Bruce, V.C.).

43. Restatement (Second) of Torts §652D.

44. *Id.* at § 652D cmt. d.

45. *Id.* at § 652D cmt. h.

46. See Michaels v. Internet Entertainment Group, Inc., 5 F. Supp. 2d 823, 837 (C.D. Cal. 1998) (acknowledging the president of Internet Entertainment Group's estimate that the company would lose one third of its $1,495,000 subscription revenue without the Bret Michaels and Pamela Anderson sex video).

47. Barber v. Time, Inc. 159 S.W.2d 291, 295 (Mo. 1942).

48. Shulman v. Group W. Productions, Inc., 955 P.2d 469 (Cal. 1998).

49. Zimmerman, *Requiem, supra,* at 357 (recognizing the argument that editors of an article have a right to strengthen the force of their evidence by naming names).

50. Bonome v. Kaysen, 32 Media L. Rep. 1520 (Mass. Super. 2004).

51. *Id.*

52. http://underneaththeirrobes.blogs.com/.

53. Article III Groupie, *Hotties in the Holding Pen: Untimely SFJ Nominations,* Underneath Their Robes, July 17, 2004, http://underneaththeirrobes.blogs.com/main/2004/06/greetings_welco.html.

54. Jeffrey Toobin, *SCOTUS Watch,* New Yorker, Nov. 21, 2005, http://www.newyorker.com/talk/content/articles/051121ta_talk_toobin.

55. Jonathan Miller, *He Fought the Law. They Both Won,* N.Y. Times, Jan. 22, 2006, at sec. 14NJ, at 1.

56. Will Baude, *The Other 10 Questions for Article III Groupie,* Crescat Sententia, Aug. 29, 2005, http://www.crescatsententia.org/archives/2005_08_29.html#005865.

57. Comment to Orin Kerr, *Article III Groupie Comes Out of the Closet,* Volokh Conspiracy, Nov. 14, 2005, http://volokh.com/posts/1131979281.shtml.

58. Miller, *He Fought the Law, supra.*

59. Amanda Lenhart & Susannah Fox, *Bloggers: A Portrait of the Internet's New Storytellers,* Pew Internet & American Life Project, July 19, 2006, http://www.pewinternet.org/pdfs/PIP%20Bloggers%20Report%20July%2019%202006.pdf.

60. Talley v. California, 362 U.S. 60 (1960).

61. SMITH, BEN FRANKLIN'S WEB SITE, *supra,* at 41–43.

62. McIntyre v. Ohio Elect. Comm'n, 514 U.S. 334, 342–43 (1995).

63. Gary T. Marx, *Identity and Anonymity: Some Conceptual Distinctions and Issues for Research,* in DOCUMENTING INDIVIDUAL IDENTITY 311, 316, 318 (Jane Caplan and John Torpey, eds. 2001).

64. A. Michael Froomkin, *Flood Control on the Information Ocean: Living with Anonymity, Digital Cash, and Distributed Databases,* 15 J.L. & Comm. 395, 408 (1996).

65. ADAM SMITH, THE WEALTH OF NATIONS 854 (Modern Library edition 1994) (originally published in 1776).

66. McIntyre v. Ohio Election Comm'n, 514 U.S. 334, 382 (1995) (Scalia, J. dissenting).

67. http://harrietmiers.blogspot.com/.

68. http://jmluttig.blogspot.com/.

69. Joyce Pellino Crane, *Internet Bullying Hits Home for Teen: Anonymous Attacks a Growing Concern,* Boston Globe, June 30, 2005.

70. Margaret K. Collins, *Push to Criminalize False Info on Web,* NorthJersey.com, Sept. 20, 2006/.

71. Denise Grady, *Faking Pain and Suffering on the Internet,* N.Y. Times, Apr. 23, 1998, at G1.

72. ROBERT D. PUTNAM, BOWLING ALONE: THE COLLAPSE AND REVIVAL OF AMERICAN COMMUNITY 177 (2000).

73. Katharine Q. Seelye, *Rewriting History: Snared in the Web of a Wikipedia Liar,* N.Y. Times, Dec. 4, 2005. Wikipedia is located at http://en.wikipedia.org/.

74. Ken S. Myers, *Wikimmunity: Fitting the Communications Decency Act to Wikipedia,* 20 Harv. J.L. & Tech. 163 (2006).

75. Alexa.com keeps track of the current most visited websites around the world. See http://www.alexa.com/site/ds/top_500.

76. John Seigenthaler, *A False Wikipedia "Biography,"* USA Today, Nov. 29, 2005, http://www.usatoday.com/news/opinion/editorials/2005-11-29-wikipedia-edit_x.htm.

77. *Id.*

78. Katharine Q. Seelye, *A Little Sleuthing Unmasks Writer of Wikipedia Prank,* N.Y. Times, Dec. 11, 2005.

79. Seigenthaler, *False Wikipedia "Biography," supra.*

80. Seelye, *A Little Sleuthing, supra.*

81. *John Seigenthaler, Sr.,* Wikipedia, Sept. 30, 2006, http://en.wikipedia.org/wiki/John _Seigenthaler_Sr.

82. Simon Freeman, *Wikipedia Hit By Surge in Spoof Articles,* The Times (London), Dec. 15, 2005, http://www.timesonline.co.uk/article/0,,3-1933568,00.html.

83. Comment to Daniel J. Solove, *Fake Biographies on Wikipedia,* Concurring Opinions, Dec. 1, 2006, http://www.concurringopinions.com/archives/2005/12/fake_biographie.html.

84. Yuki Noguchi, *On Capitol Hill, Playing WikiPolitics,* Wash. Post, Feb. 4, 2006, at A1.

85. Evan Hansen, *Wikipedia Founder Edits Own Bio,* Wired News, Dec. 15, 2005, http:// www.wired.com/news/culture/0,1284,69880,00.html.

86. Orin Kerr, *More on Wikipedia (Plus Updates),* Volokh Conspiracy, Oct. 18, 2004, http://volokh.com/posts/1098119066.shtml.

87. Wikipedia, *Wikipedia: Replies to Common Objections,* Dec. 20, 2006, http://en .wikipedia.org/wiki/Wikipedia:Replies_to_common_objections.

88. Tal Z. Zarsky, *Thinking Outside the Box: Considering Transparency, Anonymity, and Pseudonymity as Overall Solutions to the Problems of Information Privacy in the Internet Society,* 58 U. Miami L. Rev. 991, 1028, 1032, 1044 (2004).

89. The Electronic Frontier Foundation, a digital rights organization, created a manual to help people better protect themselves from being traced. Electronic Frontier Foundation, *How to Blog Safely (About Work or Anything Else),* Apr. 6, 2005, http://www.eff .org/Privacy/Anonymity/blog-anonymously.php.

90. Ralph Gross & Alessandro Acquisti, *Information Revelation and Privacy in Online Social Networks (The Facebook Case),* ACM Workshop on Privacy in the Electronic Society, Nov. 7, 2005, at §4.2.

91. Michael Barbaro & Tom Zeller, Jr., *A Face Is Exposed for AOL Searcher No. 4417749,* N.Y. Times, Aug. 9, 2006, at A1.

92. *See* Talley v. State of California, 362 U.S. 60, 64 (1960).

93. McIntyre v. Ohio Elections Comm'n, 514 U.S. 334, 342 (1994).

94. *See, e.g.,* Columbia Insurance Co. v. Seescandy.com, 185 F.R.D. 573 (N.D. Cal. 1999); Dendrite International, Inc. v. John Doe No. 3, 775 A.2d 756 (N.J. Super. A.D. 2001); Doe v. Cahill, 884 A.2d 451 (Del. 2005).

95. In some cases, courts have required that people demonstrate that their case is strong enough to defeat a summary judgment motion. The plaintiff "must introduce evidence creating a genuine issue of material fact for all elements of a defamation claim *within the plaintiff's control." See* Doe v. Cahill, 884 A.2d 451, 462–63 (Del. 2005).

96. The facts are taken from the complaint in Clifton Swiger v. Allegheny Energy, Inc. (E.D. Pa.).

97. The facts in this section are taken from Zeran v. America Online, Inc., 129 F.3d 327 (4th Cir. 1997); Zeran v. America Online, Inc., 958 F. Supp. 1124 (E.D. Va. 1997); and Zeran v. Diamond Broadcasting, Inc., 203 F.3d 714 (10th Cir. 2000).

98. Zeran v. America Online, Inc., 129 F.3d 327 (4th Cir. 1997).

99. 47 U.S.C. §230(c)(1).

100. Zeran v. America Online, Inc., 129 F.3d 327, 330 (4th Cir. 1997).

101. *Id.*

102. Barnes v. Yahoo! Inc., 2005 WL 3005602 (D. Oregon 2005).

103. The Digital Millennium Copyright Act, 17 U.S.C. §512.

104. Carafano v. Metrosplash.com, Inc., 339 F.3d 1119 (9th Cir. 2003).

105. Appellants Reply Brief, *Carafano v. Metrosplash.com, Inc.* No. 02-55658, 2003 WL 22023295 (Feb. 11, 2003).

106. Carafano v. Metrosplash.com, Inc., 339 F.3d 1119, 1125 (9th Cir. 2003).

107. The facts are taken from Jori Finkel, *The Case of the Forwarded E-mail,* Salon.com, July 13, 2001, http://archive.salon.com/tech/feature/2001/07/13/museum_security_net work/index.html; Batzel v. Smith, 333 F.3d 1018 (9th Cir. 2003).

108. Batzel v. Smith, 333 F.3d 1018, 1035 (9th Cir. 2003).

109. *Id.* at 1038, 1040 (Gould, J. dissenting).

CHAPTER 7. PRIVACY IN AN OVEREXPOSED WORLD

1. Jerome Burdi, *Burning Man Gets Hot over Steamy Videos,* Court TV, Aug. 26, 2002, http://archives.cnn.com/2002/LAW/08/26/ctv.burning.man/.

2. Evelyn Nieves, *A Festival with Nudity Sues a Sex Web Site,* N.Y. Times, July 5, 2002. Burning Man's suit was filed before the Video Voyeurism Prevention Act was introduced. Among the claims were intrusion, appropriation, public disclosure, breach of contract, and trespass.

3. *Id.*

4. Gill v. Hearst Pub. Co., 253 P.2d 441 (Cal. 1953).

5. Restatement (Second) of Torts §652D (comment c).

6. Cefalu v. Globe Newspaper Co., 391 N.E.2d 935, 939 (Mass. App. 1979).

7. Penwell v. Taft Broadcasting, 469 N.E.2d 1025 (Ohio App. 1984).

8. http://www.earthcam.com/.

9. http://flickr.com/.

10. *YouTube Serves Up 100 Million Videos a Day Online,* Reuters, July 16, 2006.

11. http://en.wikipedia.org/wiki/Moblog.

12. Katie Dean, *Blogging + Video = Vlogging,* Wired.com, July 13, 2005, http://www.wired .com/news/digiwood/0,1412,68171,00.html.

13. Andrew Jay McClurg, *Bringing Privacy Law Out of the Closet: A Tort Theory of Liability for Intrusions in Public Places,* 73 N.C. L. Rev. 989, 1041–42 (1995).

14. Nader v. General Motors Corp., 255 N.E.2d 765, 772 (N.Y. App. 1970) (Brietel, J. concurring).

15. Helen Nissenbaum, *Privacy as Contextual Integrity,* 79 Wash. L. Rev. 119, 144–45 (2004).

16. McClurg, *Privacy Law, supra,* at 1041–43.

17. Marcia Chambers, *Colleges: Secret Videotapes Unnerve Athletes,* N.Y. Times, Aug. 9, 1999, at D4.

18. Clay Calvert, Voyeur Nation: Media, Privacy, and Peering in Modern Culture (2000).

19. *See, e.g.,* La. Rev. Stat. Ann. §14:283; N.J. Stat. Ann. §2C:18-3; N.Y. Penal Law §250.45.

20. RCW 9A.44.115.

21. Washington v. Glas, 54 P.3d 147 (Wash. 2002)

22. 18 U.S.C. §1801.

23. Quoted in Anick Jesdanun, *Facebook Feature Draws Privacy Conerns,* Associated Press, Sept. 7, 2006.

24. Dave Wischnowsky, *Facebook Alienates Users,* Chicago Tribune, Sept. 8, 2006.

25. Peter Meredith, *Facebook and the Politics of Privacy,* Mother Jones, Sept. 14, 2006.

26. Quoted in Jesdanun, *Facebook Feature, supra.*

27. Wischnowsky, *Facebook Alienates Users, supra.*

28. Mark Zuckerberg, *An Open Letter from Mark Zuckerberg: Creator of Facebook,* Sept. 8, 2006. The letter appeared on the Facebook website when users logged in. It has since been removed.

29. Bruce Schneier, *Lessons from the Facebook Riots,* Wired, Sept. 21, 2006.

30. Lisa Lerer, *How Not to Get a Job,* Forbes, Oct. 13, 2006.

31. *The Greatest CV Ever Filmed,* Oct. 10, 2006, http://www.metro.co.uk/weird/article .html?in_article_id=20878&in_page_id=2&expand rue.

32. Paul Tharp, *Wannabe Banker's Video Resume Backfires,* N.Y. Post, Oct. 12, 2006.

33. Michael J. de la Merced, *A Student's Video Résumé Gets Attention (Some of It Un-wanted),* N.Y. Times, Oct. 21, 2006.

34. Comments to Andrew Ross Sorkin, *The Resume Mocked Around the World,* DealBook, Oct. 19, 2006, http://dealbook.blogs.nytimes.com/2006/10/19/the-resume-mocked -round-the-world-vayner-speaks/.

35. Interview with Aleksey, Rita Cosby Live, MSNBC, Oct. 23, 2006.

36. *Creepy Orwellian Trance of Aleksey Vayner Fails to Generate Fun,* IvyGate Blog, Nov. 20, 2006, http://ivygateblog.com/blog/2006/11/creepy_orwellian_trance_of_aleksey_ vayner_fails_to_translate_into_fun.html.

37. *Douchebag Hall of Fame: The Inevitable Charter Member,* Gawker, Oct. 16, 2006, http://www.gawker.com/news/douchebag-hall-of-fame/douchebag-hall-of-fame-the -inevitable-charter-member-207845.php.

38. Interview with Aleksey on ABC, *20/20,* Dec. 29, 2006.

39. Merced, *Student's Video Résumé, supra.*

40. "Whatsoever things I see or hear concerning the life of men, in my attendance on the sick or even apart therefrom, which ought not to be noised abroad, I will keep silence thereon, counting such things to be as sacred secrets." Hippocratic Oath, quoted in DANIEL J. SOLOVE, MARC ROTENBERG & PAUL M. SCHWARTZ, INFORMATION PRIVACY LAW 350 (2d ed. 2006).

41. MARK TWAIN, THE AUTOBIOGRAPHY OF MARK TWAIN xxxv (Charles Neider, ed.).

42. Hammonds v. AETNA Casualty & Surety Co., 243 F. Supp. 793, 801 (D. Ohio 1965).

43. Upjohn Co. v. United States, 449 U.S. 383, 389 (1981).

44. Wendy Meredith Watts, *The Parent-Child Privileges: Hardly a New or Revolutionary Concept,* 28 Wm. & Mary L. Rev. 583, 592 (1987); GLEN WEISSENBERGER, FEDERAL EV-IDENCE §501.6, at 205–9 (1996).

45. In re Grand Jury, 103 F.3d 1140, 1146 (3d Cir. 1997) ("The overwhelming majority of all courts—federal and state—have rejected such a privilege.").

46. *See, e.g.,* State v. DeLong, 456 A.2d 877 (Me. 1983) (refusal to testify against father); Port

v. Heard, 594 F. Supp. 1212 (S.D. Tex. 1984) (refusal to testify against son); United States v. Jones, 683 F.2d 817 (4th Cir. 1982) (refusal to testify against father in grand jury).

47. In re A&M, 61 A.2d 426 (N.Y. 1978).

48. The Supreme Court has held that in Fourth Amendment law, people lack a reasonable expectation of privacy when they trust others with their information. *See, e.g.,* Smith v. Maryland, 442 U.S. 735, 744 (1979) (a person "assumes the risk that the [phone] company [will] reveal to the police the numbers he dialed."). Undercover agents are not regulated by the Fourth Amendment because people assume the risk of betrayal. *See* Hoffa v. United States, 385 U.S. 293, 302 (1966); Lewis v. United States, 385 U.S. 206, 210–11 (1966).

49. Nader v. General Motors, Inc., 225 N.E.2d 765, 770 (N.Y. 1970).

50. See, e.g., Argyll v. Argyll [1967] 1 Ch. 302 (1964) (spouse liable for breach of confidence); Stephens v. Avery, [1988] 1 Ch. 449 (1988) (friend liable for breach of confidence); Barrymore v. News Group Newspapers, [1997] F.S.R. 600 (1997) (lover liable for breach of confidence).

51. Barrymore, *supra,* at 602.

52. *Id.* at 600, 601.

53. Douglas v. *Hello!* Ltd, [2003] 3 All Eng. Rep. 996.

54. Neil M. Richards & Daniel J. Solove, *Privacy's Other Path: Recovering the Law of Confidentiality,* 96 Geo. L.J. (forthcoming Nov. 2007). The article is available online at http://ssrn.com/abstract=969495.

55. BENJAMIN FRANKLIN, POOR RICHARD'S ALMANAC (July 1735) quoted in JOHN BARTLETT, BARTLETT'S FAMILIAR QUOTATIONS 309:15 (Justin Kaplan, ed., Little Brown, 16th ed. 1992).

56. Times Mirror Co. v. Superior Court, 244 Cal. Rptr. 556 (Cal. Ct. App. 1988).

57. Y.G. v. Jewish Hospital, 795 S.W.2d 488 (Mo. Ct. App. 1990).

58. Multimedia WMAZ, Inc. v. Kubach, 443 S.E.2d 491 (Ga. 1994).

59. Duran v. Detroit News, Inc., 504 N.W.2d 715 (Mich. Ct. App. 1993).

60. Fisher v. Ohio Department of Rehabilitation and Correction, 578 N.E.2d 901 (Ohio Ct. Cl. 1988).

61. Lior Jacob Strahilevitz, *A Social Networks Theory of Privacy,* 72 U. Chi. L. Rev. 919 (2005).

62. *Id.* at 952, 967.

63. Joanne B. Freeman, *Slander, Poison, Whispers, and Fame: Jefferson's "Anas" and Political Gossip in the Early Republic,* 15 Journal of the Early Republic 25, 33 (1995).

64. *Id.*

65. Giannecchini v. Hospital of St. Raphael, 780 A.2d 1006 (Conn. Super. 2000).

66. Dr. Laura Schlessinger, *Men Leave Because Liberal Feminism Gives Permission,* New Orleans Times Picayune, July 11, 1999, at E7; *Dr. Laura's Anti-Female Rant,* N.Y. Post, Sept. 14, 2006.

67. Patrizia DiLucchio, *Dr. Laura, How Could You?,* Salon.com, Nov. 3, 1998, http://archive.salon.com/21st/feature/1998/11/03feature.html.

68. *Id.*

69. Polly Sprenger, *Dr. Laura Drops Her Suit,* Wired, Dec. 15, 1998, http://wired-vig.wired.com/news/politics/0,1283,16843,00.html.

70. Marcus Errico, *Dr. Laura Dishes on Nude Photos,* E Online, Nov. 4, 1998, http://www
.eonline.com/print/index.jsp?uuid=3159acb0-ee3e-454a-ab74-ac7f972390c6&content
Type=newsStory.

71. DiLucchio, *Dr. Laura, supra.*

72. 17 U.S.C. §102(a).

73. Jonathan Zittrain, *What the Publisher Can Teach the Patient: Intellectual Property and
Privacy in an Era of Trusted Privication,* 52 Stan. L. Rev. 1201, 1203 (2002).

74. Lawrence Lessig, *Privacy as Property,* 69 Social Research 247, 250 (2002).

75. Zittrain, *What the Publisher Can Teach the Patient, supra,* at 1206–12.

76. *See, e.g.,* LAWRENCE LESSIG, THE FUTURE OF IDEAS 107–11 (2001); Raymond Shih Ray Ku,
Consumers and Creative Destruction: Fair Use Beyond Market Failure, 18 Berkeley Tech.
L.J. 539, 567 (2003) ("[C]onsumer copying does little to reduce the incentives for creation
because, for the most part, the creation of music is not funded by the sale of copies of
that music."); Mark A. Lemley, *Beyond Preemption: The Law and Policy of Intellectual
Property Licensing,* 87 Cal. L. Rev. 113, 124–25 (1999) ("[G]ranting property rights to original creators allows them to prevent subsequent creators from building on their works,
which means that a law designed to encourage the creation of first-generation works may
actually risk stifling second-generation creative works."); Neil Weinstock Netanel, *Copyright and a Democratic Civil Society,* 106 Yale L.J. 283, 295 (1996) ("An overly expanded
copyright also constitutes a material disincentive to the production and dissemination of
creative, transformative uses of preexisting expression.").

77. Eldred v. Ashcroft, 537 U.S. 186, 190 (2003) (declaring that copyright is "compatible
with free speech principles.").

78. Restatement (Second) of Torts §652C.

79. Jonathan Kahn, *Bringing Dignity Back to Light: Publicity Rights and the Eclipse of the
Tort of Appropriation of Identity,* 17 Cardozo Arts & Ent. L.J. 213, 223 (1999).

80. Pavesich v. New England Life Insurance Co., 50 S.E. 68, 70 (Ga. 1905).

81. *Id.* at 80.

82. William Prosser, *Privacy,* 48 Cal. L. Rev. 383, 406 (1960).

83. Paulsen v. Personality Posters, Inc., 299 NYS2d 501 (1968).

84. Rosemont Enterprises, Inc. v. Random House, Inc., 294 N.Y.S.2d 122 (1968).

85. *See* Hosking v. Runting, [2004] NZCA 34, at [46] ("As the law currently stands, a successful action requires information that is confidential, communication of that information to another in circumstances importing an obligation of confidence and unau-
thorised use or disclosure."); International Corona v. Lac Minerals, [1989] 2 S.C.R. 574
(stating elements of breach-of-confidentiality tort); ABC v. Lenah, [2004] HCA 63, at
[34] (discussing the breach-of-confidentiality tort).

CHAPTER 8. CONCLUSION

1. Google keeps a cache of old versions of websites, so even after a name is removed from
a website, it still exists in Google's cache and is accessible to a person doing a search. But
the cache is refreshed at regular intervals, so it will eventually disappear. There is also a
project called the Internet Archive that saves old versions of the Internet. *See* http://

www.archive.org. But information can be removed from the Internet Archive upon request. *See* Frequently Asked Questions, http://www.archive.org/about/faqs.php.

2. ReputationDefender, http://www.reputationdefender.com/. For more about the company, see Ellen Nakashima, *Harsh Words Die Hard on the Web,* Wash. Post, Mar. 7,
2007, at A1.

3. ROBERT C. ELLICKSON, ORDER WITHOUT LAW: HOW NEIGHBORS SETTLE DISPUTES
62, 54, 5 (1991).

4. Tracey Meares, *Drugs: It's a Question of Connections,* 31 Val. L. Rev. 579, 594 (1997).

5. John H. Summers, *What Happened to Sex Scandals? Politics and Peccadilloes, Jefferson to
Kennedy,* 87 Journal of American History 825, 825 (2000).

6. *Id.* at 835.

7. *Id.* at 842.

8. *See* RODNEY A. SMOLLA, FREE SPEECH IN AN OPEN SOCIETY 134 (1992) ("When the
press avoided reporting on the sexual liaisons of John Kennedy, however, it engaged in
a paternalistic decision that the behavior was not probative of Kennedy's fitness for
public life."); Jeffrey B. Abramson, *Four Criticisms of Press Ethics, in* DEMOCRACY AND
THE MASS MEDIA 229, 234 (Judith Lichtenberg, ed. 1990) ("There was also the nonre-
porting of the love lives of Lloyd George, Franklin Roosevelt, Dwight Eisenhower,
John Kennedy, and Martin Luther King, Jr.").

9. *See* Ellen O'Brien, *Chelsea Comes of Age, but Not Before Our Eyes,* Boston Globe, Sept.
4, 1994, at 1; Joan Ryan, *Clintons Let Go—Chelsea Enters Stanford,* S.F. Chron., Sept.
20, 1997, at A1; *see* Howard Kurtz, *First Daughter's Privacy No Longer Off Limits,* Chi.
Sun-Times, Nov. 27, 1998, at 32 ("For six years the media followed an unspoken pact to
avoid coverage of Chelsea Clinton, allowing the president's daughter to grow up outside the harsh glare of publicity.").

10. Ryan, *Clintons Let Go, supra.*

11. *See, e.g.,* Gail Collins, *The Children's Crusade,* N.Y. Times, May 1, 2001, at A23 (arguing that "it's always news when the offspring of important elected officials break the
law," but noting that when "there's no legal issue involved, it's a judgment call");
Joanne Ostrow, *Don't Beat About the Bush Kids,* Denver Post, June 10, 2001, at K1
(questioning whether "the media [went] overboard in reporting Jenna Bush's recent
underage drinking citation").

12. David Bauder, *Identifying Rape Victims Troubles Media,* Sun-Sentinel (Ft. Lauderdale),
Aug. 3, 2002, at 3A; Richard Roeper, *Case Shows Absurdity of Media's Rape ID Policy,*
Chi. Sun-Times, Aug. 5, 2002, at 11.

13. *See id.* ("So the media were tripping all over themselves trying to stick to policy—but
hardly anyone questioned whether the policy itself is outdated."); Chris Frates, *L.A.
Radio Show Names Bryant's Accuser,* Denver Post, July 24, 2003, at B1.

14. J. M. Balkin, *How Mass Media Simulate Political Transparency,* 3 Cultural Values 393,
402 (1999).

15. JOHN STUART MILL, ON LIBERTY 11 (Norton edition, David Spitz, ed. 1975) (originally
published in 1859).

16. Anita L. Allen, *Coercing Privacy,* 40 Wm. & Mary L. Rev. 723, 737 (1999).

17. Harvey Jones & José Hiram Soltren, *Facebook: Threats to Privacy,* Dec. 14, 2005, at 20–21,

http://ocw.mit.edu/NR/rdonlyres/Electrical-Engineering-and-Computer-Science/6-805 Fall-2005/8EE6D1CB-A269-434E-BEF9-D5C4B4C67895/0/facebook.pdf.

18. *Id.* at 20.

19. Ralph Gross & Alessandro Acquisti, *Information Revelation and Privacy in Online Social Networks (The Facebook Case)*, ACM Workshop on Privacy in the Electronic Society, Nov. 7, 2005, at §4.4.

20. Emily Nussbaum, *My So-Called Blog*, N.Y. Times Magazine, Jan. 11, 2004.

21. Marie-Chantale Turgeon, *10 Reasons to Blog*, http://www.meidia.ca/archives/2005/06/10_reasons_to_b.php?l=en.

22. Electronic Frontier Foundation, *How to Blog Safely (About Work or Anything Else)*, May 31, 2005, http://www.eff.org/Privacy/Anonymity/blog-anonymously.php.

23. Quoted in Brian Leiter, *Top Law School Warns Students: Watch What You Post!* Sept. 1, 2005, http://leiterlawschool.typepad.com/leiter/2005/09/top_law_school_.html.

24. Nussbaum, *So-Called Blog, supra.*

25. *See* Lawrence Lessig, Code and Other Laws of Cyberspace 5–6, 236 (1999); Joel R. Reidenberg, *Rules of the Road for Global Electronic Highways: Merging Trade and Technical Paradigms*, 6 Harv. J. L. & Tech. 287, 296 (1993); *see also* Joel R. Reidenberg, *Lex Informatica: The Formulation of Information Policy Rules Through Technology*, 76 Tex. L. Rev. 553 (1998).

26. Lessig, Code, *supra*, at 5–6, 236. For a discussion of how physical architecture can influence behavior, see Neal Kumar Katyal, *Architecture as Crime Control*, 111 Yale L.J. 1039 (2002).

27. Jones & Soltren, *Facebook, supra*, at 6.

28. Gross & Acquisti, *Information Revelation, supra*, at §3.5.

29. Jones & Soltren, *Facebook, supra*, at 20.

30. Judith Donath & danah boyd, *Public Displays of Connection*, 22 BT Technology Journal 71, 78 (2004).

31. Conversation with Chris Hoofnagle, December 2006.

32. Fair Credit Reporting Act, 15 U.S.C. §1681b(b).

33. Alessandro Acquisti & Ralph Gross, *Imagined Communities: Awareness, Information Sharing, and Privacy on the Facebook*, Privacy Enhancing Technologies Workshop (PET), 2006, §4.4, at 13.

34. Michelle Andrews, *Decoding Myspace*, U.S. News & World Report, Sept. 18, 2006.

35. Jorge Luis Borges, *The Library of Babel*, in Collected Fictions 112, 112, 115 (Andrew Hurley, trans. 1998) (story originally published in 1941).

36. John Battelle, The Search: How Google and Its Rivals Rewrote the Rules of Business and Transformed Our Culture 65–93 (2005).

37. *Id.* at 252.

38. *Id.* at 254.

39. Albert-László Barabási, Linked 164–65 (2002). For more about search engines, see Frank Pasquale, *Rankings, Reductionism, and Responsibility*, 54 Clev. St. L. Rev. 115 (2006).

40. Ellen Lee, *Social Sites Becoming Too Much of a Good Thing*, S.F. Chron., Nov. 2, 2006 at A1 (discussing creation of Facebook); Battelle, Search, *supra*, at 77–90.

Index

Note: **Boldface** page numbers refer to illustrations.

About the Author

Daniel J. Solove is associate professor, George Washington University Law School, and an internationally known expert in privacy law. He is frequently interviewed and featured in media broadcasts and articles, and he is the author of *The Digital Person: Technology and Privacy in the Information Age*. He lives in Washington, D.C., and blogs at the popular law blog http://www.concurringopinions.com.